# Very Close
# to Trouble

# Very Close to Trouble

## THE JOHNNY GRANT MEMOIR

Edited with historical annotations by

Lyndel Meikle

Grant-Kohrs Ranch National Historic Site

WSU
PRESS

Washington State University Press
PO Box 645910
Pullman, WA 99164-5910
(800) 354-7360

Washington State University Press, Pullman, WA 99164-5910
©1996 by the Board of Regents of Washington State University
All rights reserved
First printing 1996

*Library of Congress Cataloging-in-Publication Data*
Grant, Johnny.
    Very close to trouble : the Johnny Grant memoir / edited with historical annotations by Lyndel Meikle, at Grant-Kohrs Ranch National Historic Site.
        p. cm.
    Includes bibliographical references and index.
    ISBN 0-87422-140-4 (hardcover). — ISBN 0-87422-139-0 (pbk.)
    1. Grant, Johnny. 2. Frontier and pioneer life—Montana. 3. Frontier and pioneer life—Idaho. 4. Pioneers—Montana—Deer Lodge—Biography. 5. Deer Lodge (Mont.)—Biography. 6. Montana—History. 7. Idaho—History. I. Meikle, Lyndel, 1946- . II. Title.
    F731.G72 1996
    978.6'87—dc20
    [B]                                                                                      96-34898
                                                                                                    CIP

# CONTENTS

# PREFACE

John Francis Grant (1831-1907) was born at Fort des Pairies, located at present-day Edmonton, in Alberta, Canada. His father, Richard Grant, was a high-ranking trader with the Hudson's Bay Company. After the early death of his mother (Marie Ann de Breland Grant), 1½-year-old "Johnny" was sent to Quebec to be raised by relatives in the populous lower St. Lawrence River area.

In 1847, at the age of sixteen, he returned to the far West to join his father, who then was in charge of the HBC's Fort Hall near modern-day Pocatello, Idaho. Despite a difficult relationship with his father, Grant grew into a competent frontiersman, and married Quarra, a Shoshoni Indian, who was a descendant of Sacagawea's family. Quarra died in 1867, and he formed alliances with other women as well, raising a large family.

Realizing that good money was to be had by dealing in livestock, he became a skilled trader along the Oregon Trail. Consequently, he played a key role in developing the livestock trade in Montana in the 1850s, as well as the settlement of the Deer Lodge Valley beginning in 1859. A house and ranch he began in 1861-62, and later sold to pioneer cattleman Conrad Kohrs in 1866-67, now are part of the Grant-Kohrs Ranch National Historic Site, at Deer Lodge, Montana.

In 1867, Johnny Grant migrated back to Canada, settling in Manitoba's Red River Valley, where he soon found himself locked in entanglements with Louis Riel and the Metis rebellion of 1869. In 1892, after suffering severe financial losses in land speculation, Grant relocated in Alberta. In the last months of his life, 1906-07, Grant dictated a memoir of his many experiences to his wife, Clothild, whom he had married in 1868. He died May 1, 1907, at the age of seventy-six.

In *Very Close to Trouble*, the Washington State University Press presents the portion of the Grant memoir that focuses on his years in Montana, Idaho, Wyoming, and Oregon, from 1847 to 1867. In many ways, the manuscript is reminiscent of, and complements, another well-known contemporary account of early Montana—Granville Stuart's *Forty Years on the Frontier*.

Come, then, and ride along with Johnny Grant on his many travels and adventurous encounters in an era when the West was yet untamed.

## ACKNOWLEDGMENTS

The Johnny Grant memoir is a rare and valuable addition to the frontier literature of the northwestern United States, but its publication has been long in coming. The narrative's existence is due to Johnny Grant's wife, Clothild Bruneau Grant (1850-1919), who painstakingly wrote it down in longhand (in English) at her husband's dictation in 1906-07. After Clothild's death, family descendants continued to serve as guardians of the unpublished manuscript for another seventy-five years.

Clothild had intentions of publishing the memoir. In her introduction to the text, she wrote: "Oh! How I dreaded the criticism of the public, and now I might be less able to perform such an undertaking. I am getting old, past my fifty-fifth birthday, and perhaps by the time my book is finished and published I might be in my grave, when the worst criticism will not annoy me."

The manuscript was not published in her lifetime, of course, and it passed on to a grandson, William Nutt, who with his wife, Marigold, undertook the challenge of making it into a book. Their transcription of the narrative into typed form made it more readable, but nearly another fifty years passed before the Nutts' transcript finally would reach the public in this WSU Press edition. During many of those years, the fragile, original handwritten manuscript was carefully tended by William Nutt's daughter, Audrey (Nutt) MacLeod.

Interest in Grant revived after 1972, with the establishment of the Grant-Kohrs Ranch National Historic Site to commemorate the frontier cattle era and tell the story of Johnny Grant and cattle baron Conrad Kohrs. Remarkable as it now seems, historians, scholars, and the National Park Service did not realize at the time that a full-length Johnny Grant manuscript even existed. However, it was known that, in 1952, twelve pages of reminiscences attributed to Grant had been sent by William Nutt to Con Warren, a grandson of Conrad Kohrs, on the occasion of Montana's Gold Centennial.

As a Park Ranger at the national historic site, I began conducting extensive research into the Grant story in about 1983 or 1984. As opportunity arose, I visited and wrote to archival and museum collections all across Canada and the United States. I cannot now recall at what point in time it occurred to me that if there were twelve pages of excerpts from William Nutt, Johnny's grandson, then there could very well be a longer document. I had yet to learn that there is buried historical treasure in attics and archives all across the continent. My search included sending letters of inquiry to everyone I could locate in Alberta having the surname of Nutt.

Several years would pass, however, before I finally held the valuable memoir in my own hands, cordially sent to me by William Nutt's son, Brian. Although the truth of the work now is obvious to me, at the time I feared it could be a gigantic hoax. I could not believe such a wonderful narrative had not been published. There followed a long period during which I went through much of the memoir with a fine-tooth comb, searching for incidents that I could confirm through independent sources. It is Nutt's transcription that the Washington State University Press then began undertaking to publish.

I had, however, located only William Nutt's typed transcript, and not Clothild's original handwritten text. At this point, a suggestion arose that Grant must have dictated the memoir in French, and that we should be calling him Jean Francois Grant. This put me back on the track of locating the handwritten original, and I was successful. A frantic wintery drive to visit Johnny's great granddaughter, Audrey MacLeod, in British Columbia finally gave me my first glimpse of the actual manuscript—a volume twice as long as the typed transcript and definitely written in English! Besides Grant's early years, 1831-47, and his two decades in Montana and Idaho, 1847-67 (which already had been transcribed by William Nutt), it included Grant's four decades in Canada, 1867-1907, as well.

This was followed by a visit to the Grant-Kohrs ranch by Audrey MacLeod. She graciously brought the memoir with her and let me copy it, providing new material and creating new problems: i.e., the William Nutt transcript included some editing for clarity, and it was apparent that Clothild also had done some editing on the original manuscript itself.

What is the responsibility of an editor in such a case? It is nearly impossible in the handwritten manuscript to tell which corrections Clothild made at her husband's behest, and which she may have done on her own initiative. Furthermore, should the text follow the sometimes awkward "stream of consciousness" flow of Grant's original dictation, or should those corrections in punctuation, spelling, and sentence structure be made which certainly would have been required had Johnny and Clothild prepared a final manuscript for publication?

A careful comparison of the handwritten and typed versions revealed that changes were rarely made, and usually for the purpose of clarification. Therefore, it was decided to use the Nutt transcription, so the reader could concentrate on the subject matter without being distracted by a sometimes difficult syntax. In cooperation with the WSU Press, a few other types of editing changes have been carefully undertaken for consistency and clarity. These mainly entail minor corrections in punctuation, spelling, and capitalization, plus the addition of paragraph indentations to accommodate a clearer presentation of the extensive conversational dialogue that Johnny dictated from memory. Also, brackets indicate factual information that has been inserted for the benefit of the reader.

The decision not to include Grant's years in Canada (1867-1907) in the WSU Press edition was a difficult one, since his account of the transfer of the Hudson's Bay Company's holdings to the Canadian government is as important as his adventures in Montana. Such a volume, however, would have more than doubled the length of the book and added months—if not years—to the preparation of the work for publication. There can be no doubt that the Canadian portion of the manuscript eventually will be edited and published—and the sooner the better!

Meanwhile, here are twenty years of early Northwest history to interest, enlighten, amuse, and challenge the student of that era. Grant's memory was not perfect. He tends to be most accurate in telling his own story, and less reliable when passing along the accounts of others.

Some of these tales are new. Others confirm or contradict other published histories. But whether a particular tale is perfectly accurate or not, there is a greater truth to this memoir: it is Montana, Idaho, Washington, and Oregon history as Grant saw it, and he saw it all, from the last days of the fur trade through the wild, early days of Montana's gold rush.

In addition to the debt owed to Johnny and Clothild Grant and their descendants for the preservation of this remarkable story, I would like to acknowledge others who have played a role in its eventual publication.

Dave Walter of the Montana Historical Society provided endless guidance, support, and optimism during my initial search for the manuscript. Thanks also go to Clyde Lockwood and the Glacier Natural History Association, which put the text onto disks, making it acceptable for submission to the Washington State University Press in this computer age. Glen Lindeman, my editor at the WSU Press, not only did much of the basic editing, but added important endnotes on military matters and tribes of the Northwest, particularly regarding Columbia Plateau history. Glen also compiled the index.

Will Bagley provided valuable information on Johnny's father, Richard Grant. Others who have supplied material to verify and amplify Grant's account include Deane and Peggy Robertson, Kenneth N. Owens, Anita Steele, Sandra Woodruff, and Irene Ardies. Thanks also to Brian Nutt, who sent me the typed transcript while I was still seeking the original manuscript. I am likewise grateful to the many archivists from southern California to Winnipeg, Manitoba, who responded to my queries.

Finally, thanks to all of those who will take this book, dissect it, challenge it, analyze it, and use it in ways not yet thought of to bring to others a fuller understanding of an extraordinary man and his extraordinary times.

Lyndel Meikle
Grant-Kohrs Ranch National Historic Site
Deer Lodge, Montana

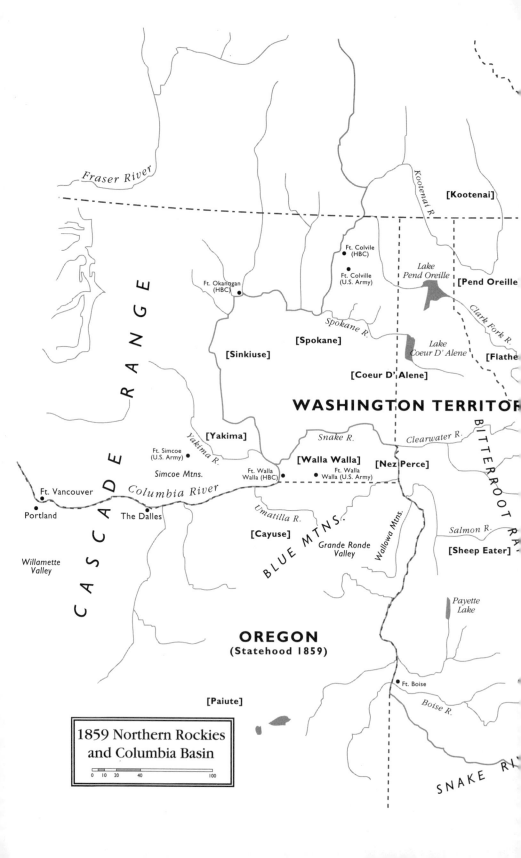

Fraser River

[Kootenai]

Kootenai R.

Ft. Colvile
(HBC)

Ft. Colville
(U.S. Army)

Lake
Pend Oreille

[Pend Oreille]

Ft. Okanogan
(HBC)

Clark Fork R.

Spokane R.

[Spokane]

Lake
Coeur D' Alene

[Flathe

C A S C A D E   R A N G E

[Sinkiuse]

[Coeur D' Alene]

WASHINGTON TERRITOR

[Yakima]

Snake R.

Clearwater R.

Ft. Simcoe
(U.S. Army)

Yakima R.

[Walla Walla]

[Nez Perce]

B I T T E R R O O T   R A

Simcoe Mtns.

Ft. Walla
Walla (HBC)

Ft. Walla
Walla (U.S. Army)

Ft. Vancouver

Columbia River

Portland

The Dalles

Umatilla R.

[Cayuse]

B L U E   M T N S.

Grande Ronde
Valley

Wallowa Mtns.

Salmon R.

[Sheep Eater]

Willamette
Valley

OREGON
(Statehood 1859)

Payette
Lake

Ft. Boise

[Paiute]

Boise R.

1859 Northern Rockies
and Columbia Basin

0   10   20    40                    100

S N A K E   RI

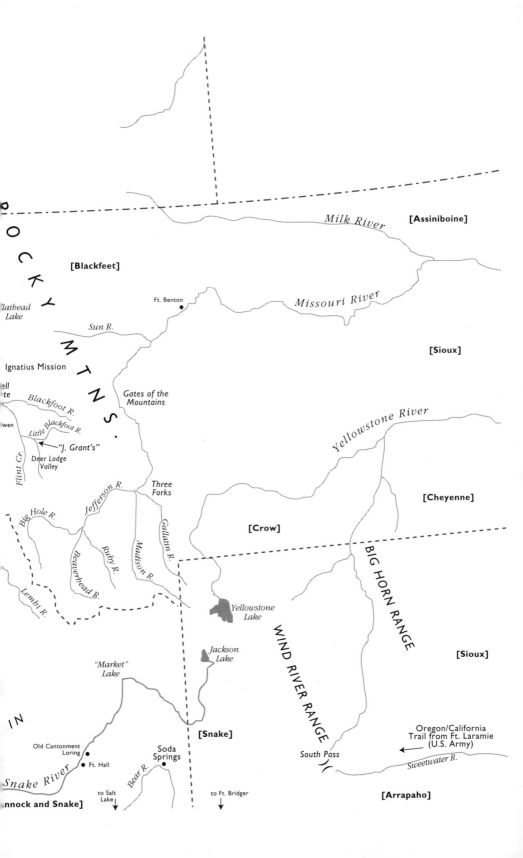

# VERY CLOSE TO TROUBLE

## Introduction

There was company in the parlor, several ladies being there. I was watching them for some time, ashamed to go in, although I wanted to go. At last I could not stand the temptation any longer, so I ran in on tiptoe and kissed one of the ladies on the neck and ran back so fast she had no time to catch me. I could not help doing it, for it seemed as though my whole nature forced me to go in. I may reflect here about this part of my nature, this great fondness for women which has followed me through life, that it has brought me very close to trouble at times, but I always got out of it without any serious consequences.

—*John Francis Grant*

John Francis (Johnny) Grant was three years old when he succumbed to the temptation to kiss the lady in his grandmother's parlor. He was seventy-six when he dictated his memoirs[1] to his last (and possibly seventh) wife, Clothild Bruneau Grant. In the intervening 73 years, he did, indeed, come very close to trouble—not only with women, but with horse thieves, gamblers, road agents, unscrupulous business partners, Native Americans, and a major Canadian rebellion.

He was born at the Hudson's Bay Company post at Edmonton, Alberta, on January 7, 1831. His father, Richard Grant, had started working for the North West Company at the age of eighteen. It united with its rival, the Hudson's Bay Company (HBC) in 1821, and Richard Grant spent the next three decades at HBC posts throughout the northern Great Plains and the Northwest. During that time he rose from the office of Clerk to the rank of Chief Trader.[2]

Johnny Grant's mother, Marie Ann de Breland Grant (also spelled Berland),[3] died when he was eighteen months old. When he was three, he, his two older brothers, (Charles) William and (Stanislas) Richard, and his sister, Jane, were taken by their father to live at the home of their paternal grandmother in Three Rivers, Quebec, on the St. Lawrence River, about midway between the cities of Montreal and Quebec. The first part of the journey was by birch bark canoe, but eventually they left the wilderness behind and the toddler had his first glimpse of a big city:

> When we passed through Montreal we spent a day in that City. My father took us around the city and as we passed the market he said to us to take the kind of fruit we wanted. So I picked a large turnip, not knowing the difference between fruit and vegetables for I had never seen any fruit. My father told me to leave it and gave me some fruit, but the bystanders had a good laugh at my expense.

Richard Grant returned to his duties with the HBC.[4] In 1842 he was assigned to Fort Hall in the Snake country near present-day Pocatello, Idaho.[5] The children stayed on in Three Rivers.

The four Grant children seem to have had a comfortable childhood, and the adventurous Johnny launched his trading career at an early age:

> I was a little gamin [. . .] when a bull dog pup took my fancy, and which I felt I must have, for which I paid a dollar that I had saved as well as a pair of gaily beaded moccasins which my father had sent me from Edmonton. These were worth a dollar and a half, so that in all I paid well for my dog [. . .] After a while my bull dog became unruly and I had so little pleasure in him that I decided to sell him [. . .] getting only Sixty cents for the dog and speedily spent it on my beloved sucre d'orge.

Johnny's school days were notable for the number of ways he found to play hooky. His teacher's notions of corporal punishment caused the boy to coax his grandmother to allow him to wear a long-tailed coat, though she wished he would wear the short Eton jacket more suitable to his age. Johnny did this because of the method of punishment utilized by Mr. Scannell, the teacher:

> [Mr. Scannell] generally wore slippers with the heels flattened down, so that he could slip them off easily and whip the scholars if they did not behave as they should. He would come behind them in his stocking feet in such a sneaking way and hit them on the back with a little leather strap. I was always very careful to pull the tail of my coat under me [. . .] It cut worse when you had no coat tails.

Johnny's education came to an abrupt end when he quit school rather than be punished when he felt he had committed no wrong. Meanwhile, his beloved brother, William, died, and his sister, Jane, was married.

In April 1847, Johnny (now sixteen) and his brother, Richard, began their long journey to join their father at Fort Hall on the other side of the continent.[6] From Montreal, their route took them to New York City, and, by the time they arrived in Kansas, they had traveled by stagecoach, railway car, steamboat, and canal boat:

> I thought everything wonderful, especially the canal boats. But when we arrived at Kansas I was more astonished to see the big covered wagons with two and three yoke of oxen hauling each [. . .] We joined a party of 28 waggons. There were in the party Bishop [A.M.A.] Blanchet[7] of Oregon, a couple of priests, some brothers and two nieces of the Bishop. We had six mules; my brother had four drawing a waggon and I rode another [. . .] I often stayed behind with some immigrant boys bound for Oregon.[8] Then we would run to catch up to the waggons. A few days after we left Kansas I got a good fright. We were at dinner when about fifteen wild looking Indians—Pawnees— came to the camp. The top of their heads were all shaved except a strip one inch wide from the forehead to the nape of the neck and the hair on that strip was left about two inches long and stood straight up like a mule's mane trimmed. The back part of their hair being long was plaited and hung down their backs. Their faces were painted red and black in stripes. The sight of them was enough to terrify anyone, but they were not hostile and there was no danger.
>
> Our trip was monotonous for a time after we got to the Platte River. The plain was level as a floor, not a twig was to be seen and the only fuel available was dried buffalo chips. Some of the party, particularly the ladies, did not like the idea of using that kind of fuel. They would say we cannot use that dirty stuff, but it was a matter of compulsion not choice. At first the ladies wore gloves and used tongs, not to soil their hands, but they soon got used to it. They would gather the chips with their naked hands and put them in their aprons. We all learned to rough it.

With his arrival at Fort Hall, the adventures of John Francis Grant really began. In her preface, when beginning to take down her husband's memoirs, Clothild wrote:

> I will endeavor to do my best in the following pages to relate the incidents in my husband's life [. . .] It will be written in plain language, but it will be the truth; although some passages might look like fiction. I will pass over many, but I will not add. My only hope to make progress in this manuscript, is to adhere to the truth, as my husband relates the incidents to me. I hope it may be a warning against the indiscretions of youth, which you will see in this book have been the cause of many failures.

Clothild may have passed over some incidents. Johnny Grant definitely did, as he freely admitted:

> If any of my old friends read the story of my life and are surprised to find little about the escapades and errors of my younger days let them not believe for one moment that I am a hypocrite; for I do not intend to reveal all of my private life here. It might not be interesting to the general public and some passages might not be justly suited to the taste of my fair readers.

Here then, suitably edited for the taste of his "fair readers" are the memoirs of John Francis Grant.[9]

1. Billie Nutt, a grandson, recalled Johnny Grant as he appeared shortly after the turn of the century. Nutt wrote down this observation in the 1950s: "I remember Granddad [Johnny Grant] very well though it is over forty-five years ago that he used to take us children on his knee and tell stories of his youth and warn us not to do some of the foolish things he had done. He was a big man and always wore his hair, which was snow white, down to his shoulders. He said it was the custom, when he was a mountain man, for the white men to wear their hair in that manner to show their Indian friends that, though they let their hair grow so that it would make a very good scalp lock, they were quite able to defend it should the occasion arise."
2. After the two fur trading firms combined in 1821, Richard Grant remained with the Hudson's Bay Company until 1853, resigning at the age of about 59. Afterward, "Captain Grant" took up the life of a free roaming "mountaineer" in the northern Rockies. Fur trade historian T.C. Elliott gives his birth date as January 20, 1794. ("Richard . . . Grant," *Oregon Historical Quarterly* 36 [March 1935]: 3) See Harvey Fleming, ed., *Minutes of Council, Northern Department of Rupert Land, 1821-31*, 442, for a synopsis of Richard Grant's assigned stations on the Canadian Plains from 1820 until 1841, after which time he was posted to the Columbia department and Fort Hall.
3. Throughout Johnny Grant's writings and in his family's histories, his mother's last name appears variously as De Breland, de Breland, Breland, or Berland.
4. Richard Grant, writing from Oxford House on January 3, 1839, exclaimed to James Hargrave: "The only advantage I have here over what a prisoner has in the civilized World is that besides being the prisoner I am also the Gaoler, a man alone in this great big barn of a house can be compared to nothing else." *(The Hargrave Correspondence)*
5. Richard Grant's taking of an Indian woman as a new wife at Oxford House caused his associate, James Hargrave, displeasure. According to Sylvia Van Kirk, in *Many Tender Ties:* "When in 1837 former Nor'Wester Richard Grant endeavoured to continue in the old ways and took an Indian wife *a la façon du pays* [in the manner of the country] at Oxford House, Hargrave was appalled. Considering the woman to be totally unsuitable to Grant's station, Hargrave applied considerable pressure to bring about their separation and was much relieved when 'the erring fellow' was posted to the Columbia [Fort Hall] in 1842: '. . . for his own sake I am truly glad he is gone, for his ideas about love and the sex were too primative to suite the atmosphere of the world as it is now about Oxford and Norway House.'" (Hargrave to George Barnston, 12/1/1842)

Richard Grant had a son by the Indian woman at Oxford House. This was James Cuthbert Grant, born in the late 1830s. In a March 1845 letter to Sir George Simpson at Fort Vancouver, Grant wrote, "besides the family I have in Canada [Johnny and a brother and sister], I have also a little son on the east side of the Mountains, in the neighborhood of Oxford House, Knowing that he was residing among the Indians, since I have been appointed to this side, I requested Mr. Dougald McTavish to apply to you for liberty to bring him to me. This request like the other was not granted [. . .] the little fellow is between six and seven." (HBCA D.5/13 fos 289-292)

6. In 1845, Richard Grant asked Sir George Simpson for assistance from the Hudson's Bay Company in bringing his children from Three Rivers to Fort Hall: "if you decline granting me your aid, and protection, I must make up My Mind to expend every farthing of my earnings to save My three children, two Sons, and a Daughter, besides a Sister from becoming vagrants the Moment the Almighty thinks proper to call from this world My aged Mother and if it should be myself then they are left destitute in a strange land without Money or friends." (Richard Grant to Sir George Simpson, 1/2/1845, HBCA D.5/16 fos 23-25) Johnny's older brother, Stanislas Richard Grant, came out temporarily to Fort Hall and returned to Canada in 1846. (Louise Barry, *The Beginning of the West*, 649)

7. A.M.A. Blanchet was the brother of Father F.N. (Francois Norbert) Blanchet, the well-known Pacific Northwest missionary. Beginning in the late 1830s, F.N. Blanchet helped initiate the earliest Catholic missionary activity in the Oregon Country among the Indians and, in particular, the HBC's French Canadians of the Willamette Valley. F.N. Blanchet eventually was declared Archbishop of Oregon, while his brother, A.M.A. Blanchet, received appointment as Bishop of Walla Walla. The Blanchets were a family long noted for service to the church. F.N. Blanchet personally traveled to Europe to raise funds, and to promote and gain support, for church activities in Oregon.

8. A daily record of this journey was kept by A.M.A. Blanchet, who was traveling to Oregon to assume his duties in the newly created post as Bishop of Walla Walla. The train, including both Oregon Trail immigrants and the Catholic party, consisted of 172 persons, forty-three wagons, and a corresponding number of livestock. Richard Grant at Fort Hall sent a man (Marigouin) eastward over the immigrant trail to Fort Bridger with horses and "provisions to meet his sons." Consequently, after crossing the Great Plains to Fort Bridger, Johnny Grant, his brother (Stanislas Richard Grant), Bishop Blanchet, and some others set out in advance of the train, reaching Fort Hall several days before the others arrived. On August 7, 1847, Blanchet wrote in his diary: "The Fort is a long square made of clay (bricks) baked in the sun. Mr. Grant, who is the bourgeois, is a kind gentleman who welcomes us with that courtesy which is remarkable among all of the gentlemen of the Hudson's Bay Company." (A.M.A. Blanchet, *Journal of a Catholic Bishop on the Oregon Trail*, 58, 61, 126)

9. This Introduction is a synopsis and condensation of the original chapters 1 through 8 of Johnny's and Clothild's manuscript, which deal with Johnny's early years in Canada. Consequently, in this WSU Press edition, the following chapters dealing with Grant's years in the American West have been renumbered.

# 1

## WHEREIN IT IS CLEAR THAT HE AND HIS FATHER WERE NOT MADE TO AGREE.

I was glad when we arrived at Fort Hall. It was one of the Hudson Bay Co's posts in the United States and my father was in charge of it. My father had married again, his second wife [Helene[1]]being the widow of Mr. [William] Kittson,[2] a brother of Comodore Kittson of St. Paul, Minn. She had one daughter, Jemima.[3] I will have occasion to speak of her more than once. Of my father's second marriage[4] there were three daughters:[5] Julia, who afterwards married Captain C.P. Higgins, the father of the late [Lt.] Governor Higgins; Helen, who died unmarried; [6] and Adeline who married Laughlin McLaren, a Hudson Bay Co's clerk.

My father was glad to see us, so was my stepmother. They welcomed me, but did not believe in keeping me idle. The first work my father set me at was to haul hay with a man by the name of Paquette, a man of two rations (that is a man who does the work of two men and gets two rations accordingly) so that it was very hard for a boy of sixteen who had never worked, not even carried an armful of wood in the house, to be compelled to work with such a man. I had to drive two yoke of oxen and Paquette drove three yoke on a waggon. We had to cross a creek every morning and evening. How I was afraid to ride going down the hill by the creek, so I would get down and walk. The oxen would go so fast that I could not get on again and I had to wade knee deep in the cold water every morning. I had to pitch on those two loads of hay, for I was afraid to get on the loads and they were loads! It was lucky for me Paquette was a kind hearted man and had consideration for me. When I would be pitching the last of the load it was almost too much for me.

I could hardly pitch high enough for him, but he would say, "A little higher, my Johnny, a little higher" and encourage me.

I did not require any rocking to set me to sleep when night came, yet I used to lie awake for some time thinking of the easy time I had at my Grandmother's where I had my own way, was petted and slept on a clean soft bed. Now all I had for a bed was an old buffalo robe under me and a three-point blanket to cover me.

I was treated like a stranger in that family. I did all kinds of work, such as washing dishes, nursing children, smoking skins; but what I disliked to do most was to sweep the Indian store. The company sold tobacco which was in rolls and retailed it by the foot. It would crumble when being cut and fall on the floor and when I swept it the dust from it would almost choke me. I did not even know enough to sprinkle the floor before I swept it. Now and then my father told me to shake the furs and beat the bear skins ready for packing to send to England. I liked this part of the work.

I began to get interested in furs, so I tried to get some of my own. The first winter [1847-48] I borrowed traps from my father and caught some foxes and wolves. One day I had a hearty laugh. There was in the fort a white boy about my age, named McIntyre. He was rather dressy and one day he came with me to see my traps. There was a skunk in one of them. We were both inexperienced in handling that animal. I was conceited enough to think that I was stronger then he was, so in taking it out of the trap I told him to hold the tail and I held its head. Poor fellow! His nice clothes were ruined as may be imagined when tenderfeet take liberties with a skunk, and always after that we gave skunks a wide berth. I continued to trap from time to time, but in the spring I could not get a very large trading outfit with my furs.

I found a brass spur which I sold for one dollar and fifty cents, and as the old Scotch saying is, "Every mickle makes a muckle" so I put this along with my furs.

I could only buy a two and a half point blanket, one shirt, two feet of red cloth for leggings, one knife, one paper backed looking glass, ten balls and powder.

I went to Salt Lake two hundred miles away with my father, who was taking tea and tobacco there to the Mormons. With my outfit I bought a horse from the Ute Indians. That was the first horse I ever owned.

At Salt Lake I saw Brigham Young who received us well. He was a very pleasant man to talk to, a stout man, light haired, fair of skin and freckled and rather plain looking. The Mormons at first had houses built with [a]dobe (a brick made of earth and dried in the sun), but it was not long before they were replaced by stone houses. They were a thrifty class of people, energetic and industrious. They had been very unfortunate the first years after they came there. The first year their crops were frozen, the second they were eaten up by grasshoppers and crickets, but they dug ditches which they filled with water, then the women and children took young willows and drove the crickets into them. The grasshoppers flew away and fell into Salt Lake where the waves afterward washed them ashore where they lay in a pile a foot deep, in some places more than a foot wide.

The Mormons believed that it was Brigham Young who banished the crickets. They finally had so much faith in him that they believed he could perform any miracle. The third year they had a good crop of every kind. After that they raised every kind of fruit. The fourth year they were selling peaches for fifteen cents a dozen. After harvest one could see the Mormon women and children each with a basket going round the fields gathering the few heads of grain that were left after stacking. After the Mormon women were through the Indian women went over the fields. So that the birds got very little after that.

There was no timber around Salt Lake so that fuel was scarce. It took them two days to get a load of wood from the mountains, one day to go and one to come back. Nevertheless there was always a pile of wood at every house. Water was also scarce and had to be brought from a distance. In the town there were little ditches along the streets lined with gravel and trees planted along the walk. Water brought down from the mountain streams flowed into those ditches, so that water was kept running all the time.

It was a very pretty town. Brigham Young must have been a clever man to rule over one hundred thousand souls without a soldier or police-man. He had full control over them and whatever he said was law. They gave the tenth of all they raised to the Mormon Church. At that time Brigham Young had forty-seven wives.[7] His main house was a very large one built something like the old convent at St. Boniface. I went every year to Salt Lake for supplies and I was well acquainted with many Mormons. They invited me to join their church; I did not object to having the wives, but I objected to giving the tenth of my horses to the church, so I did not join.

After I returned from that trip with my father I remained with him the balance of the summer [1848].

That summer they were branding calves at the fort [Fort Hall].[8] It took three or four men to handle a calf. I was presumptuous enough to think I could hold one myself.[9] The men had one down and I caught him by the hind legs, but he soon landed them on my forehead between the eyes. I saw millions of stars.

The men laughed at me. It was not easy to get accustomed to their ways. They would laugh at a person's mistakes, even if he was badly hurt, and on this occasion I did not like it.

Of course, my father wanted to know what was the trouble.

I replied, "Nothing."

Then he said, "What caused that lump on your forehead?"

I didn't say anything, but got out of the yard. I nearly cried with vexation. I was more careful in the future. But I learned after a time how to handle cattle and calves, and I raised large herds.[10]

The first summer I stayed with my father, I was afraid of him. I looked for love and affection from him because he was my father; and when I did not find it, I think it did me harm. After having passed my childhood with two kind old ladies—my grandmother and my aunt—it was not easy to be under a man who stood six feet and two inches in height and weighing two hundred and twenty-five pounds, and who had a voice like thunder when he was vexed. I scarcely knew what words he said when he got cross with me. It made me so nervous. When he sent me anyplace, I would start running.

One day there was a train of [Oregon/California Trail] immigrants at the door. He called out to me to go upstairs and get something that was in the cupboard. I started as usual climbing the stairs, two steps at a time. Once up, I could not see the cupboard.

I told him so, and he called out to me swearing, "There is one right at the top of the stairs."

"Father, you swear so much at me you make me nervous."

The cupboard was there, but I was so excited I could not see it. I lived in perpetual fear of him. I often wished my grandmother had been living; and if I had any means to get to her, I would not have remained long there.

What made me so scared of him was that he knew everything that happened, and I was at a loss to know how he found it out. There was one thing he expected of me which I did not like to do. It was to watch the hired men at the fort and report everything to him. I worked with them every day, and I did not want to act the spy. He sent me every morning to wake up the men. Some of them would not get up, and I did not report it to my father. But he always knew what was going on. I could not imagine how he knew.

At last I found out the secret. It was that little Jemima, my stepmother's daughter, who followed me and found everything out. She would report to her mother; and, she, of course, posted my father. My stepmother never said anything to me, but I had reason to suspect that she was the cause of much of the trouble that grew between my father and me.

I thought my father was needlessly harsh to me when he would tell me I was a very bad boy.

One day he said to me, "I cannot do anything with you. I will have to send you to Vancouver to Mr. [James] Douglas. He will train you."

Mr. Douglas was the head of the Hudson's Bay Co. fort at Fort Vancouver. I went to my brother Richard, who lived five miles away, and cried to him. "Oh, brother! What will I do? Father says he cannot do anything with me. He will send me to Mr. Douglas; and if he is worse than father, then I am a dead boy."

My brother said to me with kindness, "Never mind. Do not say anything but go on; and when you get to Vancouver, you take the first ship to California or some other place."

I thought my brother was very clever. I kept his advice in mind and I did not say anything, but got ready.

A few days later my father said to me, "Which do you prefer—to go now on the tenth of January with the winter express or wait till spring for me?"

I said, "I will go now."

"Remember it will be a hard trip, harder than you imagine," he said.

I replied, "Can the others stand it?"

"Yes," he said, "But they are good men."

"Well," I said, "I am as good a man as any of them. I will go now."

"Just as you please," he said. "You will have to endure hardships, but please yourself."

Now that I had made up my mind to go and after getting my brother's advice, I would have faced any hardship to get away from there, where it seemed to me I was so much despised.

1. Helene McDonald, born June 19, 1811, "was the daughter of Finan McDonald and an Indian woman, Charlotte 'Pond d'Oreille.' Helene's father, a huge, red-haired Scotsman, helped guide David Thompson's Northwest explorations in 1808-09. He built a temporary trading post at Kootenai Falls in 1808, and in 1810 or 1811 helped construct Spokane House, where he served as clerk for several years." (Glen Lindeman and Keith Petersen, "The Kittson Legacy," 4)
2. William Kittson (b. 1794), who served as a clerk with the North West Company and the Hudson's Bay Company during the heyday of the far western fur trade, died at Fort Vancouver on Christmas Day, 1841. (*Ibid*, 1, 4)
3. Eloisa Jemima Kittson was born June 25, 1836. A brother, Edwin Kittson, was born in December 1839. (*Ibid*, 4, family chart)

4. "The 29 March, 1845, in view of the dispensation of 3 bans of marriage granted by us Priest Missionary Apostolic between Richard Grant member of the Honorable Company of Hudson's Bay, Chief Trader and Commander in Chief at Fort Hall in the country of the Snakes . . . and Dame Helene McDonald widow of the late Guillaume Kitson [Kittson] on the other part, both members of the Sacred Catholic Church, Apostolic and Roman; nor any impediment being discovered, we priest Missionary undersigned have been a witness of their marriage and have received their mutual consent." (*Catholic Church Records of the Pacific Northwest*).

Johnny Grant, of course, in claiming that this was his father's second marriage, overlooked his father's liaison with an Indian woman at Oxford House, which resulted in the birth of a son, James "Jimmy" Cuthbert Grant, in the late 1830s. Young "Jimmy" also eventually came to stay with his father at Fort Hall. An 1846 immigrant recalled: "The boy was evidently the pride of the Captain. He was about 10 years old, spoke good English, and took me all over the quarters and was full of fire and energy as live boys are." (T.C. Elliott, "Richard . . . Grant," *Oregon Historical Quarterly* 36 [March 1935]: 3, 5)

Years later, Jimmie was killed in a quarrel with an Indian north of Choteau, Montana. The *Weekly Missoulian* of 8/17/1883 reported his demise as follows: "Jimmy Grant, a half-breed, well and favorably known in the county in years past and a man of considerable prominence in Choteau County, where he has lived for several years, was killed in an affray with an Indian about three miles from his ranch on the night of August 7. His wife, a half-breed, was engaged in a liaison with an Indian paramour, and the fact being reported to Grant, he armed himself and repaired to the spot where the fatal [shooting?] took place. Grant was a noted shot and it was the merest accident that he failed to kill his man at first fire, as he was within eight feet, his bullet glancing off the man's ribs. The Indian returned the fire, hitting Grant on the wrist and shoulder, and probably disabling him as his [Grant's] second shot had no effect. The Indian's second shot pierced Grant's heart and he fell dead. A squad of his neighbors gathered, searched the woods and 'returned to search no more.' The Indian's body was afterward found, riddled with bullets. Mr. Grant has done considerable business for Missoula people, having been until last fall in charge of Higgins and McClain's band of cattle, and also having had charge of W.J. McCormick's cattle. He was honest, sober and highly respected by all who knew him. He was well known at Flathead Agency and also in the Bitter Root Valley.

*The New Northwest* of Deer Lodge likewise presented an account of the incident in its 8/17/1883 edition: "JAMES C. GRANT KILLED / Shot Through the Heart by His Wife's Paramour / Special to Independent / Depuyer, Choteau Co., Montana, Aug. 8 / James C. Grant, the pioneer of this valley, was killed last night by the Indian paramour of his wife. The latter, a half-breed, and the Indian were coming from Birch, and at a point three miles from Depuyer had gone a short distance from the road to rest. Grant having come home from the hayfield, heard the situation by one who saw them. He armed himself with a Winchester and six-shooter, and mounting a fleet horse repaired to the scene. When within eight feet of the Indian he opened fire, the bullet taking effect in the fleshy part of the man's breast, and striking a rib glanced off. The Indian returned the fire, hitting Grant in the wrist and shoulder. Each fired twice, and the Indian's second shot penetrated Grant's heart.

"A party of six citizens of Depuyer started this morning at daybreak, separating into three squads, and searched the adjacent country. They returned at about nine o'clock and did not renew the search.

"By a squaw just up from Birch Creek the report comes that the Indian residents in that Valley have all left for the agency for protection and also that the murderer was found completely riddled with bullets.

"'Jimmy' Grant was a half-breed about forty-five years old, a son of Captain Grant, an old Hudson Bay trader, and a resident of Montana before its settlement by whites. James Grant's brother 'Johnny' was for a long time a resident of Cottonwood, now Deer Lodge City, and was quite wealthy, but left with a number of Indians for the Red River of the North in '67, when white settlers began to locate in Deer Lodge. Jimmy Grant lived for a long time in Deer Lodge where he was highly regarded as an honest, industrious and sober citizen. At the time of his death he had charge of Maj. W.J. McCormick and Capt. C.P. Higgins cattle. His many friends will be sorry to learn of his tragic death."

5. Helene Wilhelmina Grant was born January 28, 1846; Julia Priscilla Grant, December 20, 1848; and Adeline Grant, September 11, 1850 ("The Kittson Legacy," family chart).

6. Helene, the first born, died at the same time as her father, Richard Grant, while camped near Walla Walla in 1862. She was then but sixteen years old (see chapter 20).

7. It is generally accepted that Brigham Young had 27 wives.

8. John Prichet, a traveler, recorded the following observation of the post two years after Johnny Grant had arrived there at his father's beckoning: "At about 4 o'clock [July 12, 1849] we came to the Fort [Hall] which is situated immediately on the east bank of Snake river. It is a small establishment . . . under the immediate charge of Capt. Grant, an old Englishman, as rough as a grizly bear, but as full of hospitality as an old English lord. He treated us most kindly. He had his bread and cheese of his own make brought out and his 'home brewed drink' and we partook of it with a free good will. He is a fine specimen of an ancient Englishman. At the other posts we have passed we have scarcely been treated with politeness and civility. There is a good deal of business down here in the fur and [?] trade. We got some very good fresh beef for from 10 to 25 cents per pound." (Diary of John Prichet)

Thus, Richard Grant met the immigrants with a mixture of friendliness and business. T.C. Elliott lists a number of examples of favorable reports about Richard Grant's hospitality and kindness to American immigrants and travelers (See "Richard . . . Grant," *Oregon Historical Quarterly* 36 [March 1935]: 5-7, 9-13)

9. Johnny Grant was but seventeen years of age at the time.

10. More than 1½ decades later (in 1865), a newspaper correspondent described his visit to Johnny Grant's ranch in the Deer Lodge Valley: "Mounted on the top rail of a long corral, I also witnessed the skillful use of the lasso, by the vaqueros, who were branding a lot of wild Spanish cattle. Over the horns and the hind-legs flew the nooses, and the bellowing beeve was thrown and branded 'G' by Johnny himself." (12/16/1865, *Montana Post* [Virginia City, MT])

# 2

## WHEREIN HE PREFERS THE HARDSHIPS OF
## THE VANCOUVER TRAIL TO HIS HOME.

I got ready, and we started on the tenth of January 1849.[1] It looked as though we were to have a severe winter. That was one time I thought if my mother had been living I would not have had so hard a trip before me, nor have to leave my own home.

The express[2] consisted of ten men and thirty head of horses, the best that the Hudson's Bay Company could get—the choice of two hundred that the company owned. One fine team of white horses were called the snow horses. They had been out all summer doing nothing; they did not even have a halter on, till we reached the foot of the Blue Mountains. Then a man put on snow shoes and led them ahead, each in turn, to break the road through the snow which was very deep. The rest of the horses would follow.

All the provisions we started with was dried meat. A couple of the bales of meat were from a domestic bull that had been killed by another bull. It was very tough; it must have been given to us by mistake. Whether this was the case or not we had no other food to eat—no salt or flour, nor tea. We had a very hard time and a severe winter, as we anticipated. It generally took a month, but this winter I have reference to, it took us all winter to go.

It was on that trip that I witnessed such misery and poverty among Digger Indians[3] on the Salmon [Snake] River. They are a very poor band of Indians living on roots, ants, crickets, wild sunflowers and wild rye grass seed. They gather the seeds in the fall for the winter, while they get the crickets in the latter part of the summer. When the nights are cool, the crickets get on the sage bushes; then the Indians gather them in a basket in which there were hot coals. They sweep them in with a fan made of willows, and they shake the basket to scorch them; then they empty them into another basket and repeat the operation until they have enough. After that they dig a hole in the ground and make a fire and then put stones in it. As soon as they were hot, they took the coals out and put in the crickets and covered them with green grass and made a big fire over them, and let them cook for twenty-four hours. When they took them out they looked like dates in appearance, but not in flavor. .

The ants were gathered in a somewhat different way. Wild sunflowers generally grow about the anthills and in the fall are dry. The Indians gather and break them up and place the sticks around the anthills and set fire to them. Before lighting the fire they stick upright stakes in the center of the anthills; and as soon as the fire begins to heat [up], the ants crawl up the sticks. As soon as the stick was covered with ants, it was pulled up and the ants shaken into a basket in which there were coals which scorched them. They were then ready for serving as food. The wild rye grass was simply pulled up and the seeds gathered.

Wild sunflower seed was gathered and crushed on a broad flat stone by means of another stone, round like a roller. This ground the seed into meal which was used to thicken a kind of stew made out of crickets and ants. It is looked upon as a delicious dish. I have eaten sunflower seeds; they are good, but the crickets and ants I always refused.

As to the roots, there was one kind which was good and I have eaten it. It was like a small white onion,[4] poisonous they said when raw, but good when cooked in the same way as the crickets. Sometimes they were cooked in hot ashes; and when they were finished, they were yellow and shining as though they had been cooked in syrup. Another root they called yams was something like a carrot, but tasted like almonds. These are eaten raw or cooked. They are also dried for winter use and are ground into a meal. Another kind they called kowse [couse] was round about the size of a pigeon egg; one kind was cream colored and another white, but they taste about alike.

The only meat they generally used was that of a small kind of a grey rabbit about eight inches in length. They were very good to eat and they made robes out of the pelt[s]. They killed an antelope occasionally with poisoned arrows. They made this poison out of roots or herbs and dipped the arrows in it. As soon as the arrows reached the blood of the victim, it was doomed. Then the Indians would follow the track of the antelope and get them.

But that winter on account of the severe weather, their provisions had got low and they were on the verge of starvation. When they saw us coming, they would go ahead of us and reach the camping place first, for they knew every camping spot in their country. They would gather a supply of dry sage bushes for one campfire, with the expectation of something to eat; and when we were through with a meal, we would hand them what we had left. It was a sight to see them dip their fingertips into our kettle, then hold them up skimming the fat on the broth.

The first horses we killed were in a fairly good condition and they could get some fat, but with later ones, the broth was like water. We were compelled to eat horse flesh, for our provisions were done. I will never forget my first meal of horse flesh. It was on the Snake River near the Salmon Falls. I think these falls are among the highest in America. The Indians generally go there every spring to kill salmon and sturgeon, for they are very plentiful in spring and summer. They dry them for future use.

1. The date "1848" on the original handwritten manuscript was crossed off and replaced with "1849."
2. The route taken by the "winter express" led westward across the Snake River Plain of present-day southern Idaho, over northeast Oregon's Blue Mountains to Fort Walla Walla on the Columbia River, and down the latter stream through the Cascade Range to Fort Vancouver. This line of communication had been established in the first years of the Pacific Northwest fur trade era (1810s). By the 1840s, it was, with some variations, also the westernmost portion of the famous Oregon Trail of the immigrant era. By 1849, more than 13,000 pioneers already had passed this way to settle in the Willamette Valley and the Puget Sound country.
3. Classified by anthropologists as Western Shoshoni (or Shoshone), the semi-nomadic "Diggers" largely lacked horses and were loosely affiliated in family units. The Western Shoshoni occupied vast expanses of the drier inter-mountain West, extending from southeastern California, across the Great Basin, and as far north as southern Idaho and southeastern Oregon.
4. Grant apparently is describing "white" camas, which is distinguished by its white flower. It lost its poisonous effects when prepared properly by Native Americans. Blue-flowered camas, which is non-poisonous and more widely found throughout the Pacific Northwest region, was harvested extensively by tribes in the Columbia Plateau.

# 3

## IN WHICH THE WINTER EXPRESS WAS REDUCED TO EATING HORSEFLESH.

One evening I went along with two young half-breeds to the falls to see if we could not get some ducks, for the river never freezes there. When we came back to camp, they had killed a horse and already had their supper. The only piece of cooked meat that was left for me was a piece of the entrails. I do not know whether this was intended as a joke on me, being the factor's son; but whatever was their object, I did not give them the satisfaction to turn up my nose at it. I ate it without saying a word, although it was hard to swallow. I made up my mind not to let anyone know that I couldn't take it. After that I could eat my share of horse flesh, which was not a trifle, for I helped to eat eleven head of horses on that trip. The first ones we ate were not bad, for they were the eldest and were in good order. But soon the young horses had to be killed, many of them fine young horses that had been sent on that trip to be broken in. I was sorry, but we could not do otherwise for we had nothing else to eat.

My saddle horse was one of the first they decided to kill, for he was not known, having been bought the summer before from immigrants passing through the country. I liked the horse, however; and every time they spoke of killing him, I begged to have his life spared. They left him to me, and he turned out to be a very fine horse—a valuable blood horse. I tried to get him afterwards from my father and told him how I had begged to have his life spared; but he was considered too fine a horse for me. He gave it to his step-daughter, Jemima. It was not the only time she was preferred to me.

The last horses we killed were not very palatable. The last one was tired out the day before and could not reach camp, so the men went back for him in the morning and killed him. He was very tough. We had to boil the meat for some time to make it eatable. Even then the more we chewed the meat, the larger and more elastic it got. It was like a piece of sponge in the mouth. The poor Indians could not find fat on that broth. They must have suffered from the intense cold too, for all the clothing they had on consisted of a breech cloth and a rabbit skin robe about four feet square on their backs. They made a pitiful sight. Some of the old men had burns on them from sitting too close to the fire. Their huts were made of hay and bark.

When we got to the foot of the Blue Mountains, we could not go any further on account of the snow in the mountains. So some of the men went on snow shoes to take the express to [Fort] Walla Walla.[1] The rest of the party waited until the snow softened. We had been waiting about ten days when my father caught up to us with the spring outfit. There were sixteen in his party, my brother Richard with them. They had 100 head of horses to get the supplies from Fort Vancouver for the inland posts.

There were so many men and horses now, we undertook to cross the [Blue] mountains.[2] When we reached the Malad [Umatilla] River, my father bought a cow and a horse from the Cayuse Indians[3] to butcher. The Indians had large bands of horses and cattle. The side hills from the mountains were covered with trails. There was a young Chief who owned five hundred head, all blue roans. Another called Five Crows[4] had five hundred head as well. It was common among them for one Indian to own fifty or one hundred head of horses.

When we got to Fort Walla Walla, we found everybody there eating horse flesh, even the Factor, for horses were cheaper than cattle. There also the Indians had large bands of horses. One chief called Yellow Snake had one thousand head and as many cattle. Those Indians were peaceable at that time, but that same Yellow Snake was afterwards killed by the Americans.[5]

While we were there, we heard the gold mines had been discovered in California.[6] My brother Richard wanted to go and coaxed father to let me go with him. When we got to [Fort] Vancouver, my father was very liberal towards me for he gave me a hundred dollar outfit—all I ever got from him. I suppose he thought I would need it in going to California. We were then eight hundred miles from California, eight hundred miles from Fort Hall, and it was eight hundred miles from Fort Hall to California. We decided to go back to Fort Hall for my brother's wife and bring her with us to California, so we went back.

1. In 1818, Canadian fur traders of the North West Company established Fort Walla Walla at the junction of the Walla Walla and Columbia rivers. Standing on the Columbia's east bank, the post originally was named Fort "Nez Perces," or Fort "Numipu" after the Nez Perce Indians' name for themselves ("Numipu" in the tribe's Sahaptin tongue translates as "the Real People"). In actuality, the Nez Perces' homeland was located farther east in the Columbia Basin and they were only visitors to the fort's locality. More correctly, Cayuse bands and particularly the Walla Walla tribe occupied the lands of the lower Walla Walla watershed. In recognition of this fact, the post eventually came to be called Fort Walla Walla.

   From this key geographical location, North West Company and then Hudson's Bay Company fur hunters traded for Indian horses, which abounded in the region. Brigades from here participated in the extensive exploration and exploitation of fur resources of southern Idaho and eastern Oregon, and the adjoining parts of Nevada, Utah, Wyoming, and Montana. After the Oregon Treaty of 1846 established the international boundary with Canada at the 49th parallel, this area became U.S. territory, but British traders were allowed to remain in occupation of this and other posts on American soil.

   The HBC, however, abandoned the post at the outbreak of the Yakima War (1855-58). Subsequently, it was pillaged and partially burned down by Walla Walla warriors. Today, the site is inundated by the McNary Dam reservoir. The post is commemorated at a nearby roadside pullout, where a cut-stone monument, interpretive marker, and stones from the fort's original foundation are located. (Ron Anglin, *Forgotten Trails*, 61-4, 131-32)

2. For a detailed description of a fur brigade's back-breaking efforts to tramp out a trail in deep mountain snow, see the account by Alexander Ross in *The Fur Hunters of the Far West*, 224-35. In March and April 1824, it took twenty-one agonizing days for Ross' 50 men and 240 horses to beat a similar trail through deep drifts from the headwaters of the Bitterroot River over a pass into the Big Hole Valley.

3. A little more than a year earlier, on November 29, 1847, some elements of the Cayuse tribe had destroyed the Whitman Mission, located near present-day Walla Walla, Washington. Presbyterian missionary Dr. Marcus Whitman (1802-47), his wife Narcissa, and twelve others died in this sanguinary affair. The attack was sparked by the Cayuse's alarm at the increasing rate of deadly sickness among their population, by the continuing American immigration over the Oregon Trail (which passed through Cayuse lands), and by mutual cultural misunderstanding between the Indians and the missionaries (which was further confounded by Protestant and Catholic disputes).

   At the time of the attack, American pioneers were overwhelmingly concentrated in the settlements west of the Cascade Range, especially in the Willamette Valley. Shortly, they organized militia companies to attempt to capture the Cayuse attackers. Consequently, in the spring of 1848, mounted Oregon volunteers had proceeded eastward up the Columbia River. After several armed engagements with the Cayuse, they occupied the Umatilla and Walla Walla areas, as the conflict ground down to a stalemate. The troops then largely withdrew from the region.

   Consequently, when Grant's brigade of Canadians crossed the Blue Mountains and arrived in Cayuse territory in early 1849, a state of warfare still existed between factions of the Cayuse tribe and the Americans. However, the Indians remained on good terms, or at least were not hostile, to the British and French Canadians, or "King George men" as they were called by the tribes. The HBC continued to occupy Fort Walla Walla, and Canadian travelers and Catholic priests proceeded unmolested through the region.

Eventually, in 1849-50, the tribe agreed to surrender five warriors as the perpetrators of the attack, and hostilities ended. (For an overview, see Robert H. Ruby and John A. Brown, *The Cayuse Indians*)

4. "Young Chief" (Tauitau) and Five Crows were prominent Cayuse leaders. Neither chief participated in the destruction of the Whitman Mission, though Five Crows later was wounded in early 1848 during a battle with the Oregon militia.

5. During the Cayuse War (1847-50), the Walla Wallas and their highly regarded chief, Yellow Snake (Peo Peo Mox Mox; Yellow Serpent or Yellow Bird), stood aloof from the warring Cayuse factions, while remaining on good terms with the Oregon militia. A half-decade later, however, the Walla Wallas joined in the much more consequential conflagration known as the Yakima War (1855-58), which involved numerous Columbia Basin tribes. Yellow Snake's seizure by the territorial militia in December 1855 helped instigate a four day battle in the Walla Walla drainage between volunteer troops and the Walla Wallas, during which time the captive chief was murdered. The warriors eventually withdrew from the battlefield. (Alvin M. Josephy, Jr., *The Nez Perce Indians and the Opening of the Northwest*, 346, 348-50)

6. On January 24, 1848, millwright/carpenter James W. Marshall discovered gold in a new sawmill's tailrace in California's Sierra Nevada. Within months, news of the discovery began spreading to Oregon, Mexico, Hawaii, and eventually the East and Europe, setting off California's great gold rush, particularly in 1849 and the years immediately following.

# 4

## IN WHICH SOMETHING IS RELATED OF THE DOUGLAS'S FAMILY AND LIFE AT FORT VANCOUVER.

But I must say a word about Fort Vancouver,[1] where we stopped a couple of weeks to get the supplies. I enjoyed the life at the fort, for there were several bright young women there, the wives of the clerks and daughters of Mr. [James] Douglas and other officials. The clerks' rooms opened into the big common room that served as mess room, and the ladies teased me greatly, but I liked it.

One day Mr. Douglas came into the mess room and found four or five of them trying to take me prisoner.

"That's how you pass your time, my Johnny," he said.

They laughed very heartily at me.

I was fond of little Jane Douglas, a bright mischievous girl. She afterward married A.G. Dallas who came to Winnipeg in the sixties as Governor of the Company. I did not find Mr. Douglas the terrible, strict man I had expected from what my father said, but perhaps that was because I was only a visitor and not working for him.

That was an historic year for Fort Vancouver, because that summer [1849] the company moved its stores across the new [U.S./Canadian] boundary to Victoria [on Vancouver Island], where Mr. Douglas was again in charge. This man is the same officer of the company who afterward did so much in building up British Columbia and became Sir James Douglas.

When all the supplies were ready, my father sent the train of pack horses ahead to The Dalles to meet the boats in which we brought the supplies up the river. We had to pull on the oars for two hundred miles up the Columbia River, something I had never done before. My hands soon blistered even between the fingers, so that they stood wide apart, dry and painful. We had to portage over many places.

I remember at the first place we had to portage, big Johnny Whiteford loaded me with my father's kitchen (which consisted of cooking utensils and provisions) and which weighed about seventy-five pounds.

Then he took two little bags and put them over my head saying, "You are a big boy and strong."

I was big and weighed one hundred and sixty-four pounds at that age—seventeen years—but I was not strong enough for that load, because I did not go more than two hundred yards with it. It was pulling my head down, so I backed up against the bank and let the bags fall down. Then I found they were two sacks of gun balls weighing each eighty-two pounds. When we got to The Dalles, I was obliged to help pack the horses that were going to Fort Hall. Every morning I had to catch nine horses and pack them. It was no child's play to handle those packs with my sore hands.

On my way back I traded with the Indians. In that outfit my father had given me there were six pairs of blankets. I traded these and a few other trinkets for eleven head of horses. When we got back to Fort Hall, we went out along the [Oregon/California] trail to trade with the immigrants. We did not go to California.

I said to myself, "This country is good enough for me."

Sometimes we had quite a bit of sport with the immigrants, for there were some that were very green and very inquisitive. They would come into the Indian store and take a look around and ask what is this or what is that. On one occasion, a big tall Missourian who came in got interested in several bunches of castorums hanging in the store. These are certain glands taken from the beavers and used by the trappers as bait. He asked so many questions about them that my father told him they were prairie figs, and he actually wanted to eat one and broke it, but the odorous gum and oil running out of it soon undeceived him.[2]

My father was always ready to spring some joke on them.

That summer was my first on the immigrant road. I did not trade much for the very good reason that I did not have much to trade with. I had only a few head of oxen, so I went back with my father to Fort Hall in the autumn.

1. Established by the Hudson's Bay Company in 1824-25, Fort Vancouver stood on the north bank of the Columbia River, a few miles upstream from the mouth of the Willamette River and north of present-day Portland, Oregon. For more than two decades, this agriculturally and commercially diverse outpost served as headquarters of the HBC's vast operations west of the Rocky Mountains. British occupation continued after the Oregon Treaty of 1846, and the last vestiges of the HBC's long presence here were not removed until 1860.

2. The original passage in the Johnny Grant manuscript describing this prank was crossed out and replaced by the above refined version rewritten by someone with delicate sensibilities. The original (and livelier) entry read as follows:

"On one occasion, although I laughed at the poor fellow like the others, I pitied him. He was a big tall Missourian. He came in and as usual looked around the store. There was quite a few bunches of Castorums hanging in the store. These are certain glands taken from the beavers and used by the trappers as bait.

"He said to my father, 'Cap.' pointing at them, 'what are those?'

"My father replied, 'Why don't you know what they are? Why those are prairie figs.'

"'Prairie figs,' he said, 'I declare I never saw any. Are they good to eat?'

"'For those that like them.'

"'Can I taste one?' he said.

"My father said, 'Certainly you may.'

He picked one, a good full one, and took a bite in the centre of it. As he did so the gum and oil was running down on each side of his mouth. It was comical to see him making faces and trying to spit out the prairie fig he had tried to eat. For some time he could not speak.

"At last he exclaimed, 'They might be good for those who like them, but I declare I do not.'"

# 5

## WHEREIN HIS FRIENDS AT THE GARRISON INTRODUCE EGG-NOGG TO HIM WITH FATEFUL RESULTS.

In the winter of 1848 and 1849 [1849-50] there were two companies [Regiment of Mounted Riflemen] of American soldiers—Company "B" and Company "F"—who wintered near Fort Hall.[1] Their teams, having got tired out, they built winter quarters and wintered there about five miles from the fort. I was the white-headed boy of the garrison. I was the only young man around there then and the only one who could get liquor at the settler's store. The soldiers sent me off with their leather canteens and when I came around they would catch hold of me. If I had those canteens, full under my arms, they would play with me and put their mouths to the canteens. Then I would give first one and then another canteen a squeeze. That was my way of treating the soldier boys.

On Christmas my father sent me with some horses to the officers for them to come and spend Christmas with him. My father was jolly and liked to have others enjoy themselves too. When I got to the garrison, they offered me a bowl of some kind of drink. I did not know what it was. I drank some and handed back the bowl, but they told me to drink it all; so I did. It made me good and drunk. That was the first time I tasted liquor. It was eggnog, and I will never forget it. The officers started for the fort. I rode around with the soldiers for awhile; then I went home.

I lived inside the fort, with an interesting old character named Laurent, in a house made of adobe with one parchment window; so it was never very light inside. When I got to the door, I heard a noise inside.

I felt very brave all of a sudden and said without meaning any harm and just to hear myself talk, "What is all this noise about? I will clear the house."

I was caught by the coat collar.

I naturally tried to free myself.

Someone struck me and, of course, I struck back saying, "Oh! it is hit all around," and I had the misfortune to hit my father.

I did not even know he was there, but he knew it was me who struck him.

He said in a loud voice, "What, you hit your father?"

That blunder nearly sobered me. For a few minutes there was quite an uproar. In the melee they forgot me. I slipped out quietly and got my horse and went back to the barracks. I rode back and forward the balance of the night. It was a cold night, and my coat held together only at the collar; it was torn in two. The officers and my father kept up their frolic until morning. When everything was quiet, I went to my own quarters. Afraid to lay down on the bed, I crawled under it.

I was not long there, trembling with fear and feeling sick, when someone called me, "Johnny!"

I knew it was a friendly voice, so I answered.

It was the quartermaster and he said, "Come to the barracks with us. Your father swears he will kill you."

I accepted his invitation and ran out to find my horse ready, waiting for me.

While I was at the garrison, I went to see a man named Nadeau and told him my trouble.

He said, "Never mind, my Johnny. If he comes here I will kill him."

After that I thought I was safe. After I had a sleep, I went to my brother Richard. He was camped half-way between the fort and the soldiers' barracks. I was sitting in his home planning for the future, when the sound of horses galloping aroused me from my plans. I looked out of the door.

It was my father with one of his hired men. He was riding a large roan horse; and although he was over sixty years then,[2] he rode as straight as a rush.

He called out, "Johnny!"

One thinks quickly at such a time. I knew I had turned out my horse, so I could not get away. I simply had to face the situation.

I ran out saying, "Yes, sir."

"Hold my horse," he said in a stern voice.

I obeyed. He dismounted, reached over the saddle, and drew his pistol, an old fashioned English pistol that carried an ounce ball. I fancied I could see the ball coming. Poor old father. If he did that to frighten me, he succeeded, for I really thought he meant it. I did not stop to consider. I let the horse go and ran.

There was a spring close by in the direction I ran; and instead of going around, I went across it. I got drenched, for it was not frozen. I ran on without looking back. I had on a leather shirt, and the fringes, being wet, rattled. I heard that noise and fancied it was the noise of horses galloping, so I imagined my father was at my heels. Coming to a bunch of bushes, I stopped to rest for I was tired. I did not see anyone following me. I turned back and went on, not to my brother's home first, but to the barracks; on my way there hiding behind every bunch of willows until I got out of sight of the house.

I went to my sympathizing friend Nadeau and told him my fresh troubles. I wanted to be sure if he would keep his promise, for I was certain my father wanted to kill me. I thought if one of us must die, it was better that my father should. Nadeau told me that he meant to keep his word. I was terror stricken. I thought I was the most miserable boy in the world.

I passed the night there, but did not sleep much. Anyone can imagine the state I was in the next morning. I went to my brother's to get news, for I was uneasy. My brother told me that my father wanted me to go home.

He added, "He wants you to go to Salt Lake with him."

"I will not go," I said. "Father says that only to induce me to go back."

He replied, "You know he cannot go to Salt Lake alone without a guide."

"Well, if he really wants me to go with him," I said to Richard, "come with me."

He came.

When I got home, I went to my father's room and I said, "Good morning, father. How are you?"

"That is not the way to come," he said, "after hitting your father. You should beg his pardon."

I replied, "I do not see why I should ask your pardon. I did not mean to strike you, for I did not imagine you were there."

He did not say much more, but told me he wanted me to go with him to Salt Lake. After I returned home he never mentioned that row.[3]

Shortly after, an Indian made me a present of a mare. I was so glad, I went to tell my father of my good fortune. Instead of congratulating me on my good fortune, he was vexed and told me I had no right to trade within a mile of the fort.

I answered, "I did not trade; the Indian gave me the horse."

He asked me, "What did you give him?"

I said, "My old blanket and one of my shirts."

"What will you sleep on yourself now?" he said.

"There are many blankets in the store," I said.

"But they are not for you. They belong to the Hudson's Bay Company."

"There are plenty robes about."

"Yes, sleep on a robe like an Indian," he said scornfully.

That was all I had slept on since I came back to him.

"Well Father," I said to him at last, "what do you want me to do? You say I will never be worth my salt. How can I here, working for the company, while you do not pay me anything? I would not mind it, if it was for yourself, but you do not want me to trade. What can I do here?"

"Well," he replied slowly, "if you do not like this place, you can go."

I went then, feeling as though I had nothing to hope for on earth.

1. In the summer of 1849, soldiers of the U.S. Army's Regiment of Mounted Riflemen established a temporary military post (Cantonment Loring) four miles northeast of Fort Hall. The post was named after the regiment's one-armed commander, Colonel William Loring. The veteran regiment recently had served with distinction in the Mexican War (1846-48), participating in Scott's Vera Cruz campaign and the capture of Mexico City. In 1849, the regiment undertook its historic journey over the Oregon Trail from Fort Leavenworth to Fort Vancouver and Oregon City, becoming the first U.S. troops to be billeted in the Old Oregon Country—five companies were assigned to the lower Columbia area, while four companies established quarters at Fort Laramie and near Fort Hall. (See Raymond W. Settle, ed., *The March of the Mounted Riflemen*)

2. Johnny Grant is mistaken about his father's age; Richard Grant was yet in his mid 50s. Johnny thought his father was four years older than he was, and frequently mistook the ages of other family members as well.

3. In early 1849, Richard Grant wrote to Governor George Simpson, overseer of the vast HBC holdings in North America, about the possibilities of the Grant boys entering the company's service. Richard Grant felt Stanislas Richard was too old to join the HBC, but he had hopes for Johnny: "As to Johnny he has not want of life & I believe will hold his own, with either Indians or whites. He already understands the Snake Language, sufficient to serve as my Interpreter when no better is at hand. Whoever has informed you that John has taken to himself a wife, has imposed on you, the Lad is only now a little above 15 years of age, women are the least of his thoughts." (Richard Grant to Sir George Simpson, 1/4/1849, HBCA, D.5/24 fos 26-29)

# 6

## WHEREIN HE LEAVES HIS FATHER'S HOME AND
## TAKES UP LIFE WITH THE TRAPPERS.

I gave an Indian a horse for a leather lodge and went to live in the cedars about eight miles from the fort with some trappers. I killed a big ox, and my little dog and I lived on it all winter. I was away from home half of the time. I would go to the barracks and stay there three or four days or sometimes at my brother's house. Then I came home thinking of my lot, of the present, the past, and the future. I remembered that the only thought which comforted me when I left my dear sister [in eastern Canada] was that I should again see my father, my only parent. I got hot with anger when I remembered how I had been treated since I came home; perhaps because other children had taken my place in my father's affection. And now I was driven away from home by my own father! He did not care where I went. If my dear mother had been living, it would have been different. She would not have nagged me as my father's wife did, and she would never have let my father turn me out because I wanted to make a living for myself.

I turned to drink some then. Grief and vexation were the cause of my taking to drink; it surely was not the love of it, for if I drank one day, the next day I was sick and could not touch it. I had to pay two dollars and a half for a pint and it was bad at that price. I was the only one who could get any liquor at the settler's store. So drinking and visiting was the way I passed the winter among the trappers with whom I was living.

There was one trapper named Michand Leclair, a Creole from St. Louis, Missouri. He had been in the country for thirty-two years before my time. I liked the old man and we were the best of friends. He told me many stories of the early days. Some were very interesting and I only wish I could have remembered them all. He said in the early days the Indians were very hostile and warlike. The white trappers had to organize in a body with a captain as leader and had to be always on their guard, ready in case of an attack by the Indians.

One time he said there were twenty white trappers who came to the camp of a band of the Snake tribe, whose chief was called Mauvais Gauché (which means the Wicked Left-handed One). He invited the trappers to sit down and have a friendly smoke with him. When they accepted the invitation, he told them the Indians were afraid of their guns, so the trappers laid down their guns. An Indian was sitting beside each trapper. The moment the trappers were disarmed a signal was given by the chief and each Indian stabbed his man. There was only one trapper who escaped.

Leclair told me also a story about a man named [Louis] Vasquez, a Creole, a partner of [Jim] Bridger after whom Ft. Bridger was named. He was very fond of drink and spent freely so that he would often get hardup. When any noted Indian died, as it was customary to mourn the dead, he would put an old robe on his back and go up on a hill and cry and yell in the true Indian style. The Indians would go to him and ask him the cause of his grief. He would tell them he was so sorry for his departed brother and keep on crying. That would soften their hearts toward him, and they would give him robes and skins to comfort him. He would still continue to cry until he had enough robes and skins; then he would dry his tears and go home.

On another occasion he had been to St. Louis and spent nearly all his money. On leaving he bought a stock of needles.

After he returned, he went to the Indian camp and said to them, "My brothers," showing them the needles, "see how I like you. The man who makes needles is dead, so I thought of you and bought all the needles I could get for my friends."

The poor simple Indians believed him, and got a robe for every buckskin needle he had. Vasquez knew that if you show an Indian that you think something of him or do him a favor, he will not forget it. He will do anything for you even years after. But it is the same with a wrong. He will not forget it and he will retaliate years after.

Indians have different ways of punishing their victims. They do not always kill them. The Crow Indians, old Michand told me, would play with their prisoners and tease them. He said one time there was an old Creole named Regis who was very ugly and blind in one eye. He also had a very bad temper. It appears he was taken prisoner by the Crow Indians. Then the Indians stood in two files and compelled the old man to pass between them. Each Indian would strike him, some with an arrow, others with a ramrod, while some would whip him. The old man got angry and could not control his temper.

He said to them in French, "Hurry up, I will get angry in a minute."

The Indians did not understand him and it made them laugh, for he was twisting his body in all shapes and making faces. This only made them tease him more, and the unfortunate old man had to bear it. If he could have retaliated, he certainly would have done so, for he was no coward.

There is another story of a Ute named Anthorope, a mean contemptible rascal. If a white man did not trade with him as he wished, he would spill their ammunition on the grass. One time he tried to take old Regis' powder sack to spill it, but Regis objected and struck him on the head with the stock of his gun. The Indian saw that Regis was not afraid of him, but he would not give in.

He began to lament in the way Indians do, and said, "If you were not so ugly I would kill you, but your parents would not cry for you, you are so ugly."

So Regis struck him again.

Another of this Indian's tricks was to refuse to pay his bets. He would sulk and men would let him alone. One day he was camped in the neighborhood where I was. He came and challenged me to run horses with him, and I won several deer skins from him. When the races were over, he took the skins and sat on them, putting his blanket over his head and sulked.

David Contois, who was with me, said, "He does not intend to give them up; that is his way."

I replied, "I will see."

I went to him and pulled the skins from under him saying, "Get off from there."

He rolled off, but did not get up. He did not say a word. I got my skins. I knew if I had asked him for them he would not give them. You must never let an Indian see that you are afraid of him.

# 7

## IN WHICH IS RELATED TALES OF ONE OLD TRAPPER, AND HOW A NEW LODGE WAS SET UP.

Old Michand told me that when he first came to the country the people bought and sold their wives, and sometimes these were sold for a high price. There was one squaw who sold for two hundred beavers, which means over five hundred dollars. That was not long before my time, for I saw this woman. One Jack Robinson had her and her sister for wives.[1] She was called Antelope. I could not see why, for I am certain she was not as swift as one, and she was very short and stout. I cannot think why she brought such a high price. I do not think it was on account of her beauty, but I suppose that depends on one's fancy.

Michand had been in many places in the Indian country. One time when he was with the Pawnee Indians,[2] a preacher came to preach the gospel to them. He was telling them about the cruel men who had crucified our Saviour.

They asked him who these men were.

He said, "The Jews."

"Well," they replied, "we are not Jews. We are the Pawnees, so go on, old man."

Old Michand had had some rough encounters in his day. He had scars on his face which, when I asked about them, he said he got in a scrap with a grizzly bear. One day in the woods he shot a bear, wounding him, and he began to follow it very carefully along a little path. The bear at last circled around the man on the path. Michand turned as quickly as he saw this, but the bear was upon him. He tried to shoot, but his rifle caught in the bushes; and while he was trying to get it loosened, the bear caught him and tore the skin of his head close to his eyes. He also bit him in one shoulder and hip, and laid down beside him. It must have been a trying sensation to find oneself lying down all torn with a grizzly beside you waiting for your death. He said he moved a little to see if the bear was dead, but he was not. The bear got up and caught Michand by the loins and tried to drag him into the bushes. Michand grabbed the bushes and hung on for his life. The bear tugged at him, getting weaker and weaker, and at last sank down and died, so Michand was free.

Old as he was when I knew him, Michand was still brave and daring. I know when I lived near him, if he saw a bear he would make a circle around to meet it, then shoot it when he was very close.

He was quite a singer. He would take a book, lay on his back, and sing French hymns. He held the book upside down, and it was a German book at that, but he did not care for he did not even know his alphabet. Nevertheless, he was a nice old man and played with me like a young boy. He was quite a comfort to me during my bachelor life that winter, especially when I felt so much forsaken by my friends.

I did not hold a grudge against my father. I suppose he thought he was right, and he was my father. I went to the fort occasionally to see him.[3] I often saw Jemima, whom I hated so much at first, but now, when she had come back from school in Oregon, I thought something of her for she did not trouble me any. Besides that, within the last two years, she had grown to be quite a nice young lady. She seemed to suit my fancy in every way, and I was her choice among the men there. So we both came to the conclusion that we should get married.

I asked my father's consent, but he flatly refused to give it. He gave me to understand that I was no match of Jemima and for one reason he gave that I drank. I had been drinking that winter, but who was to blame for it?

He said to me, "And if you marry her, the Hudson's Bay officers will say that I married my son to my step-daughter because she had money."

A curious idea for refusing. Just what would make other people advise their son or daughter to marry?[4] So I thought if your step-daughter is too good for me, sir, I will take a squaw. And I did. I took a woman who had been the wife of a chief's son, but who had left him.

My father soon sent me a note by the woman's husband, saying if I did not want himself and the Indians to be against me, I must give up that squaw.

I answered back that she was welcome to go if she wished, but she wanted to remain. "Neither you nor the Indians can take her from me."

She did not want to go, for she did not like her husband. I kept her; but my father, thinking to conquer me, sent that same Indian to steal my horses, and he brought them to the fort. I lost some time looking for them. I never imagined they would be at the fort; but when I heard they were there, I went and without any trouble brought them home with me. I also kept the squaw.

The Indians did not trouble me. I kept the woman, not because I cared for her, but for spite. She was a good woman, a faithful wife and a kind mother. She was industrious, clean and saving and in all a great help to me, for I was poor, young and inexperienced. She was very handy at leather work, and every kind of it sold well then to the immigrants.

Every summer we went on the road to trade with these newcomers at Soda Springs.[5] I traded for lame cattle and they were always the best, because somehow the best got lame the quickest. I raised my cattle from that stock, and after some years I had over one thousand head of the best bred cattle that ever came to Montana. Every winter we went to the mountains, five hundred miles from Fort Hall, to trade with the Indians. In the spring we had to hurry back before the Indians began to move, for they would steal our horses. We would come back to Fort Hall; and as soon as the immigrants were on the road, we were there to trade. I led that life for nine years, camping with the Indians and on the move all the time like them. I liked it. I once thought I would always live with the Indians. I would not have exchanged my leather lodge for the finest residence in any city; still, I left it.

1. Sororal polygyny (i.e., sisters married to the same man) was a traditional form of polygynous marriage among a number of Great Plains and Rocky Mountain tribes.
2. The traditional homeland of the Pawnee was the vast Platte River country in what is now Nebraska.
3. Richard Grant reported to Sir George Simpson,: "My Sons Richard and John have Now left Me and are trying what they can do on their own hooks. They have placed themselves in the neighborhood of the Troops Stationed a few miles from this Establishment. I believe one or both intend going to California Ensuing Summer." (Richard Grant to Sir George Simpson, 2/22/1850, HBCA, D.5/27 fos 335-337)

   Governor Simpson, in his usually caustic style, replied: "I notice that your sons Richard & John have both left you to seek their fortunes in California, in which I shall be glad to learn that they are successful, thereby relieving you of the burden of their maintenance." (Sir George Simpson to Richard Grant, 6/18/1850, HBCA, D.4/71)

   The Grant boys, however, did not go to California.

4. Johnny Grant was 5½ years older than his stepsister, to whom, of course, he was not related by blood. Jemima eventually married William Sinclair III (Glen Lindeman and Keith Petersen, "The Kittson Legacy," 4, family chart). She resided for many years at Victoria, British Columbia, and spoke "of her pet beaver as playmate on the bank of the Snake River, when a girl at Fort Hall." An early traveler, Judge John R. McBride, described fifteen-year-old Jemima, wearing a "scrupulously clean and neat" Indian deer skin dress, as "strikingly beautiful, with her long dark hair falling around her bare neck and shoulders." (T.C. Elliott, "Richard . . . Grant," *Oregon Historical Quarterly* 36 [March 1935]: 4-5)

5. In this period, "mountaineers" at "road ranches" frequently traded for worn out or lame horses, mules, oxen, and cattle from westward bound immigrants on the Oregon/California Trail. When given rest and time to heal, these animals usually returned to prime condition, and were valuable additions to the mountaineers' herds for trading purposes.

# 8

## WHEREIN VARIOUS INDIANS, TRIBES, AND THE
## SIOUX MASSACRES ARE DEALT WITH.

Living among the Indians and traveling with them, I learned their way of living. The tribe I lived with were the Snake Indians, to which tribe my wife belonged. They were divided into several small bands, of necessity, because they lived principally on small game. Those I lived with were called the Northern Snakes,[1] and they had a band of Bannock[2] Indians living with them also. They were peaceable, generous, and honest Indians. The women made good affectionate wives and mothers, quick to learn the ways of the whites.

This tribe fought with the whites, and I was not the only white man with them. There were several others, traders who had taken Snake wives. We always advised them to be peaceful with the whites, that it was to their advantage, as it was to the whites, for we could trade peaceable. As I said before, there were several bands, who lived in different ways according to the locality they lived in. The Snake country was a large one, extending from the Sweet Waters [Sweetwater River, Wyoming] on the immigrant road toward California for six hundred miles in length and four hundred miles wide in some places. Some of them traveled very far to hunt buffalo, which was their mainstay while it lasted, furnishing them with food, clothes and lodges. When the buffalo disappeared, it can be imagined how terrible their loss was.

There was another band, the Diggers of Akayteka, (Salmon Eaters), whom I mentioned before, when I met them on my first trip to Vancouver. They were very poor. They had a clever way of carrying fire from an old camp to a new one some miles away. They took dry sage bark and twisted it very hard; then they would light one end and carry it like a torch all the way to the next camp, so that they always had fire. They did not go very far at one time, for the Diggers rarely had horses and the women and children could not walk very far. There was a band of those Diggers on the Humboldt River called Shoshoko (The Walkers). They gave the immigrants a great deal of trouble, for they stole their horses and cattle. The others who lived on the Salmon River had salmon and mountain sheep for food, and they were called Shkoriket (Sheep Eaters).

All those Indians in general were good until the mines were discovered; then they learnt the whites' bad habits quicker than the good ones, and the miners' good habits were few indeed. Of course, there were some bad Diggers as there are bad men in every nation, and they were hard and cruel to their enemies; but often the trouble between the whites and the Indians was brought about by the whites, like the beginning of the war between the whites and the Sioux.

Some immigrants while traveling west lost a cow one year [1854]. They went back to Fort Laramie and complained to the garrison that the Sioux Indians had stolen the animal. They were not sure if it was the Indians; the cow might have only strayed away. Even if such had been the case, it was only a cow; nevertheless, thirty soldiers and a French Canadian guide commanded by a young officer [Second Lieutenant John L. Grattan], went after the Indians. They even had two cannons with them. They found a camp of Indians at Chimney Rock early in the morning at daylight [August, 19, 1854]. They fired [the cannons] at it, but they only cut down the lodge poles. The noise, however, awakened the Indians; and as they were always prepared for war, they ran out and killed every one of the soldiers except Rouleau, the guide. He was mounted on a very fast horse he had bought from me, and he escaped. [3]

Now the Indians could hardly be blamed in this case; they were only defending their lives, yet that was the way the war began between the Sioux Indians and the Americans.

The next year [on September 3, 1855] General [William S.] Harney with a regiment of soldiers came to revenge [near Ash Hollow, in Nebraska] the killing of the thirty soldiers; but the Indians would not fight. They sent two men with the white flag, the sign of peace. General Harney told them it was not peace he wanted, but war.

"Go back and tell your young men to get ready to fight," he said, and as the two Indians turned to go, his soldiers fired at them.

As might be expected, the shots startled the camps; the Indians were soon out and ready, beginning to fight.

I never heard how many soldiers were killed, but General Harney said that they had killed eight hundred Indians and that would be the last of the trouble with the Sioux. Nevertheless, the war lasted thirty years; and during that time, the Sioux killed many parties of whites. I heard some blood-curdling tales from eyewitnesses, not only in the Rocky Mountains, but even in Minnesota. General Harney said that they had killed eight hundred at the first fight; they only killed forty-two, and these were old men and women and children who could not get out of the camp.[4] There were very few warriors killed. I heard that from the whites at Fort Laramie. Personally I did not see much of the Sioux.

In the winter of 1851 I wintered at Salmon River.[5] A Mormon by the name of Bennett came to me and asked me to go in partnership with him to trade with the Indians, because I could speak Indian and was friendly with the tribes. I told him I did not have a great quantity of goods to go and trade with the Indians. Well to tell the truth, I never believed in partnership, and my life story will prove that every time I had a partner I always had the misfortune to come out a loser, as in the present instance.

Bennett said, however, "You come and we will trade your goods first, and I will give you a fifth of what I trade of mine."

So we went and traded some of my goods for about fifteen head of horses. The Indians were then going to the Flathead country. Bennett followed the Indians, and I took the horses home. Every winter in that part of the country we always had a very cold snap, generally in January, more intense cold than I have ever felt in Manitoba in the Northwest. That year was no exception, and as we were coming home across the divide, it was bitter cold. One mule got tired out so we were compelled to leave it behind on the top of the hill. My companions were in a hurry to get down in the canyon into shelter. I was left alone behind with an Indian boy poorly clad, having only a cotton shirt and two thread-bare blankets. It was not only cold, but very slippery and sliding, and the horses were tender-footed and timid about going.

There was one Indian who had a mare loaded with meat. She slipped and rolled down the mountain; it was a sight to see the meat flying in all directions. When we got to the camp, it was too late to go for the mule. The next morning I went for him, but the snow had drifted around him, and he was buried to the flanks, frozen stiff. All that were in the party were more or less frost bitten, some on their hands; others their noses or ears. One poor American trader fairly cried, suffering so much. Myself and the Indian boy with me were the only two who escaped without being frostbitten. I was very hardy in the hands, and I could stand a great deal of cold anyway.

After we got to Salmon River where my camp was, I remained a couple of days, but I had to move out of there quickly on account of the [Blackfeet] Indians, whose war parties were just beginning to roam. There was a camp of Nez Perce Indians near us. They delayed a couple of days behind us and had their horses stolen by the Blackfeet.

Mr. Bennett came back only in the spring. He had traded one hundred and twenty-seven horses, and he wanted to give me only five instead of the fifth of the number. He said he had got only seventeen head from the Indians, the balance from the whites and half-breeds. I told him I wanted my share or none. He refused to give it to me. So I told him I would wait, and that I would get even with him. I did, although I had to wait eleven years.

1. The Northern Shoshoni (or Shoshone) ranged across southern Idaho and northern Utah, whereas the Wind River Shoshoni occupied western Wyoming. Mounted bands of Shoshoni hunted buffalo and adopted other Plains Indian traits, such as the use of tipis, ceremonial clothing and accoutrements, and the warrior's urge for glory and the chase.
2. Related culturally and linguistically to the Northern Paiute of eastern Oregon, the Bannock (or Bannack) had moved to southern Idaho to live among the Shoshoni "horse" Indians, where they too had adopted a Plains-like lifestyle.
3. The famous Grattan massacre occurred 7½ miles southeast of Fort Laramie, Wyoming. A dispute over an Indian's killing of a Mormon immigrant's strayed cow escalated into a pitched fight, resulting in the deaths of Lt. Grattan, an interpreter, and all 29 soldiers of the detachment. A Brule Sioux chief also died from the exchange of gunfire. Grant was mistaken in believing that the battle occurred at Chimney Rock, which is located much farther to the east, in what is now Nebraska. (For a brief reliable account, see Robert M. Utley, *Frontiersmen in Blue*, 113-15)
4. Two days after the battle, Bvt. Brig. Gen. William S. Harney recorded, "86 killed, 5 wounded, about 70 women and children captured, 50 mules and ponies taken, besides an indefinite number killed and disabled . . . The casualties of the command amount to 4 killed, 4 severely wounded, 3 slightly wounded, and one missing, supposed to be killed or captured by the enemy." (Report of General Harney . . . Camp on Blue Water Creek, N.T., September 5, 1855, *34th Congress, 1st Session, House of Representatives, Ex. Doc. 1, Part II*, pp. 49-51)
5. Given Grant's close connections with the Snake tribe, it appears he wintered in the Lemhi/upper Salmon country of what is now east-central Idaho, where a Mormon presence also developed. Bands of Flathead, Nez Perce, Pend d'Oreille, and other wide-ranging Columbia Plateau Indians likewise frequented and wintered in this locality in their forays to and from the Great Plains to hunt buffalo.

# 9

## WHEREIN HIS FATHER RETIRES AFTER 45 [32] YEARS SERVICE WITH THE HUDSON['S] BAY COMPANY.

In the spring of 1851 my father was ordered by the company to go away north to a post called Les Porteurs. My father was getting old. He had three young daughters, so he felt unable to go so far and accordingly sent in his resignation.

Some years earlier, the company thought that post [Fort Hall] was not paying, and they sent my father there to see what he could do with it. He put the company's interests before anything in the world, and he soon put trade at Fort Hall on a paying basis. The first year he sent to England five thousand beavers, which cost the company twenty balls and powder, the equivalent of about thirty-five cents, [for] each [pelt]. In England the furs brought eighteen shilling sterling ($4.50) per pound, and some large pelts weighed as much as three pounds each. He made about the same profit on the rest of the furs he sent and averaged about the same amount every year while he was in charge of Fort Hall.

After my father left, a Mr. Maxwell was placed in charge for one year; then a Mr. McArthur replaced him. This man did not remain any longer, and at last the company abandoned the post [1856]. After my father left the fort, he went like the rest of us to trade with the immigrants in the summer and with the Indians in the mountains in the winter.[1] There was no other way of making a living.

That same spring my first child, a girl, was born. That day we had camped at a place about a day's travel from Fort Hall; and the next day we set out riding again, my wife carrying the child with her on her pony. I had begun to drink the winter before, as I have already stated; and although it made me sick, I did not mind it. It was one way of punishing my father. Foolish boy that I was. In the winter I drank and in the summer I played cards, but I never gambled a mare or cow because that would lessen too greatly the hope of increasing my stock.

It made no difference how much I was interested in a game that year or how much money I was winning. When the thought of my baby came to my mind, I instantly dropped the cards and could not be coaxed to remain to play. I was very fond of her. When she was only a few months old, I went to Salt Lake to get my supplies, and I did not forget to buy something for my baby. I bought a box of candies and one of raisins, but when I got home her mother had to eat them for the child had no teeth yet.

In 1852, my brother Richard died after a three-month illness.[2] I was now all alone and realized it. I missed him, for when I had any trouble with my father, I went to see Richard and told him about it. He was my comforter; we loved one another. What was Richard's was mine, and what was mine was his. We always agreed together; and while he was sick, I traded for him. I had to see to his business and mine. He left a wife[3] and two sons, who went home to Montreal the following year. His death left me very lonely; although since I had gone away from my father, we had been on better terms, especially after he resigned from the Hudson's Bay Company. We traveled together there and traded close to one another on the immigrant road. We were never any farther than a mile apart.

Generally the Indians were healthy, but one summer a smallpox epidemic broke out among them. There was an Old Country doctor, Sir Wm. Scifort, there at the time making a tour of the West. He vaccinated some Indians, and they went to hunt buffalo as usual that fall. But they died by hundreds. The sick were left behind lying in their lodges. Their horses and belongings were left too, and the well people fled for their lives. There were quite a number of orphans left, and my brother Richard's wife adopted two of them, a Ute boy and a Bannock girl. She took them both to Montreal; but though they were healthy, the change of climate and the diet did not agree with them. They both died young, but not before each one had proved to be very bright and skillful and of a pleasant disposition.

The winter after my brother died, in 1852 and 1853, I wintered at Salmon River. Coming back in the spring, we saw a herd of elk—at least sixty of them. It was the first time that I saw so many together. John Collins and I started after them, more for the sake of running than of killing them, for John had only an old rifle which was almost useless, and I had a bow and three arrows. I caught a race horse that I had bought from an Indian (Capote Rouge) the year before. He was a thoroughbred Indian horse. He had been crippled by running a snag in his foot, and I had given an American horse and twenty dollars for him. I had cured him, but never used him, so I thought I would try him now.

We started in pursuit of those elk. It was a fine sight to see them run. Three of them got tired and went along the river in the bushes, and the Indians killed them with stones. I separated five from the herd and ran them to the mountains; but I never shot one, although I was close to them, for I was afraid to lose my arrows. I ran just to see what my horse could do, for this cream horse could run. He was never beaten. The last time I ran him it was against six American horses, and he beat them all. The race was to be for one mile, but we ran three hundred yards more than the mile. If we had run only one mile, I might not have been so fortunate, for my cream was particularly long-winded.

1. Though Richard Grant ceased being active in HBC affairs in 1851, his resignation became official two years later. On December 13, 1853, Lieutenant John Mullan of the U.S. Army found Richard Grant, recently retired from HBC service, near Fort Hall wintering at the encampment the U.S. Army had built and occupied in 1849-50: "Arriving at Cantonment Loring, we were most kindly received by Captain Grant, formerly of the Hudson's Bay Company at Fort Hall, who, inviting us into his house, spread before us all the comforts and many of the luxuries of life, and gave us a comfortable bed under his hospitable roof—all of which none more than ourselves could appreciate; and we thus passed the night once more near the abodes of civilization. Here Captain Grant is comfortably situated, surrounded by a happy family, and . . . lives as happily and contentedly as he so well deserves." (*Pacific Railroad Explorations and Surveys*, Vol. 1, 1855, 335)

2. Many years later, Frederick John Shaw, who was Stanislas Richard Grant's grandson-in-law, stated in a letter to the Montana Historical Society that Stanislas Richard Grant was ambushed and shot in the back by a young "Buck" when crossing a river near Soda Springs. He died there from his wound several days later. Shaw, it must be noted, is not a consistently reliable source of information. (FJS to Anne McDonnell, 9/8/1935, Richard Grant file, Montana Historical Society)

   In a letter, Shaw also told historian T.C. Elliott: "Reconstructing the story it would appear that Stanislas Richard Grant, following his having been grievously wounded by the Indian was headed towards his father then at Cantonment Loring but got no further than Soda Springs where he died of his wound." (FJS to T.C. Elliott, 4/14/1935, National Park Service copy)

3. Frederick John Shaw provided additional details about the woman: "Emelie Levreau de Langi, the wife of Stanislas Richard Grant . . . following the death of her husband in 1852 . . . journeyed overland to California. There she took unto herself a second husband Don Vasquez . . . at Half Moon Bay. Don Vasquez was murdered by Indians and his wife narrowly escaped death on several occasions at the hands of the Red Men. Following much adventure this woman finally made her way to St. Louis and from there back to Three Rivers her birthplace. Later she went to Prince Edward Island, married for the third time, this time a Scotchman, and ultimately passed away in Winnipeg, Manitoba at a ripe old age. (FJS to Anne McDonnell, 9/8/1935, Richard Grant file, Montana Historical Society)

# 10

**WHEREIN HE MAKES THE ACQUAINTANCE
OF SEVERAL GAMBLERS AND DESPERADOES,
WHO HAUNTED THE TRADERS' CAMPS
ALONG THE OREGON TRAIL.**

I have already said that I gambled in the summer on the immigrant road with the other traders. In the spring of 1853 when I got back to Fort Hall Bottom from Salmon River, I made the acquaintance of a man named Clyde Ross who had come from Salt Lake. When I moved to Soda Springs, he came there also. One day I gambled with him and an immigrant named Douglas who was cheating. I lost heavily, and Ross was the winner. He was a professional gambler, but we traders did not know it. To show the kind of men the gamblers were, I will tell of a few happenings of their stay with us on the immigrant road.

Clyde Ross and one Jeffreys were partners. It appears they had bought some cattle from a man from the south, and they agreed to meet him at a certain place to pay him for the cattle; but instead of paying him they killed him. They drove the cattle to Salt Lake and Jeffreys went to Oregon while Ross remained in Salt Lake for a time. He was a man of slight build. I do not think he weighed more than one hundred pounds, but he was a determined and overbearing man. As self-preservation is the first law of nature, Clyde Ross thought it advisable to leave Salt Lake for safety's sake and came to Fort Hall Bottom. I do not know what he did with the cattle.

I did not care about gambling with him. I did twice, however, and I was the loser both times. Sometime afterwards, three men, Tibbets, Alloway, and Hatheway, came to our trading camp where we spent most of our time in horseracing and gambling, and when the immigrants passed, in trading. They were supposed to be partners, for they were always together. They were camped near me. For two weeks they came to my tent, sometimes every day or every other day. They looked at my horses and asked the price of this or that one, but did not buy any. I knew they had not the least intention of buying any.

One day they were looking at my horses as usual, and they began to argue about two of my horses. Tibbets said that one young roan horse which was not well broken would run well; Hatheway maintained that a certain brown horse was better; neither of them were race horses. They continued their argument.

At last, Tibbets asked me if I had any objection to their running those young horses a short distance.

I told them they might, so they bet five dollars.

Hatheway asked me to go halves with him.

I told him I would.

They had their own jockey, and he rode the roan, while my Indian jockey rode the brown. The Indian was whipping his horse on both sides, kicking and yelling. Still he could not beat the roan. There was a curve in the course. The colt saw my Indian and got frightened, then bucked and threw their jockey. Tibbets was as furious at losing as if it was one thousand dollars. I felt this was only pretense and that the whole thing was a scheme.

He turned to me and said, "I will bet five hundred dollars that my Sam will beat your black horse for one-quarter of a mile."

I agreed. As soon as I replied that I would, he sat down and considered for some minutes very seriously.

He then got up and said, "I am not quite so excited as I was before. I will make you another proposition, I will bet one hundred dollars."

I knew that my horse was not a quarter-of-a-mile horse, but I did not want to let him bluff me, so I said I would take him up. He sat down a second time and did a little more meditating.

Finally he said, "Johnny, I am ashamed of myself for not keeping my word with a young boy like you, so I will stick to the five hundred dollars."

"Oh!" I said, laughing, "Mr. Tibbets, one hundred dollars is enough for me to give you."

He replied pleasantly, "You are a very shrewd boy; let it be one hundred dollars."

We went to the starting point, and on the way I told Tibbets that my horse was not a quarter-of-a-mile horse.

"Well", he says, "if your horse beats mine, I will give you five hundred for your black horse, and if mine beats yours, I will give you a chance of winning yours back by racing again."

We started [the race]. On the way there was a little pool of water; my horse went around it and Sam left him.

When the race was over Tibbets said, "I will not go back on my word. You may have the opportunity of winning your money back."

He was certain to win for his horse had beaten my horse so easily, but I took him on again. We turned and ran homewards, and I rode my own horse. I noticed every time I used the whip on the right side he bolted, so I whipped on the left side. At the first stroke, I hit myself on the toes. It felt as if I had cut them off, but it was a matter of making or losing two hundred dollars, so I made good use of the whip. My horse beat Sam by the length of his head. So I was even with Tibbets.

He said to me, "We will run again in a few days."

I replied, "No, sir. I have had enough of horseracing for some time."

Ross came to me and said, "If your black horse was well trained, he would beat Sam; let me train him." I agreed and caught the horse and tied him up.

We sat down and began to play cards. I was losing heavily when a whirlwind passed over us, which frightened my horse, and he broke loose and got away. I left the cards to go for my horse, and on my way back I was thinking that it was strange how that man could win all the time. I came to the conclusion that there was some foul play. I had lost in a short time fourteen hundred and seventy-five dollars since I began to play with him. It was not in cash, but its equivalent, for I gave him horses to that amount. We did not play any more that day, and I made up my mind not to play any more with Ross.

That same night, I was in my tent and I heard someone call, "Johnny, are you asleep?"

I answered, "No."

"Well", he said, "have you a candle?"

I had one and he told me to light it. It was Alf Tomly. He said to me, "You lost heavy today." He knew it for he was looking on.

I said, "Yes, Ross won every time I played with him. I know there was foul play somewhere, but I could not find him out."

He replied, "I will tell you, if you promise me to keep it secret; for if you do not, I am a dead man."

I promised not to tell anyone.

He took a pack of cards from his pocket and showed them to me. They were all sanded, except two, and Ross and this fellow knew which cards these were. We had been playing "Monte", a Mexican game, and

Tomly explained to me how the trick had been done, but he told me I must pretend to know nothing about it. I promised, though I knew it was much easier said than done. The next day I drove my horse into the corral and paid Mr. Ross with American horses. There were some valued at two hundred dollars, and one of them was afterwards sold for seven hundred dollars at Salt Lake. Still, American horses did not suit me for riding, as they were too heavy, and I did not have any wagons then.

I did not think much of Ross, for he had abused my confidence. I avoided his company as much as possible.

A day or two afterwards I met him. Although I tried to conceal my feelings, he noticed there was something annoying me; and I think he attributed it to my loss, for he said, "Johnny, you have been a heavy loser. I will bet my roan against a leather suit that before two months I will make you even with the game."

I said to him it will be a good investment even if I lose; I would not have the horse on any consideration, for I suspected that he had got the horse dishonestly.

I had seen the horse before in the possession of an immigrant, who told me then that he was taking him to California. The horse was a fast pacer, and at that time horses of his stamp were very valuable on the Pacific coast. I heard afterwards that Ross had hired a Mormon boy to steal the horse from the owner.

# 11

## IN WHICH HE RACES HORSES WITH
## THE DESPERADOES, ONE OF WHOM COMES
## TO A TRAGIC END.

A few days later Ross said to me, "Johnny, you have an opportunity to win back what you have lost. Stratton has arrived with a race horse."

I was acquainted with Stratton, for he had come to Fort Hall to trade two years before and I had bought his outfit. Ross suggested that I go to see Tibbets, who had moved about ten miles away and who had secured sixty-four head of cattle in about two weeks' time. I was looked upon as the best trader on the road, yet I only got six head at the same time. I had seen his cattle shortly after he got them. They were not lame. I suppose he got them when the owner was either absent or asleep; I do not think he got them honestly. Ross advised me to go to Tibbets and challenge him for the race. They would lend me Stratton's horse, and I was to bet sixty-four head of my cattle against his sixty-four. If I lost, Ross and Stratton would pay me for my cattle; if I won, I was to divide with them.

Ross said, "But do not tell him which horse you are going to run."

I had made up my mind to have nothing more to do with them, but I relented now and told him I would go. It was only ten miles away and I went over the next morning.

When I reached Tibbets' place, his horse Sam had poultices on his forelegs. I had dinner with Tibbets and after dinner we chatted for a few minutes. I did not mention anything about the horse or race.

He said to me, "Johnny come down to the flat and see Sam jump."

He took the poultices off his horse's legs; there was nothing wrong with the horse; and down on the track Tibbets had made Sam show us some fast running.

When I was ready to go, he said to me, "Wait, I will go with you."

After we got on the road he said, "Any news from Soda Springs? Any newcomer?"

I replied that Stratton had arrived.

[Tibbets said,] "Has he brought a race horse?"

"Yes, I was sent here on account of that horse. Ross told me to challenge you for a race."

"Why did you not mention it before?"

I replied, "Because I do not want to have anything to do with them."

"You are right," he said. "Do you know his reason for bringing that horse?" I told him I did not.

"Well, it was for your special benefit, for that horse is mine. I know all about this race. I just want to warn you. I take an interest in you. You are too young and honest to gamble with us. We are all thieves, robbers, and murderers; but Ross is the worst. Do not waste words with him; if you have any difficulty with him, he will shoot you; simply do not let him shoot first. I know that he and Jeffreys killed the man from whom they bought those cattle."

That was the time he told me how Ross and Jeffreys got the cattle. It made me somewhat nervous. I was only twenty-one, I had never been in the company of murderers before, that I was aware of, and I concluded to avoid Tibbets and Ross.

Tibbets also said, "If you want to bet on those horses, do not bet much, just enough to see what they will do. I will give you an opportunity to win back what you have lost. I have sixty-four head of cattle; you put the same number, and we will go to Salt Lake and get an outfit and then you can go among the Indians to trade. You know the Indians, and you are a very shrewd boy."

He thought that by praising me I would consent.

He added, "I will give you half what we make."

I told him I would consider his offer, but I did not have the least intention of accepting his offer. However, I was thankful to him that he warned me against his companions, although he acknowledged that he was no better than they were.

When they found that their first plan failed, they planned to try another. On my arrival at Soda Springs I did not let Ross know the result of my visit to Tibbets. The race came off as agreed. I bet on Sam, although Tibbets had told me that John, the fine handsome horse that Stratton had brought, was a thousand-yard horse. Sam was a quarterhorse. John left Sam on the start, but Sam won the race. So it seems I would have lost my sixty-four head of cattle if I had taken Ross' advice; and I suppose if I had found any fault, I would have had my brains blown out.

I left shortly after the race took place. I went to Oregon with Jack Collins; and after I came back, I heard that Tibbets had sold Sam and a half interest in John to Jeffreys and had gone to Old Mexico along with Alloway and Hatheway. They took John with them. Some time after, Jeffreys came back, I suppose to settle with Ross concerning the cattle. He had heard that Ross complained he was posing as an honest man, not like the rest of the gang, while he (Jeffreys) was as bad, as he was himself a partner in his deals, a thief, a robber, and a murderer.

Jeffreys, knowing how treacherous Ross was, set a trap to get rid of him. He told Ross their horses were lost, and both men went to look for them. Some time after, Jeffreys came back to the Springs alone. He said that out on the plains Ross had accused him of hiding the horses, and they quarreled. Ross fired at him, but the revolver had snapped; and as he wheeled around, Jeffreys had shot him with his shotgun. This was not the case, for I was told by a reliable man that the horse hunt was only a pretense to get Ross out. It appears one of Jeffreys friends had taken the caps off Ross' pistol and put dough in the tubes. Ross had not even shot at his partner. There was nobody to interfere with the murderer, so Jeffreys then took Ross' horses and went to Oregon, where I suppose he posed as an honest citizen.

# 12

## IN WHICH HE TELLS OF HIS SUCCESS IN TRADING WITH THE IMMIGRANTS, AND OF THE MASSACRE OF ONE PARTY BY THE INDIANS.

In the summer of 1853, there was a train of immigrants killed by Indians on the Boise River about twenty miles from Fort Boise [Ward Massacre, August 20, 1854[1]]. Jack Collins and I passed the same place on our way to Oregon a few hours before the massacre was committed, and my father passed three or four hours after. While we were in Vancouver, the soldiers went after the murderers. They only took one old man and two of his wives.[2] They took them back with them to The Dalles where they were stationed.[3] When we were coming back from Vancouver, Antoine Poirier and Jack Collins had remained behind. We were told it was not safe to go back to Fort Hall, that the road was lined with Indians. But we had to go back, for my family and stock were all there.

When we got to the Blue Mountains, we waited for William Sinclair and McArthur, Hudson's Bay clerks whom we knew to be coming, and so we had company. After we had traveled four or five days, we were nearing the place where the massacre had taken place. That night when we camped, Sinclair and McArthur camped on a ridge in their tent and lighted a candle inside. I told them I thought it was not safe—they were making targets of themselves for the Indians.

"Oh, I do not think there are any Indians around," one of them replied.

"Well," I said, "I am not very brave and I do not wish to be taken by surprise."

So I called Sinclair's Indian, Oshan, a Bannock, to come to see the horses with me. We went round the horses, talking the Snake language so that if there were any Indians nearby, they would hear us. Next morning we had just started when we saw the tracks of a couple of horses. We kept on traveling. When we were going up Boise Hills, we saw dust rising behind us. We knew it was a party of Indians, so we slackened our pace and stopped, pretending to arrange our packs as though we were afraid of nothing. The Indians caught up to us. There were seven of them, and the son of that old man whom the soldiers had taken prisoner was one of them. He inquired about his father. I told him he was well, that the soldiers were treating him kindly and they would bring him back the next summer. (I did not know anything about him.)

There was another Indian with them who had been the cause of the massacre in a way. The story, as they told it, was that an Indian had stolen a horse from an immigrant train. Next day two others were riding behind the wagons of the immigrants, as all friendly Indians do, when one of the immigrants turned round and shot at an Indian and killed him. The other escaped back to the camps and soon nine warriors returned and killed nearly every one of the immigrants, twenty-five in all, men, women, and children. Just one boy got away in the bushes.

Among the party we met there was one who had been at the massacre—a tall, fine-looking Indian and a friendly fellow, Big Man. The Hudson's Bay Company often left their horses in his charge when they got tired out traveling. He wanted to take revenge for one of his family who was killed in that fight.

At the time they caught up to us, I did not know they had any of the murderers among them, but we found it out later. We traded horses with them and parted good friends. They told us that we had been lucky the night before. It appears two of them had come quite close to Sinclair's tent, scarcely fifty yards away; but when they heard us talking Indian, they knew we were of the country, so that was the reason we had not been shot. We then parted and continued on our way to Fort Hall without any more dangerous adventure.

I had sent my cattle to Salmon River with an Indian, so I went and wintered there. In the spring I went again on the immigrant road. I was very fortunate with the immigrants. They often told me they drove their cattle a long distance after they were lame or footsore from traveling, so that they could reach my camp. This was when a returned immigrant was in their party and told them I would give more for the cattle than other traders. I never offered them less than ten dollars for a yearling, while other traders gave only one or two dollars. This would aggravate them, naturally. It was after one of those offers, I suppose, that a train passed me one day with a large drove of cattle. I went over to them to trade, but they would not listen; they were swearing and abusing the traders on the road.

I did not say anything, but joked with them and kept on traveling, all the time with my eye on the cattle. When I thought of going back, I offered one of them ten dollars for a yearling. He was surprised at the offer; and I got twelve head out of that herd before I left, as I had done in many other instances by offering what I thought was right. The other traders would always look for big oxen and cows. But they would be footsore and worn out; and it would take them a longer time to get strong, while my young cattle got well and fat more quickly. After a few years my herd so increased that I could afford to give one fat animal for two poor ones. However, I had a great deal of trouble with my lame cattle and sometimes I felt discouraged.

The other traders, when the immigrants had passed, would trade their cattle for ponies and go out hunting. I would have liked to go off too, but I remained to look after my lame cattle. I was rewarded for that in four or five years, so I could have bought out all the traders within two hundred miles. When I gave one fat animal for two poor ones, I always took care to keep the best ones. It's my belief that everyone is adapted for some particular calling, and I think for many reasons mine must have been stock raising. In any case, the result of my trading and breeding in Montana was that in eleven years, I had one thousand head of as fine cattle as ever grazed in the Deer Lodge Valley or surrounding country. I had some of the best cattle that went over the road to Oregon and California. They were always in fresh grass and moving all the time. That is what Montana cattle do not have now, nor ever will again.

1. The fatalities included eighteen men, women, and children, several of whom were captured and tortured to death. The attack by 30 or more warriors was the result of increasing long-term tension between Indians and whites in the Snake River country during the immigration era. (See Annie Laurie Bird, *Boise: The Peace Valley*, chapter v)
2. Upon receiving word of the destruction of the Ward party, Major Granville O. Haller set out from The Dalles with 26 regulars, 40 volunteers, 10 Nez Perces, and 2 Cayuses to the scene of the attack. "When the soldiers and volunteers reached Boise Valley they could not get a fight out of the Indians, but killed five men and took one man, four women, one girl and three children prisoners . . . The chief of the tribe committing the massacre . . . [was] among the prisoners. However, he had not been present at the massacre, was much opposed to it." (*Ibid*, 87) The next year, Haller returned for a second, more extensive campaign in the region, in which Johnny Grant was destined to play a part.
3. The U.S. Army's Fort Dalles (at present-day The Dalles, Oregon) stood on the south bank of the Columbia River, just east of the Cascade Range and the Columbia River gorge. In this era, The Dalles was a key commercial, military, and administrative center on the line of communication between the more populous lower Columbia region (i.e., Portland, Fort Vancouver, and the Willamette settlements) and the wilder, untamed "upper country" (i.e., the Columbia Basin, and the valleys of the Bitterroots and northern Rockies).

# 13

## IN WHICH HE BECOMES THE INTERPRETER FOR
## MAJOR HALLER, AND ACCOMPANIES
## A RUDE YOUNG LIEUTENANT.

In the summer of 1854 [1855] when I was trading on the immigrant road, I received a message from Major [Granville O.] Haller at Fort Boise. He wanted me to act as his interpreter.[1] He had come with three thousand men[2] from The Dalles to capture those Indians who had murdered the immigrants the year before. There was not much doing on the road just then, and I had been thinking of moving to Grand Round Valley[3] to settle. I decided that by going to Fort Boise I would be getting nearer that country. So I got ready to move—horses, cattle, and all. Antoine Poirier, Thomas Pambrun, and Jack Collins came with me.

When we had traveled about two hundred miles [westward] and reached the Malad River, about forty miles from Camas Prairie, where Major Haller's command were camped,[4] we stopped for the night. I had a dream that troubled me very much, so much so that Antoine Poirier, my chum, said to me next morning, "What is the matter with you? You look so troubled."

I told him I had a bad dream, which is the sign of bad luck, so I was at a loss to know what to do.

Then I added, "Antoine, what do you prefer doing? To go on, or go back? It makes no difference to me one way or the other."

Both men said they did not care whether they went on or turned back home. Then I told them to turn the oxen and outfit back and go home. I felt that my outfit and men were safer, and I continued on to Major Haller's camp.

When I got there he sent me with Lieutenant Gay[5] and forty-one soldiers to hunt the murderers. He kept the rest of his command, three thousand, there. We had to go into a country where very few white men had ever been, and we had no guide. We went to Lemhi where there were Mormons on the Salmon River. From there I went to the Snake camp about twenty-five miles in the mountains where they were hunting and got a guide.

A couple of days before we got to Lemhi, Lieutenant Gay came to me excited and cross asking, "Where are you taking us? That Indian, a prisoner we had with us, told us in signs you were taking us where there are no Indians. He says you are blinding us."

I replied, "I do not know any more than you where the Indians are. I am not your guide. You find the murderers and I will speak to them. I will tell you where I am going, to Lemhi. There are two roads there; one follows down a fork on one side and comes up on the other to Lemhi. That will take us two days. The other one where I am going now goes across the mountains and will take us only one day. You can choose which one you will take."

He took the longest. He was the most disagreeable traveling leader I ever was with; he was conceited and contrary. If we wanted to stop where there was a good camping place, he would not agree, but would camp in some rocky place full of prickly pears (cactus) just for pure meanness. All that first day I was thinking of the way Gay had spoken to me, but I managed to control my temper.

At night after we were camped, I went to him and said, "By the way you spoke to me today you seem to doubt me, while I am doing my utmost to help you get those Indians. I will let you know there is just as much honor under the leather I wear as there is under your broad cloth. If I had not promised Major Haller to come, I would leave you here."

He apologized, saying he was rather hasty and that he supposed he did not understand the Indian.

I asked the Indian what he had said. It appears the lieutenant had asked him if he knew the country, and he had answered that he was going like a blind man; he did not know the country; he did not belong to that tribe of Snakes. I interpreted what the Indian had said to the lieutenant. He acknowledged that he was wrong, but did not speak to me again until we got the Indians.

We came upon two Indian lodges. The lieutenant took one of the two men prisoner, for what reason I could not tell, unless it was to satisfy one of his whims, for the Indian (Pigate) was peaceable and good. I knew him well. He wanted me to intercede for him.

He said to me, "You know I never killed anyone or stole horses."

I told him I knew it, but that I could not do anything for him. (I had traveled long enough with that lieutenant to know it was no use to try and reason with him.) They tied his two legs together like a horse and then fastened him to a stake. A soldier kept guard over him, but they left his hands free, so of course from under his robe he loosened his legs and escaped. When the guard came back on his beat, he saw the Indian going, but did not dare to shoot him, for Pigate was cunning enough to run towards the lieutenant's tent to prevent their shooting. The tent was pitched on the edge of the bush by the river; so when the Indian got near there, he jumped aside and took to the bush. I saw him the following winter and when talking about that time, he said he had started so quickly and the night was so dark, he ran against a small poplar tree that was leaning over and it knocked him down. He lay still quite awhile; and when he saw that no one was following him, he got up and made for the river.

This staking out of a man reminds me of another Indian who was treated in the same way. Once when I was going to Salt Lake, I camped on Bear River. There were some troops camped there also. They had an Indian staked out. The commanding officer sent for me. When I got to his camp I saw Pocatello, the Ute sitting down all painted and jolly looking. The officer asked me if I knew that Indian.

I said, "Certainly I know him; he is the worst scoundrel in the Ute Nation. I do not know if he is a murderer, but he will steal horses and abuse the traders."

Pocatello looked at me and laughed; he understood some English. He did not appear to be afraid. I was not surprised next morning to learn that Pocatello had made good his escape. It was no wonder, for they had only tied his legs together and left his arms free. Later, that same Pocatello got to be a great chief.

1. It appears that Grant was trading at a considerable distance east on the immigrant trail at the time he received Haller's message sent from Fort Boise. As Grant moved west, Haller's command moved east to Camas Prairie, where Grant joined the soldiers.
2. Though Haller's campaign of 1855 included more troops than were available in the hastily organized fall 1854 expedition, Grant's claim that Haller now led "three thousand men" is inaccurate and highly inflated.
3. The broad, well-watered Grande Ronde Valley in what is now northeastern Oregon is nestled between the Blue Mountains to the west and the extremely rugged Wallowa Mountains on the east. Oregon Trail immigrants often took respite here before undertaking the difficult crossing of the Blue Mountains to the west.
4. According to an official report: "The command reached Fort Boise July 15 . . . The next day a talk was held with some two hundred Indians . . . of whom sixty-five were warriors; and it having been ascertained that four of the murderers were present, they were seized, brought before a board of officers . . . and, their guilt having been clearly

established, three were hung on the graves of their victims . . . the fourth was shot by the guard in endeavoring to escape . . . The command then continued to the great Cammish [Camas] prairie . . . upwards of sixty miles beyond Fort Boise" (Major General John E. Wool letter, 9/4/1855, *34th Congress, 1st Session, House of Representatives, Ex. Doc. No. 1, Part II*, pp. 78-79; see also, Annie Laurie Bird, *Boise: The Peace Valley*, 87-88).

5. Lieutenant "Gay" appears to be 1st Lt. Edward H. Day, of the Third Artillery, who is known to have been under Major Haller's command during this period. Research in U.S. Army records in the National Archives, no doubt, would clarify this point as well as other aspects of Grant's experiences as an army interpreter.

# 14

## WHEREIN HE NARRATES SOME PAINFUL INCIDENTS
## IN THE INDIAN WAR.

To return to my trip with Gay's party, that same day we went to Lemhi, and from there we went across the country on our way back to Fort Boise where we expected to find those murderers on their own hunting grounds. Between the Salmon River and Fort Boise there was another band of the Snake tribe who are called the Boise Indians.

After we had traveled about ten days, I noticed marks which indicated a fresh camping place. There was a fresh fireplace. I drew the attention of the lieutenant to this and said that there had been Indians here that day or late on the day before. He at once decided to follow them, but in my opinion he acted with very little judgment. He took five men, and himself and I made seven men in all. He sent the remainder with the guide to join the main body, while we were to follow the Indians without knowing how many of them there were. We traveled eight or nine miles and found the camp. There were only three Indians and some women. One woman was one of the wives of the old man they had taken prisoner. I spoke to them, but they did not wish to answer for they felt suspicious. They had not seen any white men in that neighborhood before. The old prisoner's wife told me at last that there were thirteen warriors in the party, the three whom we saw and ten others who were away undoing beaver dams [to catch beaver].

Our position was a dangerous one. There were thirteen of them and they would fight desperately. I said to the lieutenant that I would go after the others.

"Well," he said, "I will send two men with you."

"I will not go," I replied, "with two men in their present dress, for the Indians will mistrust us. I will lend one my leather shirt and the other my coat."

So with this mountaineer garb we started off and soon found the Indians busy as the old woman had said, about one-quarter of a mile from the camp. Like the first group, they did not want to answer me, for they thought that there was something wrong. I kept on talking to them, and as I found they had killed a beaver, I tried to buy it from them. A son of the old man, the prisoner at Fort Boise, was here: the same Indian I had seen the year before in the neighborhood of the massacre. I told him the soldiers were passing and that his father was with them. At last, I managed to coax them to the camp.

We had gone about two hundred yards towards it when we met the lieutenant, who had left the sergeant and one man to guard the three Indians at the camp. We got the Indians to sit down on the grass to have a chat. I called the young man aside and asked him if there were any among them who were implicated in the massacre the year before.

"Yes," he replied, "there are three."

He told me which they were. I turned my back to them and without pointing them out told the lieutenant which ones they were by their dress. I did not want to alarm them, but the lieutenant got excited, jumped up, cocked his double-barrel shot gun, and called out, "Watch them, watch them. They will run."

I asked him if he wanted to take them prisoners or kill them.

"I will not kill them if I can help it," he said.

"Well," I said, "the way you are acting you will not take any of them alive."

Even as we talked a tall Indian, who was one of the murderers, got up and ran like a deer through the pines. The second one of whom I have already spoken was a good peaceable Indian called Tewanee, who took care of the Hudson's Bay Company's horses. He started to run, but they shot him in the side. The shot was deadly, but he had strength to pick up his bow which he had dropped. He pulled the string, but there was no arrow; he was too far gone to notice it.

He leaned against a cedar tree, his arms stretched out, saying, "It is enough."

The officer shot him again, aiming at his head; but he hit him in the little finger, eighteen inches from it.

The third one in trying to escape passed me running. I caught him around the wrist and held his hand in which he was holding his bow and arrow. He was one of the murderers; and I had been watching him before sharpening his arrow and trying his bow without the arrow in it. If he had put the arrow to it, I had my hand on my pistol and I certainly would have used it.

The other Indians all started to run. I shouted to them, "Do not run. It will be worse for you, if you do so."

They all came to me. The second one whom the soldiers had shot twice already was not dead yet. He came towards me too and caught hold of his brother-in-law who was near me. One of the soldiers put an ounce ball and two buckshots into his musket and fired between the two, striking the first one, who had been shot, in the side and making a gaping wound from which his entrails protruded. Still that did not kill him at once, for he tried to walk away staggering.

I shouted, "In mercy's name, finish him."

They shot him again in the back and killed him outright. They had shot at him seven times from a distance of from six inches to ten feet.

When that Indian was dead, I told them to take charge of the one I was holding. As soon as the lieutenant fired the first shot back at the camp, the three Indians who were left in charge of the sergeant started to run. The sergeant killed one before he rose; and as the others started to run for the bush, he killed one before he reached it; and one escaped

The lieutenant told me to look under their blankets for concealed weapons. I told him they did not have any, for if they had they would have used them; but I said to him, "To satisfy you I will look."

I told them to open their blankets. They did, but did not have weapons of any kind. There was one warrior who did not open his blanket, so I opened it for him. He had no weapon, but he had got an arm broken nine months before; mortification had set in and below the elbow there was only the bare bone four inches long.

I wanted him to come to the military surgeon to have it attended to, but he refused saying, "It does not pain me except when my blanket touches it."

# 15

## WHEREIN HE ENDS HIS WORK WITH THE SOLDIERS
## AND HE IS OBLIGED TO LEAVE THE COUNTRY.

Now we had to go back to the main camp, and we did not know where they were. We were compelled to employ some of the Indians to guide us; and we let the others, who were innocent, go. If those Indians had been treacherous, they could have taken us to some larger Indian camp and got us all killed. That is what we richly deserved for making such blunders. However, we traveled all that night till we got to the first soldiers with our prisoners.

Next morning one of the soldiers put an Indian on his horse behind him and another got on a tree that was lodged against another tree over my campfire. When the Indian passed him, he put the rope around his neck and he was left hanging. He was kicking, so a Dutch ["Deutsch," or German] soldier caught him by the legs, pulling him down and twisting him till he finished him, saying at the same time, "That is the way to do it."

The other Indians who had not been [. . .] murderers and whom we took as guides were looking on. The hanging of the murderer might have been a lesson for the Indians not to murder any more whites; but the cruel act of the Dutch soldier could only incite the Indians to treat the whites with more cruelty when they would get them in their power. So the whites ought not be surprised at the cruelty of the Indians towards them after such examples.

After the soldiers cut down the body of the dead Indian, they threw it at the foot of a tree and put some leaves over it and left it; then we kept on traveling to join the main body. I had made up my mind to tell Major Haller how Lieutenant Gay had acted. He could have taken those Indians prisoners if he had taken the proper means; his orders were to take them alive, for I heard Major Haller tell him so, but he did not go about it properly.

The whites had said that we traders and mountaineers were with the Indians; that is, that we sided with them. Now I lived among them, but I would never urge them to commit any crime. However, if I had known that the soldiers would act in such a cruel manner, I would never have gone with them. If I stayed in the country now, I was left at the mercy of the Indians. Although I had done my best to help the soldiers, I did it to show Major Haller that what had been said about traders and mountaineers was false. I suppose he never heard the part I had played in the arrest of that Indian. I did not, after all, say anything to him that I knew, although I noticed all the blunders that had been made from the beginning.

What was the general's object in sending those three thousand men from The Dalles to hunt up the murderers, and then keep them at Fort Boise where Indians are seldom seen? They sent only forty-one men three hundred miles in the mountains through a country uninhabited by whites. When I showed Lieutenant Gay the tracks of the Indians, he took six of us forward, and sent the other thirty-four back instead of these men remaining nearby so that if we needed help, we would know where to get it. If those three Indians had been at their camp where they could have laid hands on their rifles, they could have killed us all. That is what the officer said himself.

When we got to Fort Boise to Major Haller's camp, Lieutenant Gay said to him, "Major, Johnny is a soldier."

From Fort Boise I had to go home alone. I rode fast. I always did, but I would have traveled still faster if I had known, as I found out later, that I was pursued by the Indians. One night I thought I heard a cow bellowing, but knowing there were no cows in that part of the country I thought it might be a bear. Next morning after traveling some time, I saw the tracks of a cow. I supposed the immigrants had lost her. The Indians also noticed the tracks and, being hungry, followed the cow and butchered her. The work delayed them, but it saved my life, for they were following me to kill me. It is a wonder they did not do it afterwards. I may thank Tyndaille [Tendoy], a Snake chief, whose sister I had for a wife.[1] I always believed I owed my life to his influence with them, although he did not belong to the same band.

The troops went back to The Dalles. They had killed one of the murderers, hung one, so that seven of the original nine escaped.[2] They never gave themselves the trouble to hunt them up afterward. While they were on their way back to The Dalles, the Columbia Indians rose in rebellion and the war began [Yakima War, 1855-58[3]].

A few years before that the Cayuse and Nez Perce Indians had a fight with the troops [Cayuse War 1847-50[4]]. There was much sickness among the Indians and the Rev. Dr. [Marcus] Whitman who was living near there gave them medical attendance; but in spite of his care, some died. An American half-breed [Joe Lewis] told the Indians that it was the doctor's medicine that killed them. So the Indians decided to kill the doctor. An Indian called Tom Sackry[5] killed him with a hatchet. The troops [Oregon provisional government militia] were [. . .] ordered out to avenge the doctor's murder, but there was not much fighting done.

In 1854[6], as I have already stated, the war began and lasted four years, and it might have lasted longer had it not been for two companies of half-breeds from Oregon under the command of a half-breed named Billy McKay. The Cayuse Indians took their horses with them towards the Nez Perce country, but the horses would always go back to the place where they had been raised. The half-breeds would then gather them together in corrals and kill them. They killed as many as seven hundred in one corral. So the Indians concluded that it was useless to continue fighting, for they were the losers, and they finally surrendered.[7]

1. Quarra, the sister of the noted Lemhi chieftain Tendoy, sometimes was referred to by the similar sounding English name, "Cora." Johnny and Quarra were married at least as early as the mid 1850s. In the late 1850s, Johnny appears to simultaneously have had three or more wives.
2. Altogether, Haller's men intentionally shot and hanged about as many warriors (i.e., "19") as the number of whites who had been killed.
3. In the opening battle of the Yakima War (October 1855), Major Haller's hard-riding command of 84 regulars from The Dalles suffered a sharp defeat at the hands of Yakima and Klickitat warriors in the Simcoe Mountains of south-central Washington. Reinforcements from The Dalles led by Lieutenant Day came to Haller's relief.
4. Grant is mistaken about the Nez Perce role during the Cayuse War. Though a few Nez Perce supported the war-faction of the Cayuse, the majority remained neutral or actively supported the capture of the Whitmans' murderers.
5. Actually, it was the Cayuse chief Tomahas who tomahawked Whitman in the back of the head while the missionary was talking to Chief Tiloukaikt in the living room of Whitman's house. Tamsucky, who Grant identifies as "Tom Sackry," was one of the leaders in the attack on the mission on November 29, 1847. (See chapter 3 endnotes)
6. Here, Grant refers to hostilities beginning with the Ward massacre and Haller's campaigns against the Snakes in southern Idaho in 1854-55, which then was followed by the Yakima War in the Columbia Basin that continued intermittently for three years, or 1855 to 1858.
7. This story about McKay's volunteers probably was distorted as it evolved through oral recounting. It appears to be partially based on an incident occurring near present-day Spokane, Washington, during the final campaign of the Yakima War, which involved regular U.S. Army troops. Following victories over the Spokanes and Coeur D'Alenes

at the battles of Four Lakes and Spokane Plains on September 1 and 5, 1858, a large column under the command of Colonel George Wright (including 700 soldiers, 33 Nez Perce scouts, and 200 civilian packers) slaughtered between 800 and 900 captured Indian horses on September 9 and 10, 1858. Ever afterward, this sanguinary site along the Spokane River near the present Washington-Idaho border has been known as "horse slaughter camp."

# 16

## IN WHICH HE JOINS HIS FATHER, AND RETURNS TO TRADE WITH IMMIGRANTS AT SODA SPRINGS.

One might think, as my father said when I turned my outfit back instead of sending it to Grand Round Valley, that I was foolish to pay any attention to a dream. I felt I was doing it for the best anyhow, and we heard of the trouble between the whites and the Indians. I did not forget to remind my father that I was right acting as I did. If I had continued, I would have been surrounded by the Indians on every side. I could not have come back to Fort Hall on account of the Snakes, against whom I had been working with the soldiers, nor go to Oregon for fear of the Chinooks and Columbia Indians.

My father said to me, "But you did not know of the danger when you sent the outfit back."

I certainly did not; but I had a presentiment of impending danger, and I was glad I heeded it.

That winter I remained at Fort Hall and hunted antelope. One day when I was herding the cattle with a young Indian, we caught sight of a band of about eight hundred antelope and started after them. The Indian had a good buffalo horse, and I had my cream horse with a Mexican saddle. We followed the herd and each killed a stag with our arrows. I fastened a rope on the one I killed and dragged it over to a bunch of willows. While I was busy with it, five more passed. I took the saddle off my horse and chased them and killed all the five with a club, for they were worn out with running. I always preferred riding without a saddle. It seemed to me to be easier on the horse, as well as on the rider; and consequently I rarely used a saddle or bridle; I used a hair rope instead of a bridle. I always rode a good horse, and I took my greatest pride in that.

As I said before, we were herding the cattle that day we saw the antelope. Our way then of herding them in the winter was to leave them out on the plains, but to open roads for them to pass from one ridge to another. If we did not do this, we would have lost them in the snowbanks.

We never saw them together all winter; they always went in separate little herds.

That winter of 1854 and 1855[1] was a very severe one, and a man I knew named Trim, who had three hundred oxen to winter for someone in Salt Lake, lost two hundred and twenty of them. He went after them every day and drove them to the camp with dogs, so that they were harried and weakened.

That same winter, besides looking after my own cattle, I had my father's also, about one hundred and fifty head in all, cows and calves. I lost twenty-five of them, nearly all old cows whose calves had run loose with them all summer, and who had been driven five hundred miles from the springs to the mountains. In the spring we went on as usual to the immigrant road. The following winter father and I wintered at Beaver Head.[2] We were obliged to leave early on account of the Blackfeet Indians.

That spring of 1856 the snow was very deep. Antoine Poirier, who was working with me, came ahead with me to break the road [from the mountains toward Fort Hall]. After we had traveled about forty miles, we waited some time, near a canyon. My father caught up to us there and camped with us.

When I sent Antoine to inquire how soon they were going to start, my father answered, "Let Johnny go ahead; he has good strong horses and he is young."

So I led. To go around the canyon was fifteen miles; but straight it was only five miles, so we went the short way. There was five feet of snow in some places, and we did not know the road; but we followed a pack trail.

The first day we drove the horses by small bunches back and forward to break the trail, then the pack horses, and last the wagons. The next day the road was so sliding at one place we were obliged to fasten a rope over the wagon bows and give it to an Indian and his two wives who were traveling with us to hold. In this way we prevented the wagons from upsetting. Fortunately it was only for a short distance that the road was so sliding.

The first night after we crossed the canyon, we heard a cow bellowing. Antoine ran out to see what was the trouble. It was the wolves devouring one of my big cows. We had to butcher her the next morning. That day we waited for the rest of the party to come up, for we had to cross a worse place than the canyon, the Blacktail Deer Divide.[3] My father's party were still away behind us.

It appears when he missed my stock on the other side of the canyon, he sent his men to see where we had passed; but they were afraid to undertake the straight road, so they went around. In that way it took them two days to get over, while we did it in less. However, we waited for them and all crossed the divide together. It was very bad, but it was not so difficult with a large party, and we used the same plan of crossing as we had at the canyon.

Fred Burr got to the divide at night after our party and father had left there in the morning. The Blackfeet came up and left Fred Burr on foot, for they stole twenty-six head of horses from him. If we had delayed just one day, the Indians would have made a big haul from us too. There must have been five hundred head of horses and seven or eight hundred head of cattle in our bunch. Fred Burr got all those cattle safe over the divide, and he had three hundred oxen. I sold him some horses. He was so anxious to get my old cream that I at last sold the horse to him for two hundred dollars. But I missed my old favorite very much later. After we got to Fort Hall, we remained there a few days; then we went to the immigrant road again at Soda Springs.

1. Johnny appears to be juggling the sequence of his chronology here; actually, if his dates are correct, he is recalling the winter prior to the outbreak of the Yakima War.
2. Louis R. Maillet, another mountaineer, recalled the following incident involving Johnny Grant in January 1856: "Johnny Grant whose camp was on Beaver head Creek, was in his Lodge making Pack Saddles. An Indian[,] a brother in law of Johnny's[,] came into the Lodge and hit Johnny over the head with a club. Saying the [sic] He had treated his sister badly & that He loved his young wife [Quarra] better than the old one. Grant caught the Indian and threw him[.] whilst He was holding the Indian down, Squaws came in with knives & would certainly have killed him but Maillet got up & knocked down a couple of Squaws, then got out his pistol and told them that He would kill them if they did not behave. for a while the row was stopped. Grant got away at night[.] another brother in law arrived[,] brother to the young wife. He was Tin-doy [Tendoy] the bravest indian He [Maillet] ever Saw. He rated the mischief makers roundly and told them that if they ever caused any more trouble, He would take a club & Knock their brains out. as the Indians feared him, everything was peaceful in camp. (Louis R. Maillet to William F. Wheeler, MS65, Montana Historical Society)
3. Blacktail Deer Creek is a southeastern tributary of the Beaverhead River. Dillon, Montana, now stands near the junction of the two streams. Travelers passing over the Blacktail Deer divide normally were going to, or coming from, the Monida Pass locality on the present-day Montana/Idaho border.

# 17

## IN WHICH HE TELLS OF SOME PIONEERS, AND OF
## THE MORMONS RISING IN 1857.

That same summer [1857¹] Colonel Lander surveyed a cutoff on the immigrant road.[2] He had as interpreter one Ned Williamson. One day they met an Indian, and the colonel said to Ned, "Ask that Indian how far it is to Johnny Grant's camp."

Ned turned to the Indian and said, "Shoshonee—Johnny Grant—Soda Springs—three o'clock—how?"

The whites were in the habit when teaching the Indians to say something in English, to say it themselves and then make the Indian repeat it. So that Indian repeated what Ned said.

"Shoshonee (that is the name the Snake Indians call themselves)—Johnny Grant—three o'clock—how?"

"Colonel," he said, "we will reach Johnny Grant's at three o'clock."

They traveled all that day and the next until night before they reached my place. The colonel said, "Ned, I do not think you understand the Snake language."

But he said, "Yes, Colonel, I do, but that Indian lied."

As a matter of fact, Ned did not understand it, but there was money in being [an] interpreter; and people at that time were just as they are now; they would do anything for the almighty dollar.

The Snake is very difficult to learn to speak. Among the traders there were only three of us who could speak it correctly: myself; Thomas Lavatta, a Mexican; and an Irishman named Dempsey, who did not forget his own brogue when he learned Indian.

Some travelers came to him one day and asked him, "Are you French Dempsey from the mountains?"

He answered, "Yes, by japers, I am."

That same Colonel Lander, while working on the road, wanted to learn the Snake language. He would write the words in English and their meaning in Snake. One day when he saw a rabbit, he said to a Snake Indian, "American rabbit?"

The Indian, thinking he wanted him to repeat it, said, "Shoshonee rabbit."

"Why it is nearly the same as in English," said the colonel. So he wrote it in his book ("American rabbit—Shoshonee rabbit"). This Colonel Lander was afterwards killed in a battle between the North and South. He was a Southerner [actually, Lander was a Northern general].

I said once before that people then used any means to make money. The following incident will prove it. There was a Mormon named Emmett, a blacksmith, who bought a crippled mule for five dollars. He killed it and hung the meat in his blacksmith shop, which was made with four posts and covered with cedar boughs. Immigrants passing by saw the fresh meat and asked him, "Trader, what have you there?"

"Moose," he answered.

The immigrant said, "Well, we have never tasted moose meat. Would you sell us some—just a few pounds to taste it?"

He sold them some at twenty-five cents a pound. The next passerby maybe would ask him if it was deer; another would say buffalo; and he always agreed. So of his mule he sold moose, deer and buffalo at the same price. The proceeds of the sale of his mule netted him about one hundred dollars.

One day one of the immigrants who had come to buy some fresh meat noticed the mule's head which was about ten yards from the shop and said, "Well, I declare. This moose had a head exactly like a mule."

Emmett was not put out, but said, "Don't you know that a moose has a head like a mule?"

The newcomer had never seen a moose and he did not doubt the Mormon's word. There were a good many tricks played on the newcomers in those days.

In 1857[-58] I went to Deer Lodge Valley[3] and wintered there. That same year the Mormons declared their independence [Mormon War, 1857-58]. Troops were then sent out to restore order, but they could not reach their destination that year.[4] The Mormons certainly did all in their power to prevent them. They watched their trains of supplies; and when they stopped to camp, the Mormons stole their stock more than once. They told the teamsters to take what they wanted and leave; then they placed all the wagons together and set fire to them. In fact, I saw three places where such disasters had taken place; there remained only the tires and other irons of the wagons after they were burnt. It was rumored that the Mormons had stolen eighteen hundred head of stock from the American government that summer. Consequently, the troops had to content themselves with what the country could afford, and that at a very high price, for everything was scarce, and it was not safe to fetch anything any distance. The Mormons were always watching to prevent it. I could have sold two hundred head of cattle to the troops, but I did not like the idea of risking my life.

Towards spring [1858] Mr. Thinkland [Benjamin Franklin Ficklin] came to me to buy cattle for the troops.[5] I sold him two hundred head. Then he went to Bitterroot to get some more, but he came back without any. He did not tell me the reason, but I imagined why he did not. He wanted me to take the cattle I was selling to him to Fort Bridger, at my own risk. I positively refused to do it; it was too much of a risk. I did not wish to give the Mormons a chance to give me any trouble, for I was certain to regret it if I attempted to take cattle to the troops, so I lost the sale of those cattle.

A few days after, I [. . . left for] Fort Bridger to sell horses to the troops.[6] I was camped about forty miles from home when Mr. Thinkland [Ficklin] came to my camp with a man named Jack [Jake] Meek. I suppose he brought him as a witness to our conversation.

He said to me in a commanding tone (thinking to frighten me), "If you go to the barracks and the officer asks you anything about the cattle, remember that I was not the party who went back on the bargain. You broke it. Now remember if you do not—I will make you sorry for it."

His threats roused my temper, and I said to him, "Mr. Thinkland, you might have heard that I was a coward, because I never quarrel with anyone nor meddle with other people's affairs; but you are not able to make me own up to what I never said. You are the party who backed out of that bargain, and you cannot deny it. You say too that I will be sorry for this if I do not take the blame. I'm ready now. Come on; we will settle the matter here."

He left me without saying another word. When I got to Fort Bridger, the officer commanding did not ask me anything about it. I sold some horses to him, but it took some time to do so. In the meantime, the inner man had to be attended to, so I bought some beef from the quartermaster at twenty-five cents a pound, and it was not very choice at that. He would only sell shanks. It was very poor beef, for the cattle were very thin, so much so that the oxen they killed could not rise without help from a swampy spot. I've seen ten or twelve soldiers drag an ox away to butcher it.

When I came to Fort Bridger, I had forty-seven horses and mules. I sold them all; then I remained there three weeks. Time seemed to slip by very quickly, for I had lots of company and plenty of sport. It was quite a town then. There were three thousand soldiers in the barracks, some stores, and a few gambling houses, all of canvas. I fear I was reckless; I gambled until I lost all but two horses and fifteen cents. But I still had a note of six hundred dollars from Colonel Lander, which was for supplies that I had furnished him the year before when he was surveying a cutoff or short cut on the immigrant road. I wanted to gamble it for half price, but no one would take it, for they said that Colonel Lander would never come back. When I ran short of funds, I sent a Mexican, Tom Lavatta, who was traveling with me, to Redford's store in Salt Lake where I had left sixteen hundred dollars that I had got for nine mules [. . .] He brought the money in a handkerchief. I bid high and was fortunate; I broke the bank; I won my money back and four thousand dollars besides.

There was not funds enough in the bank to pay me; the banker was not obliged to pay me the surplus. I was going to take back my money, but he said, "Hold on," and went out, soon bringing back a large amount of gold coin in his coat tail. He paid me every cent. I sent the same Mexican with about as much money as he had brought before in the handkerchief. I believe I placed too much confidence in that man, although he was honest. I did not count the money either time.

I should have stopped my gambling then, but I did not. It seems a gambler cannot stop, and I will say here to anyone that will take an old man's advice, "Do not begin to gamble."

I continued. We were playing Monte, which is a Mexican game with cards. There was an ace, and a deuce to bet on. I was going to bet on the deuce, but the Mexican was near the table with one knee down and his eyes on a level with the table. He said to me in French to bet on the ace. I thought he must have seen the "doir," that is, the next card which tells. I took his advice and lost. Then my money went like butter in a frying pan; I had only those two horses and fifteen cents in cash left.

As I have already stated, I had Colonel Lander's note. I was very glad that I was not able to sell that note, for on my next trip to Salt Lake, I got it cashed. Colonel Lander it seems had left the money with a man named

Lanford [Langford] in Salt Lake. I was glad to get the money, for I needed it to buy my supplies. The colonel had been misjudged by the man who said I would never be paid, but I had the utmost confidence in him; I always trusted everybody until they gave me reason not to do so. In fact, it was the usual thing to trust one another in those days; we bought and sold on credit without a scratch of the pen.

1. If Johnny Grant's chronology is correct for this period, he does not indicate where he wintered in 1856-57.
2. Frederick West Lander was a civilian engineer working for the Department of the Interior. The Lander Road, surveyed in 1857 and constructed in 1858 with government funding, extended from the vicinity of South Pass, Wyoming, to near Fort Hall. Immigrants began using the cutoff in 1859. At the outbreak of the Civil War, Lander remained loyal to the Union cause, eventually becoming the commanding general of the Eastern Division of the Army of the Potomac. He died March 2, 1862, from the effects of a battlefield wound. (E. Douglas Branch, "Frederick West Lander, Road-builder," *Mississippi Valley Historical Review* 16 [September 1929])
3. In October 1857, prior to moving to the Deer Lodge Valley to winter over, Johnny Grant was in the Beaverhead Valley with his father and other mountaineers. This is confirmed by the pioneer chronicler, Granville Stuart, who, with a small group of companions, had just arrived in Montana for the first time. Having come from Salt Lake City, they set up quarters on the Beaverhead in October 1857 where Dillon, Montana, is now located. In addition to Snakes, Bannocks, Nez Perces, and a few Flatheads wintering in the Beaverhead Valley, Stuart also recorded the presence of the mountaineers, particularly Richard and Johnny Grant's group:
   "Fifteen miles further down the Beaverhead at the mouth of the Stinking Water was . . . Captain Richard Grant, an old Scotch gentleman formerly with the Hudson's Bay Company, with his family, John F. Grant and family, James C. Grant, Thomas Pambrum and family, L.R. Maillet, John Jacobs and family, Robert Hereford and family, John W. Powell, John Saunders, Ross, Antoine Pourier, and several men in the employ of Hereford and the Grants. Captain Grant built a good, three room log house for his family to live in, but the others occupied Indian lodges made of dressed elk skins . . . The time during the winter was passed trading with the Indians and in visiting one another's camps and in hunting."
   Stuart's account presents interesting details about events in the winter lodges, such as the extensive gambling among the Indians, whiskey drinking by the mountaineers ("which fortunately was not long"), the effects of a mild smallpox epidemic, and the prevailing prices in the Indian trade:
   "The price of a common horse was two blankets, one shirt, one pair of cloth leggins, one small mirror, one knife, one paper of vermillion, and usually a few other trifles . . . The Grants . . . complained bitterly of the American hunters and adventurers for having more than doubled the price of . . . articles among the Indians in the last ten years."
   Richard Grant, always the hospitable host, invited the Stuart party to Christmas dinner: "Captain Grant invited Reece Anderson, Ross, James Stuart, Jacob Meek, and myself to dine with him. The menu consisted of buffalo meat, boiled smoked tongue,

bread, dried fruit, a preserve made from the choke-cherries, and coffee. This was an elaborate dinner for those days. Supplies were scarce and hard to get, and most of us were living on meat straight."

Shortly after Christmas, Stuart reported that Richard Grant "was getting ready to move his camp to Bitter Root valley by way of Deer Lodge valley." Johnny Grant, it appears, too left, either at about this time or earlier. Johnny appears to have spent the rest of the winter in the Deer Lodge Valley. (Granville Stuart, *Forty Years on the Frontier*, Vol. 1, 125-27, 129)

4.  Grant's description of the Mormon harassment of Colonel Albert Sydney Johnston's column of 2,500 soldiers during the "Mormon War" is fairly accurate. Johnson's westward march across Wyoming in 1857 was so hindered by these Mormon tactics that Johnson had to give up the objective of occupying Utah. Instead, his troops went into winter quarters (1857-58) in the Fort Bridger vicinity.

5.  According to Granville Stuart, who "just after Christmas" had moved with his companions from the mouth of Blacktail Deer Creek to the lower Big Hole River: "About January 1, 1858, there arrived ten men, under the command of B.F. Ficklin, who had been teamsters in the employ of Johnston's army. They were enlisted as volunteers, and sent out from the winter quarters at Fort Bridger to purchase beef cattle from the mountaineers. They were guided by Ned Williamson, and reported very little snow on the route. They could not purchase cattle on terms to suit them, and fearing to return in mid-winter, remained on the Big Hole until the general exodus in the spring, when they returned to Fort Bridger. They were compelled to eat some of their horses on their way." (*Forty Years on the Frontier*, Vol. 1, 129-30)

6.  In the spring of 1858, enterprising mountaineers, including Johnny Grant, took the opportunity to drive horses and mules to Fort Bridger to sell to the soldiers and immigrants.

# 18

## IN WHICH HE ENTERTAINS SOME INDIANS ROYALLY, AND DECIDES TO FORM A SETTLEMENT AT DEER LODGE.

That summer [1858] when I had the misfortune to lose so much at gambling, the troops got to Salt Lake and made the Mormons come to terms. I went back to Deer Lodge and from there to Bitterroot after my cattle, which I had left with a man named Jacobs.

I wintered at Henry's Fork close to Fort Bridger. In the winter of 1858 and1859 I did well, for I was the only trader who had fat cattle; the others had sold all their beef cattle the winter before to the government, so that they had left only the poor ones which they had bought that summer from the immigrants. I used to trade one fat cow for two poor ones. I had my choice of those cattle, and consequently in the spring I had a fine herd of cattle. I traded that spring with the immigrants on Ham's Fork.

Every summer the Mormons sent wagons to Kansas City to bring immigrants, mostly girls. Sometimes they sent as many as two hundred wagons. That summer quite a number of the families came, and with them two hundred girls—strong, healthy ones, barefooted, dragging little carts. There were four girls to each cart, in which they had packed belongings. Those young girls were from all parts of the world—England, Wales, Denmark, Germany and the United States[1]—the Mormons having immigration agents in all of these countries.

That summer, thinking to do better than at home, I sent a man to California with one hundred and seventy-seven head of cattle, five horses and two mules; and I paid him one thousand dollars a year. He was eighteen months away and brought me back thirteen hundred dollars.[2] I should have had nearer thirteen thousand at the price. He told me he had sold some of the cattle, but I won't judge him now. Nevertheless, I again trusted him with seventeen hundred dollars in 1861 when he went to St. Louis to buy some goods for me; and this time I received proper returns. In the fall of 1859, I went back to Deer Lodge, for there were not many immigrants coming west on the road.

I settled then at Deer Lodge, building my first house on the Little Blackfoot, a stream which comes from the summit of the Rocky Mountains. It was a very beautiful place, near the railroad junction where is now the town of Livingston [Garrison³]. I was there alone; my nearest neighbor was at Bitterroot, one hundred and thirty miles away; and Fort Benton was one hundred and eighty-five miles; Salt Lake was five hundred miles distant, but it was there I got my supplies every year. I used to take a few head of horses and trade them for what I needed.

It was not a very safe location at Deer Lodge, for there were six tribes of Indians who passed my place twice every year, in the spring and fall. One day I had quite a surprise. I heard Indians yelling, and looking up saw that the noise came from a hill. My house was at the foot of it. I saw a band of brave looking Indians, warriors mounted on horseback. I was not exactly afraid, but I was none too [remainder of sentence missing].

When they came down I saw that there were about fifty of the leading Indians among the Blackfoot. They were going to trade with the Flathead Indians, and there were some of the Snake Tribe in their party. When they came close to me, I thought it good policy to treat them like any other travelers. I made a sign to them to dismount, shook hands with them in a friendly way, and gave them all the meat they could eat and coffee to drink. I gave them some tobacco and smoked with them. They camped near my house, and in the morning I gave them their fill. They went away very well satisfied. By that friendly act I got on very well with the Indians, and it was to my advantage in after years; in fact, it was a great help to me then, for with two hundred and fifty head of horses, and over eight hundred head of cattle roaming in the valley, I was at their mercy. They did not forget my kindness.

The same fall [1859] I went to Salt Lake for my supplies as usual. When I got to Box Elder, there were some troops there, and there had been a fight a few days before. The commanding officer sent for me and asked if I knew those Indians with whom they had fought. He said they had killed one hundred and fifty and that the surgeon could take his affidavit that he had seen seventeen dead in one place. I asked him how many lodges there were in the camp. He said there were seven. I knew then it was old Chin Wisker with his sons and son-in-law, only seven warriors in all. I was well acquainted with them, for I saw them often. Chin Wisker was a peaceable old Indian, but his brother, Mauvais Gauché [Wicked Left-handed One], was a different kind of a man, a renegade rogue, as I have already stated. I told the officer if these were the same lodges I was used to seeing, that I was well acquainted with their owners, but I did not tell them there were only seven Indians in all. I was, certain, however, that his men did not kill one hundred and fifty.

I could not exactly find out at Box Elder how many of the seven they had killed, but the following winter I met some of those same Indians at Beaver Head, where I used to then go every winter to trade with the Indians. I asked one of them how many soldiers they had killed. I thought he would boast of it, but no. He answered that he did not think they had killed any or perhaps one. This one, he thought, was a great man, for all the soldiers gathered around him. I knew he was a sergeant for I heard at the time of the fight that one had been shot in the shoulder but not killed. These Indians said they had wounded seven or eight soldiers and killed nine horses. I enquired of him, too, how many Indians had been killed. He answered if we had been standing out as tall as pine trees, they would have killed us all, but we were hidden behind rocks in the mountains. They kept on driving and we slipped back from rock to rock; but there was an old man who could not get away quick enough, and they killed him. That was a very different account of the fight given to me by the commanding officer and the surgeon, who saw seventeen where there was only one.

I went to Salt Lake and back home without anything very lively happening. I wintered in Deer Lodge alone with my family, which included my new wife Quarra and my children. In the spring of 1860, I felt very lonely. My father had moved to Missoula not long before, so I concluded to go to the immigrant road to induce some families to come with me and settle where I was. I took my horses, but my cattle I left, trusting to Providence for their safety.

As I was leaving, two strangers came walking up the trail to my house. One of them said to me, "Do you want to hire a man?"

I told him I was going away and did not need any.

He said then, "Perhaps you would like to have a house made of hewed logs."

A hewed house? I had lived in a leather lodge for ten years, and the house I was living in was a very rough shack of cottonwood logs with the bark on. It was the first house I had built.

I said to the fellow, "All right, what is your name, and where do you come from?"

He said, "My name is Joe Prudhomme. We deserted from Fort Benton."

It seemed a poor recommendation, but it was honest. They had been hired by the American Fur Company; and when they reached Fort Benton, they were disappointed, for they found everything was different from what had been promised to them, so they left the company's employ. The man's honest appearance pleased me, and I hired him at twenty-five dollars a month.

Then he said, "Won't you hire my partner also?"

I agreed.

I went away then with my family, with Thomas Lavatta, and a few Indians. As I have said, I took my horses, but left my cattle with these men. I did not know them, but I trusted them and I never had reason to regret it.[4]

1. The sentence, "There were no Irish girls in the crowd," was crossed off the typed transcript of Grant's memoirs.
2. "Mr. [Louis R.] Maillet . . . returned to Ham's Fork, and from there took 400 head of beef cattle for John Grant, to California for a market, and readily sold them there." (Louis R. Maillet to William F. Wheeler, MS65, Montana Historical Society)
3. Here, Grant confuses Livingston (located on the Yellowstone River) with Garrison at the northern end of the Deer Lodge Valley. He was unfamiliar with both communities, of course, because these railroad towns were established long after Grant had left the Rockies to homestead in Manitoba.
4. According to Louis R. Maillet: "Johnny Grant had moved his stock from Ham's Fork [in] the fall of 1859 to little Black foot in Deer Lodge Valley. here he had built a couple of log Houses & corrals. the Spring of 1860 Grant returned to the Emigrant Road. In October Maillet . . . went to little Blackfoot, Johnny had not yet got in from the road. Johnny had left his large band of cattle & horses in charge of Joe Prud'homme who was putting up another hewed log House for Grant. —Maillet went to work & helped him on the house until Grant's arrival. after 10 days Grant & families came in. He had bought quite a little Stock of goods on green river. So a little Store was opened & put in charge of Maillet. (Louis R. Maillet to William F. Wheeler, MS65, Montana Historical Society)

# 19

## Wherein is related the discovery of the first gold in Montana, and the opening of new markets for the settlement in Deer Lodge Valley.

One day on our journey as we were coming close to our campingplace, we saw a grizzly bear. Thomas Lavatta fired and wounded it, but the bear got away. My Indian man and I followed him up on horseback. I fired a couple of shots, but he kept on. I distanced the Indian; and when the bear got in a small grove of poplars, I went round and round. Suddenly I saw the bear going round a bush as if he was wounded and wanted to lie down. I got ready to fire, but all at once he came the other way at me with a roar. To be sure I lost no time in riding off. I struck my horse on the jaw with my revolver, to make him turn quicker, and I urged him as much as I could to go faster.

When I got a little ways on, I thought I must not let the bear scare me so badly; so I went back very carefully, looking sharply around. At last I saw him lying down. I was certain I could see his head. I aimed between the two ears and fired - but what a disappointment! It was not the bear at all; it was a burnt poplar uprooted over an ant hill, the two roots looking like the ears.

Well I said to myself, "Johnny, it is time to go, when that bear could scare you blind."

When I got into the camp, I told them of my adventure. An Indian chief, Old Snag, made fun of me, so well he might. That afternoon again while traveling I saw two more grizzly bears. I would have liked to kill them in spite of the fright the other had given me, for they were fine animals, lazy and fat. Their fur shown like silver. I approached them, but did not get any closer than about three hundred yards. I got off my horse and fired; then I jumped on my horse and ran one way and the bears the other. I had enough of bear hunting.

I finally reached the immigration road and managed to induce ten or twelve families of traders to come with me. They were [Louis] Descheneau, Leon Quesnelle, Louis Demers, David Contois, Fred Burr, the Stuart boys[1], the Cosgrove boys, Jackson, Jack [Jake] Meek, and two sons of my old friend, Michand Leclair. They settled on Cottonwood Creek about eleven miles from the Little Blackfoot. When I was returning home, I saw quite a number of families camped near my house. I learned a little later that some came from Missouri, [and] some from Fort Union, where they had been hired to the American Fur Company.

As soon as I reached the house, Joe Prudhomme came to me and said, "Surely, Mr. Grant, I do not know whether I have done right or wrong by you. I have disposed of some of your cattle."

"How many?"

"Thirty head, I sold them for twenty-six hundred dollars."

I was sorry he had sold a yoke of oxen that were extra good leaders, but he had sold them for two hundred dollars. A few years before the other traders used to ask me what I intended to do with so many cattle; where could I market them?

I pointed to my fireplace, but they would only answer, "You cannot eat them all."

"Anyway, as long as I have them I cannot starve."

I also told them to wait awhile, that we would have plenty of people there very soon. What I had looked for had already begun. Prudhomme had sold those cattle to Captain Mullen [Mullan], who was going to survey a road from Fort Benton in Montana to Walla Walla in Washington.[2] The mines were discovered the next year,[3] and the market I hoped for was ready for me.[4]

Although I never mined, I helped out the men who found the first gold in Montana in this way: A freighter [Jacobs] who was driving some people to the Florence mine[s] on the Salmon River, four hundred miles from Deer Lodge, had the impression he could get to it by following the Salmon River. He reached one of the forks and followed it, but instead of finding its source (a small stream that he could easily cross), it ended in a canyon which they could not cross. Jacobs knew the party would be angry with him, and likely kill him, so he deserted. They were in a very trying position for people who did not know the country.

The miners then left their wagons and packed their oxen. Some took the trail to Bitterroot; others came to Deer Lodge, and I suppose were prospecting in every creek, for they found some good indications. They came to me and told of it, and they said that if they had provisions they would go back. I let them have some beef and flour and other groceries, and they went back to Bannock[5] where they found rich diggings, so it was in Montana at Bannock instead of the Salmon River in Idaho that they discovered their gold and opened up some of the first gold mines in Montana. Bannock was about one hundred miles from my place; Virginia City was about the same distance; French Gulch was about forty miles; Butte about thirty-two; Bear Gulch and Helena, about forty miles away.

In the next few years mines were discovered all over Montana. That was the time to sell cattle and all kinds of provisions. Any sort of cattle would sell for one hundred and twenty dollars; beef was twenty-five cents per pound; flour was twenty-five dollars per sack; and even went up as high as one dollar a pound in 1864.[6]

To come back to my house at the Little Blackfoot and my return to it,[7] Joe Prudhomme had built a good hewed log house with a good floor in it. He was not only a good carpenter, but a good blacksmith and a good tinsmith, and he had made a pair of dog irons for the chimney. Out of a coal oil can he made a churn and by churning the cream all summer, had sold one hundred and seventy-five dollars' worth of butter. He could have sold more cattle and pocketed the money and run away; but no, Joe was a trusty man. I never regretted having trusted him. I was well satisfied with my new house, but I remained only one year in it.[8] In 1861 I gave it away[9] and moved to Cottonwood nearby where the other traders had settled.[10]

1. James and Granville Stuart already had spent time in the Beaverhead and Deer Lodge valleys between October 1857 and June 1858. They had left Montana in the summer of 1858 and traveled to Fort Bridger, where they dealt in livestock and traded on the immigrant trail for two years, before returning to Montana in the autumn of 1860.
2. Following the conclusion of the Yakima War, Captain John Mullan resumed directing the construction of the Mullan Road, which eventually extended from the U.S. Army's Fort Walla Walla, across what is now eastern Washington, northern Idaho, and western Montana, to Fort Benton on the Great Plains. Completed in 1859-62, this overland route connected the normal head of sternwheeler navigation on the Columbia River at Wallula with the similar upper limit of steamboat activity on the Missouri River at Fort Benton.

   In the fall of 1861, while constructing the road, Mullan's men established Cantonment Wright at the junction of the Clark Fork and Big Blackfoot rivers (near modern-day Missoula). The camp was named after Colonel George Wright, of recent Yakima War fame. The Mullan route was extensively used by miners, packers, and suppliers during the great Montana gold strikes of the 1860s. In the lower Deer Lodge

Valley vicinity, the route crossed the Clark Fork, passing close by Johnny Grant's ranch, and extended eastward in the Little Blackfoot Valley.

3. The Pacific Northwest's initial wave of wealth seekers swarmed into the region's first gold fields in 1854-55 and, after the Yakima War interlude, again in 1858 when mines were discovered in northern Washington Territory around the HBC's Fort Colvile and in western Canada's vast Fraser River and Kootenai areas. The approaches to the northern placer mines were either directly northeast from Puget Sound to Canada, or eastward through the Cascade Range into the Columbia Basin and then northward.

Following shortly, in the early 1860s, came a greater surge of gold miners into the future territories of Idaho and Montana, beginning with gold strikes on the Clearwater (Orofino mines), Salmon (Florence mines), and Boise drainages in Idaho's Bitterroot Mountains, as well as in the John Day country of northeast Oregon. As in the earlier British Columbia excitement, men who had been in the California gold fields led the vanguard; usually they came either overland from the Golden State through the intermountain West, or by steamers up the Pacific Coast and then east via the Columbia corridor. As the horde of miners extensively worked the Clearwater and Salmon districts in 1860-61, discoveries in Montana quickly followed on Grasshopper Creek (Bannack) in 1862, Alder Gulch (Virginia City) in 1863, and elsewhere. It is the Montana gold rush to which Grant refers.

Key routes from the Columbia Basin and the Orofino and Florence mines across the Bitterroot Mountains to western Montana included (from north to south): the Clark Fork route, the Mullan Road, the Lolo Trail, and the Elk City road (or southern Nez Perce Trail). Other gold hunters came from the East by water up the Missouri or overland across the Great Plains. Still others traveled northward from Wyoming, Utah and the central Rockies. The gold rush stimulated extensive settlement and commercial development, which deeply affected the lifestyle of Johnny Grant and the other Montana traders.

4. On May 8, 1861, James and Granville Stuart, situated eight miles lower down on the Clark Fork from Johnny Grant, noted: "Our settlement is known as American Fork. Johnnie Grant's at the mouth of Little Blackfoot is Grantsville and the one above on Cottonwood creek is Cottonwood. We are becoming somewhat civilized as we remain long enough in one spot to give it a name." Granville Stuart also referred to Grant's settlement as "Grantsburg." Stuart's "American Fork" soon came to be known as Gold Creek, and "Cottonwood" became Deer Lodge. (*Forty Years on the Frontier*, Vol. 1, 167, 170-71)

5. The famous mining town of Bannack was established in 1862 as waves of gold hunters rushed to Grasshopper Creek following word of the strike.

6. In the bustling Alder Gulch district, swarming with thousands of wealth seekers, the cost of basic supplies rose to critical levels in the winter of 1864-65. Conrad Kohrs noted: "The winter started in early and late trains from Salt Lake were on the road snowbound . . . Prices went away up, flour to $1.50 per pound. In fact everything was sold at fabulous prices. In Virginia [City] the miners turned out in a regular riot. Hall and Alport and other freighters who owned large quantities of flour barricaded their stores and held off the rioters with guns. But the mob went all through the town and seized small lots of flour. Among others I lost 400 pounds I had stored in George Gohn's . . . There were provisions and flour enough in the country but all in the hands of a few men who were determined to make all they could and prices continued high until new supplies could be brought in." (*Conrad Kohrs: An Autobiography*, 39)

7. In their journal, the Stuart brothers, who resided but eight miles away, provided glimpses of occurrences centered on "Grantsville" during this period (1861-62). For

example, in regard to the activities of Grant's wife (or wives) and female relatives, Granville Stuart reported: "June 10. [1861] . . . I saw a party on horseback passing along the foot of the mountains . . . They proved to be a party of squaws from John Grant's on a root digging expedition." On August 5, 1861: "Thomas Pambrun passed here going to Walla Walla . . . Johnny Grant's Indian wife was with Pambrun. She is going to stop at Hell Gate canon below Flint creek and gather service berries." (*Forty Years on the Frontier*, Vol. 1, 172, 184)

With many different tribes haunting the Deer Lodge country, horse stealing raids were frequent. Granville Stuart noted: "Truly our horses have fallen among perilous times." On June 15, 1861, for example, he wrote: "Joe . . . [a] young Indian horse herder, came along and told me lots of news. He says that on the night of the eleventh there were stolen about ten head of Johnny Grant's horses, five of his mother-in-law's, (old squaw Giomman) three from Powell, one from Joe himself." On June 17: "I made a quick trip up to Johnny Grant's settlement and back to hear what was on up there. Those thieves who have lately been stealing horses were Blackfoot Indians. They came suddenly on a camp of Flatheads over the other side of the mountains. The Flathead camp outnumbered them and as they could not get away with all the stolen horses they took a few of the best and fled, leaving most of the stolen horses behind. The Flatheads (honest fellows) brought them over the mountains to Johnny Grant's and delivered them to their owners." (*Ibid*, 173-75)

Johnny Grant frequently was on the move for trading purposes during this time too, as Stuart notes: "July 15 [1861] . . .Tom Adams, John Grant, John W. Powell and party arrived from Benton." On July 22, 1861: "John Grant . . . and others passed en route for the Hudson's Bay trading post near the St. Ignatius Mission. Paid John F. Grant twenty-eight pluie of beaver skins. War parties of Bannocks have the mountains on fire in all directions. Somebody will probably lose some more horses." (*Ibid*, 182-83)

Grant continued his gambling ways as well. In December 1861, Granville Stuart noted that he and his friends from Gold Creek were "flat broke and afoot" after betting on brother James Stuart's marksmanship against a brother-in-law of Johnny Grant's, named Pushigan. "John Grant had been bragging about what his brother-in-law could do." The Indian was unbeatable, using "a long, heavy muzzle loader . . . on which he had a sight made of hoop iron." The match took place at "Grantsville." (*Ibid*, 190-91)

8. On January 1, 1862, Stuart reported: "Everybody went to grand ball given by John Grant at Grantsville and a severe blizzard blew up and raged all night. We danced all night, no outside storm could dampen the festivities." The next day, with the storm still raging, Stuart noted: "No one ventured to even try to go home . . . Johnny Grant, good hospitable soul, invited everyone to stay until the storm should cease . . . After breakfast we laid down on the floor of the several rooms, on buffalo robes that Johnny furnished, all dressed as we were and slept until about two o'clock in the afternoon, when we arose, ate a fine dinner that Johnny's wife, assisted by the other women, had prepared, then resumed dancing which we kept up with unabated pleasure until about nine in the evening, when we paused long enough to eat an excellent supper. We then began where we left off and danced until sunrise." (*Ibid*, 193)

9. Many years later in a 1922 newspaper article, Montana pioneer F.M. Thompson reminisced about "Grantsville" and Johnny Grant's domestic situation, perhaps with some exaggeration: "[In 1862] we journeyed up the Hell Gate to the mouth of the Deer Lodge, where we took possession of one of Johnny Grant's abandoned cabins, in which we set up housekeeping . . . hundreds of cattle were grazing in the valley. Seeing a couple of cows with small calves, we got them into the corral, and by gentle means

and salt, we became able to milk them . . . [I] was soon able to supply our table with Deer Lodge butter, the best brand probably for 500 miles, for Grant's squaw wives, (he had four of them) made no use of their cows [actually, Grant stated that by 1863 Quarra made "good butter"]. Grant had a wife from each surrounding tribe of Indians, and when a war party was sighted, care was taken to ascertain which tribe was to be entertained, and the other three women and their kids were secreted until danger was averted." (3/18/1922, *Gazette and Courier* [Greenfield, Massachusetts])

According to Catholic Church records, seven of Johnny Grant's children were baptized on March 19, 1864:

Aloysius, age 9 years; mother, Aloysia Larpantis
William, age 7 years; mother, Quarra
Richard, age 6 years; mother, Aloysia Larpantis
David, age 5 years; mother, Quarra
Julia, age 3 years; mother, [illegible]
John, age 2 years; mother, Quarra
Emma, age 1 year; mother, Isabella Ruis
(*Records of the Catholic Church, Diocese of Helena, MT*)

Grant's family tree is complex and, as yet, not entirely verified. The following chart of Johnny's wives and children is drawn from church records, newspaper obituaries, archival materials, descendants' recollections, etc. It accounts for "six" women and twenty-one children, though, in 1886, Johnny stated that there had been "seven" mothers of his twenty-one children. (Some accounts list another son, Phillip, who in fact may have been a son of Johnny's brother's widow by a second marriage):

Children by Louise (b. 1833)—
    Marie Agnes (b. 1851)
    Jane (b. 8/1854)
Children by Aloysia Larpantis—
    Aloysius (b. ca. 1855)
    Mary (b. 11/28/1855, d. 1/25/1933)
    Richard (b. ca. 1858)
Children by Quarra (b. ca. 1840, d. 2/24/1867)—
    William (b. 10/1/1856)
    David (b. 10/17/1858)
    Julienne (b. 1/7/1860)
    John (b. ca. 1862)
    Ellen (b. ca. 1863, d. 1/19/1868)
    Charles Henri (b. ca. 1866)
Children by Isabel Ruis (Mrs. Charley Buck)—
    Emma (b. 1863)
    James (b. 3/6/1869)
Children by Clothild Bruneau (in Canada)—
    Charles Alexandre (b. 5/30/1869)
    Margaret (or, Marguerite Marianne) (b. 12/15/1870, died as infant)
    Maria (or, Moria) (b. ca. 1874)
    Alice (b. ca. 1878, d. 2/1951)
    Marie Corinne (b. ?, d. 3/23/1883)
    Francis (baptized and interred, 5/9/1881)
Children by Lily Bruneau (Clothild's sister) (in Canada)—
    Sara (b. ca. 1870)
    Clara (b. ca.1872)

10. In the winter and spring of 1861-62, Grant suffered from squabbles due to wives and relatives. As James Stuart noted: "January 17. [1862] All the women in this part of the country have been at John Grant's, having I suppose an Indian Dorcas Society something after the manner of their white sisters, and like them it has broken up in a row. All the women have left for home. That is, they have joined their own people, leaving a goodly number of widowers. Next thing the aforesaid widowers will have to hunt up their absconding wives and the chances are most of them will have to yield up a number of good blankets or horse or two to father-in-law to persuade the lady to return." (*Forty Years on the Frontier*, Vol. 1, 194)

   A couple of months later, Grant also had troubles with Victor, the Flathead chief from the Bitterroot Valley. According to James Stuart at Gold Creek: "April 7 [1862] . . . Victor's camp passed here today . . . Maillet came from Cottonwood today to see Victor. Victor is much dissatisfied with John Grant's conduct this winter and is on his way to see Grant and try to have some settlement with him. He says Grant has Snake and Bannock wives and plenty of Indians (Snakes and Bannocks) coming to visit him and when they leave they steal horses from the Flatheads. He says Grant will have to keep the Snake and Bannocks away from his place, etc. As Deer Lodge valley and the valleys of the Big Hole, Beaverhead, and Jefferson have been, from time immemorial, a neutral ground for the Snakes, Bannocks, Nez Perces, Pend d'Oreilles, Flatheads, Spokanes, Coeur d'Alenes, and Kootenais, it looks like the old chief is too arbitrary in insisting that the Snakes and Bannocks should be forbidden to spend the winter and hunt there the same as all others, because of little squabbles common to all tribes. Maillet returned home today very much disgusted with Indians in general, and Victor in particular. Maillet also speaks Salish or Flathead." (*Ibid*, 203-4)

   Today, the exact spot where Grant's ranch stood at the mouth of the Little Blackfoot River is unknown. In a visit 25 years later (1886), Grant reported that only "a couple of feet of the old fireplace" remained from his cabin, and great "change" had occurred in the vicinity due to the large railroad yard at the new town of Garrison (see appendix B). Thus, ravages of time obliterated the "Grantsville" ranch, where Johnny had first settled in the Deer Lodge Valley in 1859.

   In ca. 1861-62, after Johnny left the mouth of the Little Blackfoot and moved the short distance to Cottonwood (Deer Lodge), he erected two structures that still stand at the Grant-Kohrs Ranch National Historic Site. The cabins are joined together as part of bunkhouse row. In late 1862, Grant began building another, larger home, the "first good house" in the Deer Lodge Valley (see chapter 21); this ranch house likewise remains today, as the focal point at the national historic site.

   While Grant's family was still utilizing the first structures that Grant erected at Cottonwood, a visitor in August 1862 recorded: "I soon reached a good sized log House, or rather two joined together, and reigning up asked permission to stay over night. To this Johnny Grant the proprietor readily assented, remarking, 'If I could put up with the fare he had to offer I was welcome.' Sending out an Indian boy to unsaddle and turn in the grass my poney, he invited me to take a drink, which I find to be pure neutral spirits, but diluting it with water, quite palatable after my long ride of nearly 40 miles that day.

   "I then set down to supper, which consisted of bread and fresh meat, served in Indian style, that is, all in a pile, to which I did ample justice . . .

   "John Grant, or as he is called here, Johnny Grant, is a man I should judge of 32 or 3 years of age, tall and well formed, with less of the Indian than American in his features, of a dark swarthy complexion, increased no doubt by exposure and his habits of life. He had, I understood, three Indian wives, and seven or Eight, perhaps more, children, that he treats with an affectionate fondness of manner that the children of many white men might envy. His little son David seemed to be the more especial pet of his father.

"Here in this luxuriant grassy valley, abounding with game and fish—the finest brook trout I ever saw—possessed of large herds of cattle and Horses, surrounded by his half breeds, Indian servants, and their families, with a half dozen old French mountaineers and Trappers who have married Indian women for his neighbors, Grant lives in as happy and free a manner as did the ancient Patriarchs.

"Let me wish, for the open hearted manner in which he bestowed his hospitality on the 'stranger within his gates,' that this pleasing life of his will not be invaded, and that he may long live in the enjoyment of the blessing with which a bountiful nature has so lavishly surrounded him." (From the diary of Edwin Ruthven Purple, *Perilous Passage: A Narrative of the Montana Gold Rush, 1862-1863*)

# 20

## WHEREIN CAPTAIN GRANT—

## "HANDSOME" GRANT—DIES WITHOUT

## LEAVING HIS SON EVEN THE PROVERBIAL SHILLING.

That same year [1861] my father went to Oregon with his family and wintered in Walla Walla.[1] He died there the following year [1862] at the age of seventy two.[2] Joe Prudhomme and Thomas Pambrun were with him at the time. They told me he was constantly calling for me, telling his wife to tell me to hurry up.[3] He got better for a few days and told these men that if he continued to improve, he would alter his will, and would leave me fifteen hundred dollars. He did not get better, so his will was not altered. It was drawn up in favor of my step-sisters, Julia and Adeline, to each of whom he gave fifteen hundred dollars, also to Jemima, his step-daughter. Sometime before he had given a generous sum to my brother's widow, but he did not leave me one cent, not even the lone shilling to buy crepe, that he used to threaten me with.

He had left some stock; but as he had lost one hundred and eighty head that winter, his herd was small. I am nearly certain that if he had changed his will in my favor, I would not have accepted anything, but would have passed it unto my stepmother, for at the time of his death I was richer than he was. I was then worth one hundred and ten thousand dollars in horses and cattle. I did not value money. I spent as freely as I made it. I did not care whether he left me any money or not, but I was very sorry to lose my only parent. I did not have even the consolation of even being at his bedside during his last hours, nor had I any chance to tell him that I was sorry for having acted as I did when I first left.[4]

Although he turned me out of my home, I never kept any spite against him. We visited one another when we were camped in the same place, and I often traded for him. If I had a good horse and he or any of his family fancied it, I made them a present of it. I did this to please my father. When he called me his son, I was ready to do anything for him. Sometimes when he was in a very good humor, he would say I was the one he loved best, but he had an odd way of expressing it.

I often thought since, if I had been more patient with him, we might have got along better, but I was young and thoughtless. I had been brought up by a very indulgent old grandmother who did not check me, but allowed me to do as I pleased. Then what a change it was to come to my father who had been in the employ of the Hudson's Bay Company from the age of eighteen, accustomed to ordering rough men. It had almost become a second nature to him to be harsh. I had none to advise me or say a kind word to me. Still I might have had more patience with him and overlooked his temper, had he not put me out and turned me loose at seventeen to live among Indians. He could not expect much good to come from me.

I was sorry I could not go with him when he went to Walla Walla. It was impossible for me to leave my stock then. My stepmother, who returned to Missoula with her daughter, felt her loss deeply.[5] She was a very clever woman of Scotch descent. She could speak several Indian languages besides English and French. Very few women were as skillful as she was in needle work, especially in embroidering leather. After I married, I was on good terms with my father, and even more so with my stepmother. She always gave me good advice on how to treat my wife and how to bring up my children. But what I most admired in her was her kindness and patience to my father during his long months of helpless suffering from rheumatism. Her daughter Julia married Captain Higgins[6] sometime after my father's death. He was not wealthy, but he was a good manager, and he invested his wife's money to good advantage. He began to keep a store; then he went into partnership with one Frank Worden. He afterwards organized a bank called the National Bank of Missoula, and he was president of it. One of his sons died a year or so ago. He had risen to be Governor of the State [actually, Lieutenant Governor].

1. The frontier commercial center of Walla Walla was strategically connected to The Dalles and Portland, Oregon, via the Columbia River corridor, and supplied the Bitterroot and northern Rockies mining camps from the west. The bustling new town stood adjacent to the U.S. Army's Fort Walla Walla, which had been established in 1856 during the Yakima War. For several decades, Walla Walla continued as the economic and social hub for eastern Washington Territory, Idaho's Bitterroot country, and parts of western Montana Territory. The post and town should not be confused with the older Canadian fur trading post (1818-55) of the same name, located 27 miles to the west at the mouth of the Walla Walla River.

2. Actually, Richard Grant was "68 years and 5 months" at the time of his death on June 21, 1862. (6/28/1862, *Washington Statesman* [Walla Walla, WT])

3. On June 24, 1862, James Stuart at Gold Creek, reported: "Word came that Captain Richard Grant is seriously ill at Walla Walla, and his sons, John and Jimmie have gone to see him. The doctors say he cannot live long. This has cast a gloom over the entire settlement. Captain Grant was a jovial kind hearted gentleman and very popular with the mountaineers." (*Forty Years on the Frontier*, Vol. 1, 211)

4. "Both he [Richard Grant] and his daughter Helene, aged sixteen, died in a tepee on Mill creek, near Walla Walla, while returning from The Dalles with a year's supply of provisions for the ranch. Later his grave (possibly that of his daughter as well) was moved to Mountain View Cemetery, Walla Walla, and marked in 1923 with a simple stone, 'Richard Grant, Chief Trader, H.B.Co.'" (*Catholic Church Records of the Pacific Northwest*)

According to the fur trade historian, T.C. Elliott: "A daughter named Helena, aged about 16 years, died at the same time and was laid beside her father . . . Grant at the time was returning home from The Dalles, where he had purchased a year's supplies for his family and cattle ranch, located on what is known yet as Grant Creek, a few miles northwest of present day Missoula." ("Richard . . . Grant," *Oregon Historical Quarterly* 36 [March 1935]: 1)

In an amazingly inaccurate and erroneous account of Richard Grant's death, pioneer George W. Goodhart later related the following story while supposedly camped with Johnny Grant and his father in the upper Snake River country: "some old squaws came down and told us that old Mr. Grant was dead.

"Johnny said, 'What will we do?'

"I said, 'Let us go and see . . . I think the best thing we can do is to lay him out on a buffalo robe, on the outside of the wickiup where the sun won't strike him early in the morning.'

". . . About nine o'clock Johnny woke me up and said his father was in the hot sun and that we ought to do something with him [they dug a grave].

"One of the men took a pencil and wrote on it: HERE LIES/JOHNNY GRANT/GENERAL SUPERINTENDENT FOR THE HUDSON'S BAY COMPANY/AGE 94 YEARS/DIED AUGUST 1862[.] Then we dug a hole and set it in solid at his head; and in 1921 it was still there, only broken a little."

Goodhart's description is a complete falsehood both in regard to location and the circumstances of Richard Grant's death, and brings into doubt the overall reliability of Goodhart's reminiscences. (George W. Goodhart, *Trails of Early Idaho*, 253-54)

5. Helene McDonald Kittson Grant survived her husband by a little more than a year, passing away at the age of 52 on August 7, 1863, at the Grant Creek ranch (Glen Lindeman and Keith Petersen, "The Kittson Legacy," family chart).

In August 1863, Major John Owen in the Bitterroot Valley noted: "Monday 10 Recd a Note from Mr. Wm Sinclair informing Me of the Death of Mrs. Grant. Poor Woman she has paid the great debt of Nature at last. Peace to her ashes. She Was a good Woman an affectionate Wife & Kind Mother. She died on friday last the day after I left Hell Gate the place of her residence" (*The Journals and Letters of Major John Owen*, Vol. I, 290).

6. On March 31, 1863, Owen received a "report of Capt. C.P. Higgins having Married Miss Julia Grant." (*Ibid*, 278)

# 21

## IN WHICH HE BUILDS THE FIRST GOOD HOUSE IN DEER LODGE VALLEY, AND WITH HIS QUARRA ENTERS ON A NEW PERIOD OF EXISTENCE.

In the fall of 1862 I built a house in Cottonwood, afterwards called Deer Lodge. It cost me a pretty penny. I hauled my lumber from the Flathead Reserve, which was one hundred and fifty miles away. The house was made of hewed logs with posts in the corner. It was sixty-four feet long, thirty feet wide, and sixteen feet high. I paid five dollars a day to McLeod, the hewer; and to the carpenter, Alexander Pambrun,[1] I paid nine dollars per day. Now came the plastering. There was no lime to be had. I did not know limestone when I saw it. Some people told me it was one color; others said it was such another; so to be certain about it I took a boy and went on the mountain and picked up some stones of different colors and put them in the stove to urn. The one that slacked I knew to be limestone.

I then went with a wagon and hauled plenty more of this kind and burnt it. Now that I had the lime, a plasterer was needed. I got one and he charged me one hundred and fifty dollars to plaster the first story, but it was very well done. I went back to the house twenty years after, and the plaster was as sound as ever.

I only had homemade furniture at first; but about four or five years after, I bought Captain Labarge's freight; and among the lot there were some parlor chairs. I paid twenty dollars each for two parlor chairs, and ten dollars each for four other chairs. I also bought ten thousand dollars' worth of flour and groceries from him. The captain gave me a receipt in full before I paid him one cent, and then he came two hundred miles with me to get the money. The year before he had brought up the Missouri on his boat some freight for a Captain Hall. He was obliged to leave it on a sandbar on account of low water, and it got damaged. Then Captain Hall sued him for thirty thousand dollars damages, and he was afraid to get his goods seized. I've sometimes thought as I look back to the old days that if I had been one of the desperados who began to come into the country then, I could have got out of paying the captain easily. For in that long drive from the Missouri, we passed over some very steep and very narrow trails on the brink of canyons when I could have [leapt from the] waggon on the hillside and let the [?] and the horses go over the brink of the canyon a couple of hundred [feet].

My house was not finished until the spring of 1863,[2] but we moved into it the year before; and Quarra, my little wife, showed a wonderful skill in taking up all the ways of white women. She had already learned to cook well, for she had worked for my people at Fort Hall, and she now made good butter. She could make my clothing as well as a tailor, and in every way she was a capable wife, as bright and as merry as a lark; and she was very proud of our new house.[3] She was a woman of the Snake tribe, and still very young—about twenty years old and the mother of two children.

One day that spring when Quarra was upstairs in the house, she called down to me, "There is old Cream coming."

I went up to the window and looked out and over the plains. Away out on the trail there was a bunch of horses with my old cream horse at the head. As he came nearer, I could see him smell the road from time to time, then raise his head and come on at a fast trot. I felt myself choking at the sight of my old horse after seven years. I ran down and out to meet him.

It was my old partner Bennett, whom I had not seen for eleven years, who had the bunch of horses. I did not know how he came by my "Cream." I had sold him to Fred Burr in 1855 [1856?], but anyhow it made no difference to me. I only wanted my horse again. I offered Bennett a big black horse, a younger one for him; but he told me he would not trade Cream for ten horses; he considered him the best horse he had.

"Mr. Bennett," I said, "you have owed me twenty-five horses for several years; but you give me Cream and you can go. We'll cry quits. Anyhow, Bennett, I warn you that I'll take him whether you are willing or not."

So when he knew I was determined on it, he took the black horse and gave me my old Cream.

In the spring of 1862 the Blackfeet Indians[4] stole one hundred head of my horses, as well as some that belonged to others. Together with five other men who had lost some horses I followed the thieves. We overtook them one hundred and fifteen miles from home, three of us getting there first. They were sitting down, I suppose preparing for a fight, while one was on horseback watching.

When we came up he rode unto a knoll. Thomas Lavatta wanted to shoot him, for he was at a good range, but I objected. I had now taken up freighting instead of trading and I had to be cautious.

"If you shoot him," I said, "when we go to Fort Benton for freight, they will follow our oxen with arrows."

When the Indian who was guard and who was coming behind us saw the dust rise before my companions, he called out to the other Blackfeet to leave in a hurry, for the Snakes were coming. He knew I lived with the Snakes, and he thought I had a party of them. The Blackfeet started with the band of horses, but when they reached the mouth of a ravine, they left the horses there and went in another direction to mislead us. If they had kept on in the same direction, I do not believe we could have overtaken them, for our horses were tired, and we had been riding a long distance, while they had been changing horses so often, their mounts were fresh.

However they got away with seven of my best horses. The one woman among them was riding a big racehorse of mine that I had run in Fort Benton the year before. I suppose they knew he was a fast horse.

Only forty-six were left when we caught up to them; the remainder were scattered all along the road, as they could not be very easily driven away from their range. Coming home we found them all. A couple of the American horses had foundered.

Three of the Blackfeet had forked off from the party before we had caught up to them and had went to the Blackfeet Agency, where Little Dog,[5] their chief, lived. Now Little Dog was my friend since the time I had given dinner to those Blackfeet Indians who had come down on the Little Blackfoot when I was living there all alone. I had treated them well and Little Dog had not forgotten. As I had said before, an Indian never forgets a good turn.

Little Dog was at the agency when the three Indians arrived there. He recognized my horses at once. He made those Indians dismount, saying those horses belonged to his friend, and he took charge of them for me.

1. "Alexandre Pambrun (1829-1912) married the beautiful daughter of Samuel Black, Angelique, who was a pupil in the Sister's School in Oregon City and called 'one of the song birds.' The two were married by the Protestant minister, Rev. G. H. Atkinson, in Oregon City on November 15, 1851. Angelique died in Vancouver a few years later. 'Unable to bear the sight of the little home where the deaf school now stands,' the family recalls, 'he placed his little daughter Harriet Emelie in the Sister's School and went with his younger brother John to work for Richard Grant on the Beaverhead

Ranch in Montana.' Presently he had a cattle ranch of his own and a part Blackfoot wife Therese, widow of one Burdeaux. After the death of his second wife, Pambrun went to live with his married daughter, Harriet Emelie Truchot. He was a forward-looking, courteous and generous man, remembered fondly for his engaging ways and consideration for others." (*Catholic Church Records of the Pacific Northwest*)

　"In 1862 he [Alexander Pambrun] started freighting with John F. Grant from Fort Benton to Fort Charles and Deer Lodge." (Obituary of A. Pambrun, 12/4/1912, *Acantha* [Choteau, Montana])

2. Exact figures and descriptions for the initial construction of the Grant home at Cottonwood, if they exist, have yet to come to light, but in 1864 Johnny entered into a contract with Louis LaFrance for the finish work on the house: "Louis LaFrance agrees to make construct and finish the following mentioned work on and in a building now in progress of erection for the said John Grant - viz - twenty three large windows, two four light windows, three transom windows. Twenty five shutters and sashes for the said windows and the frames. Six batten doors, one double Panel door with the frames and hangings. to lay down two floors, one upper and lower floor, one pair of straight Stairs with one hand rail, to put on Shingle roof, to finish [furnish?] all the necessary shingles for said roof. John Grant agrees on his part to furnish all necessary material Lumber. Nails. Screws. Locks and Hinges, and all the necessary tools to be delivered at the building. John Grant also agreeing to Board the said Louis LaFrance and his workmen during the time necessary to finish said work. Said work to be completed on or before the first day of November AD One thousand Eight hundred and Sixty Four. John Grant furthermore agrees that when said work shall be faithfully and completely finished to truly and faithfully pay to the said Louis LaFrance the sum of One thousand one hundred dollars ($1,100.00) in Gold or its equivalent.

　Signed and delivered in presence of Louis La France (signature) / F. H. [Bien] (signature) / John Grant (signature)

　(Granville Stuart Collection, Brigham Young University)

3. The house became known for lively parties, and solemn rights, as well: "The Catholic church of the Immaculate Conception was founded by Rev. R. De Ryckere, in July, 1866. Previous to this time, however, and for many years, the place [Deer Lodge] was known to the fathers of the mission, and services were held at the house of John Grant. On the first Sunday after Father De Ryckere's arrival he held service at John Grant's house, later the residence of Conrad Kohrs." (M. Leeson, *History of Montana, 1739-1885*, 561)

4. On April 30, 1862: "Johnny Grant sent Pierre Ish down to tell us that 'Tom Gold Digger' and Tom Campbell had arrived from Fort Benton and say that there is a war party of Blackfeet on the road over to steal horses from this side of the mountains" (Granville Stuart, *Forty Years on the Frontier*, Vol. 1, 205).

5. Little Dog played a prominent role in Montana history throughout this period, and his name appears frequently in the frontier literature recorded at the time.

# 22

## IN WHICH HE REWARDS THE HONESTY OF LITTLE DOG FOR RESTORING HIS STOLEN HORSES. WHEREIN HE MAKES A COUPLE OF TRIPS AMONG THE INDIANS IN SEARCH OF STOLEN HORSES; BROWN, A DISCOURAGED COMPANION, SHOOTS HIMSELF.

That same summer I went to Fort Benton and Little Dog returned my horses. He told me that if he had known the Indians had stolen more, he would have gone after them. This chief, who usually wore the coat of an American officer, was short but well built, and very intelligent. He had nine wives, one of whom was an American half-breed. Mr. Vaughan, who was the Indian agent, one day gave strict orders to Little Dog that wherever he saw any white man with liquor in his possession, he should take it and spill it.

The chief asked him, "Everyone's?"

"Yes," Mr. Vaughan said, "everyone's, without exception."

"But those who have given their money for the liquor do not like to part with it, for I suppose they must like it," said Little Dog.

Mr. Vaughan said, "That makes no difference. I tell you to spill all the liquor you see on the reserve, for they have no business to bring any there."

"I will do it," Little Dog replied, and, stooping he reached under Mr. Vaughan's bed and drew out a two gallon keg of whiskey.

Vaughan said to him, "What are you going to do with that keg?"

"Ha!" the chief said, "I am going to spill it out."

"Oh, no!", said Mr. Vaughan, "not that one."

"Well," said Little Dog, "other white men like their whiskey as well as you do. If I cannot spill that one, I will not spill their's either."

Mr. Vaughan saw that Little Dog was too shrewd for him. The chief was, like himself, too fond of the fire water to spill it, so he finally settled the agreement by treating the chief and himself with some of the contents of the keg.

On my return from Fort Benton the following summer, I went to the Bannock mines on business. While I was there some of the Blackfeet stole twenty-two of my horses. Two months after, the same chief, Little Dog, and another chief, Long Hair, who was also my friend, brought back these horses together with the other three that the Blackfeet had stolen in the spring. I rewarded them for their honesty. I gave them each a horse and one hundred and fifty dollars worth of dry goods and groceries.

I had bought a fine blood colt from my father for one hundred dollars. He was three years old then, a fine horse but very wicked. He would bite, kick, and strike with the front feet. I caught him that day the chiefs came, threw him down, bridled him, and packed him with the one hundred and fifty dollars' worth of goods. I then gave the rope to Chief Long Hair and told him to handle him as I had done.

"You see," I said, "he is very wild; but be sure to do as I have done and you will be safe."

He was well satisfied; but it appears that the next morning he bridled the horse as I had done, but instead of putting the goods on his back, he put his wife on. The horse bucked and sent the poor woman flying into the air. She fell and had an arm broken. When Long Hair reached Fort Benton, he sold him for ten buffalo robes which was equal to about twenty-five dollars.

That same summer the horse was sold to some Crow Indians for twenty buffalo robes. The next year this band came to Fort Benton, and two Crow Indians were riding the same horse. They had quite conquered him, as the Crows always can break in horses. Some of the whites at the fort offered the Indians four horses for him, but the Indian refused the offer saying, "Oh no. This horse just plays with the buffalo."

He meant by that, the horse was very fast and a good hunter.

That same horse was the cause of much merriment. One day when there were at Deer Lodge two half-breeds from Edmonton, Canada, one Charles Favel and his brother. I had this young blood horse caught, and they admired him greatly. One of them who considered himself a great rider agreed to ride the horse, and for the rest of us it was an amusing sight to see that horse buck. He bucked forward and sideways and every other way that a horse can buck. He did it all in a circle of about one hundred yards, but could not throw his rider off unless the horn of the saddle would break. It was as good as a circus for the women and children. They all came out to look.

It was comical to see him. His hair was rather long and cut broom fashion, and the bucking of the horse shook him so that his hair would fly up every time his head moved.

When he dismounted he looked at his bruised knuckles ruefully, but he only said, "Hey, boy, he jumps high."

He was a good rider, but he did not care to ride that colt a second time.

To come back to my Indians, I gave Little Dog a quiet horse and one hundred and fifty dollars' worth of goods. Both men were very well pleased and thanked me for my liberality. They went away rejoicing. I may appear to have been very liberal with those Indians, but it was good policy on my part, for it was certainly to my advantage to secure their friendship and good will, even at the cost of two or three hundred dollars. For as I have already stated, I was certainly at their mercy without the least protection, as there were no police or no other officers of the law to protect us. Everyone had to protect himself.

I had reasons to be on my guard. My horses were stolen four times in eighteen months—three times by the Blackfeet. Early in the spring of 1862 I was driving Frank Worden, Captain [C.P.] Higgins, [Thomas] Adams, [John W.] Powell, and Bolton to Fort Benton. Frank Worden and Powell were intending to go by boat to St. Louis, Missouri.

One morning after we had traveled about sixty miles, Worden went for the horses, and shortly afterwards returned, rubbing his hands excitedly, saying, "We're afoot; we're afoot."

I thought he was joking, but it was only too true. He brought us to see the tracks; the Indians had taken our horses by a path even close to where we were camped. They led them over our heads on a rock ledge projecting over the camps. The horses had been turned out to graze and had wandered onto higher ground, so that we could not see them.

I went up with Worden; and as he had said, there was not a horse left. We saw the Indians' tracks and a gun worm[1] and a wiping rod. So we knew that it was the Blackfeet who had visited us, for they use the flint lock gun.

Four of us started out on foot that day, and we had traveled only a mile when luckily we found four of our horses that had not been seen by

the Indians. I suppose they had been in the bushes. I took the horses back
to our camp and told our companions who were there to pack them and
come after us. I went on, leaving them to follow the other three [men] who
had gone ahead. That night we all camped on the Dearborn River. Next
morning we held a consultation and decided that four of us would keep on
traveling with the horses until we reached Sun River Agency, then to secure horses there and send them back to meet those who were left behind.
But we were disappointed. We could not get one horse [at Sun River
Agency], so we did the next best thing. We sent back a team of oxen.

At last we arrived at Fort Benton. I hired a Blackfoot half-breed named
Baptiste Champaigne to come with me to follow my horses that had been
stolen. None of my party would come to search.

Baptiste and I went to the Sweet Grass Hills, about seventy-five miles
from Fort Benton, to a big camp of Blackfeet, but they [the horses] were
not there; so we camped and the next day went on to another camp about
twenty miles farther. As soon as we reached that place, the Chief Big Nose
and one of his sons, to our surprise, mounted our horses and rode off, not
returning until evening. In the meantime, we were invited into a lodge and
there given a meal of the best that was in it. We certainly relished a dish of
boiled buffalo tongue and meat from the hump. While we were eating, an
Indian was standing at the door, and as soon as we had finished, he beck-
oned to us to come out and accept an invitation from him to go into his
lodge for another meal.

There was no end to their courtesy and hospitality; they would like
us to enter each lodge and take a meal in each. When the chief returned, he
had not only the horses we brought that day, but the others that had been
stolen on the Fort Benton trail.

He rode into the camp and said to his people, "This white man does
not live in our country. When we go to his place, he treats us well. He feeds
us to the eyes. When we go to the agency at Fort Benton, the white people
will eat before us and never ask us to eat. In spite of that, when you steal a
horse, you take his. It looks as if you did it for a reason."

He then turned to me and said, "My friend, there are your horses,"
pointing to them. "They are thin, but it is better to count their ribs than
their tracks."

While he was talking, I noticed his son was looking with longing
at my saddle blanket. It was a fine bright one, called the Navajo blanket. I gave it to him. He immediately went into their lodge and brought
out a very fine buffalo robe. I told him I could not take it, for my horses

were too thin, but to give me a small piece of robe to put under my saddle.

Others offered me moccasins, and other [word missing] but I could not take anything, for my horses were too poor to be burdened.

That Chief Big Nose, it seems, was one of those who had visited my house at the Little Blackfoot, and he had not forgotten my hospitality.

We struck the trail again, abandoning the next day on the road four horses that were too tired to push on.

It was all I could do to reach Fort Benton, for I could not ride any further. I had been ruptured two years before[, on] One day we were having a contest at jumping [. . .] I could not get a truss before I left home [Cottonwood]. Maillet had warned me not to go to Fort Benton with those men. He said I would have to break the road, for it was early in the spring, and there was a hard crust on the snow, which was also very deep in the mountain divides. I told him I would remain behind and follow them, but he said he knew when we got to the deep snow, I would go ahead, and that would be just the worst place for me. I said I would not.

I kept my word the first day of the trip, but I soon got tired of watching them going from one side to the other not making any headway. They were not accustomed to that kind of traveling, so I went ahead. After our horses were stolen, I walked thirty miles and carried Adams' rifle besides my own. All this with the riding after those horses had aggravated my rupture to such a degree it became almost unbearable. I was obliged to get some kind of a wagon to make the return trip.

I bought an old iron axle wagon. It looked like one that had been made in Adam's time it was so primitive. I had to hire a man to drive me home.

On one other occasion two of my horses were stolen by the Snake Indians. They stole some of the other traders horses as well, Gold Tom [Henry Thomas] and a man named Brown being the losers.[2] They were furious and threatened to kill any of the Indians that would come to town whether he was friendly or not. I asked them why they did not go for their horses.

Gold Tom replied there was no one to go with them; I told him I would go, although I was not worrying much over two horses, so then they could not very well back out. I brought a hired man by the name of White, and there were five of us in all.

We found the horses' tracks not far from this range, and we followed them. When the tracks began to look fresh, the other traders began to complain that their horses were getting tired; but it was their courage that was failing. As we pushed on, the tracks grew fresh. I told them to hurry up, that we were getting close to the Indians; but they replied that their horses were getting too tired to go farther. I showed them a bluff of timber ahead and told them to go and camp there, while I will follow the tracks, or get my horses or kill an Indian.

I then started at a fast gait. After traveling some time, I went up a ravine and then to the top of a hill to see if I could see the Indians. There were three of them down in the bottom of the ravine. They were eating and had three of the horses by them. Another Indian was with the remainder of the horses, which were about three hundred yards from them grazing. Two others were digging roots at the foot of the hills. I turned and motioned to my companions to come.

One of them distanced the others, and when he came to me, I pointed out the Indians to him and said, "Shoot that one."

He had a good rifle, but he would not shoot. He said they were Flathead Indians.

"Do you not see your horses?"

He answered, "There is a big company of Indians over yonder," pointing to the bluff of timber where I had told the others to go to and camp.

I told him it was only a bluff of dry cottonwood. "Give me your rifle," I said.

He would not. In the meantime the rest of our party caught up to us.

The Indians now noticed that they were [being] followed and mounted their horses, starting to herd the other horses. I immediately understood their drift and ran down the hill to cut them off before they reached the horses. At the same time I called out to my companions to hurry and go for the horses. There was only one Indian guarding them. My men refused. There were some willows to pass through, and they feared that there might be Indians ambushed there who would kill them. My man White was willing to come, but the others said their horses were tired. Oliver Leclair, a son of my old friend Michand Leclair, would not even come down the hill. The cowards that they were. I gave them a piece of my mind after all their boasting of what they were intending to do if they saw the Indians with their horses.

I told them, "There are your horses. If you do not want them, I do not intend to risk my life to get them for you."

They turned back. I am certain the Indians laughed at us.[3] I only had two horses among them, and my brother-in-law Tyndaille [Tendoy] got them for me the next winter. When I went to trade among the Snakes, they said that they stole my horses because they were angry with me for leaving them and going to live with other tribes. They meant my living in Deer Lodge, which was not a place they frequented, other tribes passing there, as I have already stated.

To return to our wild goose chase after the Indians who had stolen our horses, the trader Brown had all his horses stolen but two; and a few days after, the Indians came back and stole them. Poor Brown got discouraged at being so unfortunate, in fact, he tired of life.

He took his pistol one day at home saying, "This is too much bad luck," and he put it to his ear and blew out his brains.

It was about this time [September 1861] that young Michel Leclair, a son of my old friend Michand Leclair, came to his death[4] at Cottonwood in a quarrel with an American named Frank [Goodwin], who was himself shot a short time after. After shooting Michel, Frank went to Fort Benton and remained there some time, turning out his horses with the herd at the fort.

One day [in 1862] the horses were brought in, and he noticed that someone had been riding his horse. On inquiry he found out the herder, who was an Italian, had ridden his horse. Frank beat him on the head with a pistol and nearly killed him. This Italian lived upstairs in the fort. There was a gallery there over the front door and a door opening onto it from the house. The Italian saw Frank coming to the fort some time after, and he leaned over the gallery and shot him. He went down and emptied his pistol in him.[5] He then went away with another man, and I afterwards heard that he was killed by the Sioux Indians.

1. This reference is to a gun worm—a small, wired, screw-like device. When screwed into the end of a ramrod, it was utilized to extract a ball from the barrel of a muzzleloading rifle or to clean the rifling with a patch.
2. Granville Stuart's diary entry for May 8, 1862, probably refers to this incident, though Stuart writes that "Bannocks," and not "Snakes," ran off the horses: "Tom Campbell and Joe Hill came down from above and report that those Bannocks stole about twenty-five horses from Johnny Grant. Gold Tom, Brown, Ish, Chas. DeLabreche and several others are in pursuit of them and I surely hope they may overtake them and return home loaded with Bannock scalps." (*Forty Years on the Frontier*, Vol. 1, 208) As Grant noted earlier, the Bannock associated with the Shoshone, or "Snake."
3. Again, apparently in reference to this incident, Stuart reported on May 11, 1862: "Gold Tom came down from above. He says they overtook those Bannock horse thieves, but did not get their horses, because the Indians 'bluffed' them off. I suppose there were six or seven whites and but ten Indians. They should have gotten those horses." (*Ibid*, 208)

4. Stuart also wrote about this shooting: "Sunday, September 29 [1861 . . .] Frank Goodwin went up to John Grant's and got into a drunken row and shot Michel LeClaire twice, with a navy Colt's revolver, wounding him (it is supposed) mortally. Poor little Michel he was under middle size but active and strong and only twenty years old. Goodwin was much larger, weighing about one hundred and sixty-five pounds and could have handled poor Michel without shooting him. It is a shame. This is the effect of bringing whiskey into a peaceful quiet community."

Earlier in the year, on May 31, Stuart had noted: "Went up to Little Blackfoot settlement and found the majority of the inhabitants on a drunk." (*Ibid*, 169, 187)

5. Another version of this incident has the altercation arising over "a gambling game," and Frank Goodwin's death coming at the hands of a "Greek," rather than an "Italian." (*Ibid*, 208 fn.)

# 23

## WHEREIN HE TELLS OF HIS BIG FREIGHTING OUT-FIT, AND OF THE ADVENT OF "BAD MEN," THIEVES, AND MURDERERS—INTO MONTANA. IN WHICH THE VIGILANTES ARE SEEN TO TAKE THE LAW IN THEIR OWN HANDS, AND THE RASCALLY SHERIFF IS ONE OF THE FIRST TO BE HANGED.

I was now satisfied that the Snakes would not trouble me any more, for Tyndaille [Tendoy], I was certain, would protect me; and as to the Blackfeet, I had three of the principal chiefs as friends. There was no danger of my horses being molested by any of that tribe. I could now go to Fort Benton and not be afraid to be left on foot.

I had a large quantity of freight, partly for my own store and also for others to bring from Benton to Deer Lodge. I had a freight train which consisted of twenty-eight wagons.

There were ten wagons drawn by horses. Two of these were drawn by six horses in each, my wagon master driving one, and the other, I myself in charge. Eight other horse wagons had four horses on each; the remaining eighteen wagons were drawn by six yokes of oxen in each. I also had some extra oxen for relays. I was as proud of my oxen as a good teamster is of his horses. I had them all well matched, the six yokes in each wagon being of the same color. I had thirty-two hired men and paid five dollars a day to Alex Pambrun and as much to two carpenters and seventy-five per month to my teamsters.

All my accounts I kept in my head. Sometimes I would get a little mixed up and it gave me some trouble, so I got a book and pencil to keep my accounts; but after putting them down, I could not understand my own writing. I concluded to hire a bookkeeper. The first one was James Arnold. He was not a competent man, for I could reckon mentally quicker than he could with a pen. But I had no choice. I soon learned, however, that as soon as I had to depend on others I lost money.

I freighted in those days for others and got ten dollars per hundred for hauling freight one hundred and eighty miles. There was more money made freighting then than there is at the present time. Freight from St. Louis, Missouri, to Fort Benton by boat was twenty-five cents per pound. In 1862 I ordered goods from St. Louis for the first time to the amount of four thousand two hundred dollars, but the boat sunk at Sioux City and I lost all except twenty large ox chains, which weighed one hundred pounds each. They cost me delivered in Deer Lodge twenty-five dollars each for freight only from Sioux City by land.

If I had had more experience and placed more value on money, I would not have taken them. I wrote about my loss to Mr. Campbell, the dry goods merchant at St. Louis with whom I had invested my money. He had paid the freight and insurance, he answered, but he could not get any indemnity for me, as the insurance company blamed the steam boat company, and they blamed the company. It seems that the boat had been hired to bring corn from Sioux City for the government, but they failed to do so. Then the government compelled them to go back for the corn. While turning, the boat struck a snag in the river. It sprung a leak and sunk, so between them I never was paid. If I had been more used to doing business and had kept pressing my claim, I would have got my insurance, but I trusted to others and the result was as usual—I lost all.

My mind was scarcely at rest about the safety of my horses from Indian thieves when I had to reckon with white men who were also robbers and murderers.[1] They were more to be feared than Indians, for they were living right in among us in our settlements. In the fall of 1863 a well-to-do German who lived in Virginia City in Montana sent his hired man [Nicholas Tiebalt, or Tbalt] for two mules that were in a herd kept by a man called Long John [John Franck]. It was about twenty miles from his home. His man not returning, he became uneasy and suspected that he had deserted with the mules. He enquired of everyone he saw coming from Denver if they had met a man with two mules and at the same time giving description of the man and the mules; but no one had seen them, so he suspected foul play. He was not mistaken.

A few days afterwards a man [William Palmer] hunting in that neighborhood shot a pheasant which fell in a bunch of willows. He went to pick up his bird, but imagine his surprise on finding the dead body of a man close to where his bird lay. He at once reported this at the mines, giving a description of the man he had found. The German, hearing of the murder, went to see the body and recognized his man. He had been found near

Long John's cabin, so John was arrested on suspicion and accused of being the murderer or an accomplice.

He was threatened with lynching if he would not give some information in regard to the murder. He told them that if they gave him his liberty, he would tell who had murdered the man. They released him on those conditions, and he told them that George Ives and Whiskey Bill [William Graves] had killed him and robbed the man of two hundred dollars and the two mules.

The citizens of Virginia City, nearly all miners, then formed a committee called the Vigilance Committee with one [Wilbur F.] Sanders as leader, for the protection of the public against highwaymen who were keeping the country in a state of terror. The Vigilantes began to search for George Ives.

In the meantime Conrad Kohrs, a butcher from Virginia mines, came and bought cattle from me. The day after he left I went to meet my wagons which were coming from Salt Lake loaded with flour and groceries. I wanted to send one half to Virginia City and the other to Deer Lodge. Fifteen miles from home at Warm Spring Creek I caught up to Con [Conrad Kohrs] who could not make his cattle cross the ice. I had a strong horse and went ahead to break the ice for him, but I ruined my horse, a fine pacer. It bruised his front legs, but I did not notice it till next morning when he was quite stiff. I thought when he would get warmed up he would be all right, but instead he became worse, and by the time I had traveled fifteen miles he could scarcely walk. I was all day getting back to Spence's place.

That evening before dark George Ives and Whiskey Bill came up the trail laughing and chatting and went into Long John's tent which was near [James] Spence's. After supper Long John came into Spence's tent.

He talked for a few minutes before he said coolly, "George Ives killed a man today."

No one spoke, for among such ruffians the less said the better.

After he had gone a few minutes, George Ives came in and chatted for some time.

At last he said, swearing, "I killed the toughest white man I ever killed, I emptied my revolver on him and had to finish him with my shotgun."[2]

No one said a word. I looked at him to see if there was any change in the countenance of a man who had committed such a cold-blooded murder, but there was not the slightest.

He added, "Dead men tell no tales."

He then began to talk of how he had once held up a stage. This stage had been held up on its way to Salt Lake not long before.

[Bill] Bunton, one of the passengers, was known to be a very brave man, but this time he lost his nerve; and when the robbers held up the stage, he gave over his little sack of gold and his revolver quietly. "That is all I have boys, do not spill any blood," he said.[3]

The other passengers on the stage seeing Bunton give in so easily followed his example and gave up their gold and other valuables. Long after[ward,] some of them learned what Bunton was up to that night. One fellow there named Bummer Dan [Dan McFadden] had been a reckless harum-scarum fellow, fond of drink, a good miner who made money only for the pleasure of spending it. But for some time before, he had been getting more careful and had saved five thousand dollars which he was bringing to Salt Lake to invest. He knew there was danger of being robbed on the way, so he had enquired where he had better carry his gold; and someone in league with the robbers must have heard of it, for they knew exactly where he had hidden the gold. When they called on him to hand it over, he gave up four sacks. They ordered him to hand out the other two he had around his belt, and he gave up his last dollar.

No one knew who had robbed the stage. Some time after that there was a man loafing around the camp [Nevada City], a shiftless fellow who never seemed to work. He stole some underwear from one of the miners and was arrested. They threatened to hang him to frighten him.

He said scornfully, "You want to hang a man for stealing underwear, but you never touched those who robbed the stage."

With threats they ordered him to tell the names of those who had held up the stage, and he promised to do so if they gave him his liberty. They agreed, and he told them it was George Ives and his chum Doc who had done it.

George Ives heard about this and that man was doomed. That same day this poor fellow was walking down the road when George Ives shot him.

So that night in Spence's tent after talking about the man he had killed, Ives said, "I have three more men to kill here, and then I will gather my horses and go among the Blood Indians. Then let every Yankee[4] look out who comes in my way."

He went away from Spence's, but coming back later asked me when I was going back to Deer Lodge.

I told him I would leave the next day.

Well, he said, "I will travel with you."

I was not very anxious to travel with him after hearing him say that he intended to kill three more men, for perhaps I was one of the men he meant. So I added, ["]I must go to Virginia City first["], and [I] went, but I did not get any money.

So Ives changed his mind. He asked me if anyone had said anything about the man that was killed on the road. I had heard nothing of it. I started home, for I was anxious to leave his company. He stayed at Long John's till at last he was arrested by the Vigilantes with Doc and Bohn Olham [Boone Helm]. They were taken to Virginia City, and on the way George Ives attempted to escape to the mountains, but he was followed; and when his horse put his foot in a badger hole and fell, Ives was recaptured.

On their arrival at Virginia City they were hanged. One of them, Bohn Olham [Boone Helm] was asked when he had the rope around his neck if he had anything to say before his death.

He shouted defiantly, "Hurrah for Jeff Davis, you Yankee sons of b!" He then swung into eternity.[5]

That same Olham [Boone Helm], I was told, five years before was going to Fort Bridger with three other men when they lost their horses at the foot of the hill on Bear River. They were snowed in, their provisions ran out, and afterwards were obliged to live on human flesh like cannibals. Olham [Helm] survived his companions. In the spring he was found by an Indian in the Fort Hall Bottom. He still had a human thigh left which he was devouring like a wild beast. It is not surprising that he was such a desperate character.

The Vigilantes, I think, strung up five more of the robbers. There was at that time in Virginia City a lawyer named [H.P.A.] Smith who wanted to defend those desperados. He appeared to take a great deal of interest in their welfare, so much so that the Vigilantes began to suspect that he was in the ring with the robbers; so they arrested him and told him they were going to hang him. Their threats had the desired effect. He begged to be released and told them that if they gave him his freedom he would tell them where the rest of the robbers were to be found. They agreed. He then told them to go to Bannock [Bannack] and they would find the list of names in the possession of Henry Plummer, the sheriff.[6]

They went to Mr. Plummer's and found the list. There were eighty-two members in the gang. The sheriff was the leader of the robbers, so the safety of the public was in poor hands. When Plummer saw that he was to be hanged, he went wild. He cried and begged for his life. Although he was looked upon as a desperado, he was at heart a miserable coward. He promised the Vigilantes to walk to Salt Lake if they would give him his liberty, but they believed that such a notorious character had already lived too long and the world was better rid of him. The robbers could not have [had] a better leader for he had the law in his own hands. If a robbery was committed, it was reported to him; but he made no arrest. He got his share of the spoils, and let the robber free. He was a villain of the worst type, as this story will show:

He and a man [Jack Cleveland] whom he pretended to befriend came from Florence one year and wintered at Snow River. They lived, together, in fact and shared one bed. Plummer's companion looked upon him as a warm friend. One day they were in a saloon together at Bannock, and Plummer deliberately shot his companion without the least cause. I suppose the man knew too much of his past life and he was afraid that perhaps he might get him in trouble, for the man he shot did not belong to the gang of robbers.

After shooting that man in such a cowardly way, he turned around and treated the crowd, telling the bartender to charge the drinks to Henry Plummer. He appeared as unconcerned as if he had bid the time of day to a friend. No one said anything to him, he being the sheriff, but that did not save him when the Vigilantes made up their minds to lynch him [January 10, 1864]. They also hanged one Buck Stinson, and they tried to arrest a Mexican [Joe Pizanthia], but he fought desperately so they shot him. After he was dead, they hung him and riddled him full of bullet holes. The next to be lynched were John Baker [Dutch John Wagner] and his companion Steeves [Steve Marshland[7]].

1. Johnny Grant here refers to the infamous "road agents" who infested the bustling Montana and Idaho mining camps during the first years of the gold excitement. Some of what Johnny says is hearsay, and it should be obvious to the reader by now that his hearsay narratives of some other topics have missed the mark by a bit (e.g., in regard to dates, names, and other specifics). However, Grant also presents here valuable testimony about the heyday of the "bad men" and "vigilantes" in Montana history. The standard works describing vigilantism in Montana and Idaho include: Thomas J. Dimsdale, *The Vigilantes of Montana* (1866); Nathaniel P. Langford, *Vigilante Days and Ways* (1890); and Hoffman Birney, *Vigilantes* (1929). Several recent book-length studies also have been published, including Ladd Hamilton, *This Bloody Deed: The Magruder Incident* (1995), and articles on frontier violence have appeared in *Montana: The Magazine of Western History*.

2. Here, Ives is referring to an informer he had just murdered, and not Tbalt, as will shortly become evident in Grant's narrative.

3. Unbeknownst to the other passengers, Bill Bunton was one of the road agents carrying out his part of a carefully rehearsed robbery plan.

4. During these years, as the Civil War raged in the East, several of the road agents in Montana and Idaho were in the habit of freely expressing their contempt of the Union cause.

5. In 1865-66, Professor Thomas J. Dimsdale of Virginia City recorded Boone Helm's last words as: "Every man for his principles—hurrah for Jeff Davis! Let her rip!" (*The Vigilantes of Montana*, 167)

6. As sheriff of Bannack, Plummer was authorized to be the chief law enforcement officer for all of the mining camps east of the Bitterroot Mountains.

7. The quick summary justice dispensed by the Vigilantes, as described by Grant in these chapters, occurred in January 1864, except for the hanging of George Ives, which took place December 21, 1863.

# 24

## In which he lends his horses to the Vigilance Committee setting out for Hell's Gate on their grim mission of death to law breakers.

That same John Baker [Dutch John Wagner] who was hanged by the Vigilantes had worked for me one winter two years before. In the spring he left to go to the Kootenay Mines. It was there I believe he learnt his profession of a highwayman. He returned to Deer Lodge with Steeves [Steve Marshland], and a few days after he came to my house and asked to board with me. I told him he could, for I thought he was an honest man. I had no reason to think otherwise, as I had always found him a good man. A couple of days later he came to board at my place.

One of my teamsters named Tom Reilly said to me, "If you keep that Baker here, it will give Steeves, his friend, the chance to go in and out of your house and they will do you some harm, for they belong to a bad set. If I were in your place, I would send him away as soon as possible."

I took his advice and told Baker [Wagner] that my wife had too much work to do and she did not like to have a stranger to cook for besides the family.

He replied, "I will go if you trade horses with me. I will give you twenty dollars to boot when I come back from Bannock."

I consented, I was glad to get rid of him; in fact, I would have traded even with him to do so. However, I never got the twenty dollars. As soon as we traded, he left.

The next day I started alone on horseback to go to Virginia City to meet Conrad Kohrs. After traveling about eighteen miles I saw Baker's [Wagner] and Steeve's [Marshland] horses grazing near a deserted cabin. I went back of it, tied my horse, and went in. They both looked surprised or pretended to be. But as I soon understood, they must have been waiting for me. They gave as an excuse that they had lost their horses, and they hurried to get ready, for they intended to travel with me. I did not care for their company, but I could not get out of it. They mounted their horses. I certainly was surprised and startled to see their equipment which consisted of a shotgun with the stock cut off just long enough for a hand hold and the barrel cut off about fifteen inches long in the style of thorough high-waymen. I did not feel at my ease, but there was no choice. I did not wish to let them notice my uneasiness, so I said little.

After we started on the road, each in turn would linger behind. I always tried to ride along with the one who was behind. I did not like the way they acted, for I suspected treachery. We had traveled three or four miles when I noticed a wagon coming from Virginia City. There were French people in it and behind them coming round a curve in the road I saw a rider. As he came closer, I recognized Con Kohrs whom I was going to meet.

I said to them, "There is Con. I will go back now."

They looked at one another terribly disappointed. I never imagined they were so bad. That made me certain that if we had not met that wagon in which there were four men they would have killed both Con and me, for they knew he was bringing the money for my cattle. I had told Baker [Wagner] at my house that I was going to Virginia City to get this money, and thirty-five hundred dollars was a temptation with only two lives in the way. I suppose our time had not come.[1] Anyway, we escaped. I went back home, and they continued their journey; but they soon came back, for those Frenchmen who were in that wagon we met and who lived twelve miles from my place said that they saw two men prowling around their place that night.

Then they went about fifty miles from Virginia City and held up five wagons of travelers who were coming from the mines and going to Salt Lake for supplies. They expected to make a big haul there, but they were sadly disappointed. On meeting the wagons they called to the men to hand out their valuables or be shot. One man in the last wagon took up his rifle and in doing so it was discharged accidentally. This shot frightened the robbers a little, and the other travelers took advantage of the scare and fired at the robbers, wounding both of them.

The two escaped, however, to the mountains and were found by the Vigilantes and hung a few days afterwards. Steeves [Marshland] was hung in an old cabin in the Big Hole Canyon. They put the rope around his neck and threw it over the door and pulled him up as high as possible, although his toes were still touching the floor. They left him hanging there without waiting till he was dead. They knew he could not get away.

Baker [Wagner] was found in the Blacktail Deer Canyon. They took him to Bannock and hung him. Before they reached Deer Lodge they caught up to a man named Irving who was taking care of the robbers' horses. They arrested him, but they could not find him guilty of anything, so he was set at liberty; and he certainly took advantage of it, for at once he left for the Kootenay Mines and then through the Canadian northwest country east to the United States.

On arriving in Deer Lodge the Vigilantes arrested one [Bill] Bunton who it appears was one of the leaders of the gang. He had not the appearance of a desperate character, for he was very popular and genteel; in fact, he was a general favorite and good company. He had been to my place several times to dances, and he behaved like a thorough gentleman always. He would be the last man to be suspected of being one of the leaders of such a murderous gang. He was a year in Deer Lodge before I could make his acquaintance.

He came then to my house with Johnny Cooper, and they wanted something to eat. I told them there was nothing cooked, for I was alone; but if they would take bread and butter with milk, they were welcome to it. So I left them to go to the milk house.

They were alone in the house and could see everything. At the time there were seven sacks of gold dust under the table, the contents of each sack being from five hundred dollars to one thousand each. These were not touched. I suppose they thought they would get it later.

They were well satisfied with the reception, they received for they came again and Bunton said to me, "Here, Johnny (most everyone called me Johnny then; in fact, most everyone was known by their first names for often a man's surname was not known). I give you this boy," pointing to Johnny Cooper.

The lad did not look to be more than twenty years old. He was small and delicate looking but plucky.

Bunton said, "You may get in trouble and you can call on him then."

I replied that I did not expect any trouble, for I had no enemies. So I did not take him.

Bunton opened a saloon afterwards alongside of Worden's store. He did a good business and was well thought of. Everybody was surprised when the Vigilantes suddenly arrested him and hung him [at Cottonwood].

They surrounded his house and broke open the door. When he caught sight of them, he called for help, but no help came. He was a doomed man. His time had come.

He had a shotgun and a revolver, but he never tried to use them. They took him out easily and hung him. From there the Vigilantes went to Hell's Gate (now Missoula), ninety miles from Deer Lodge, and before leaving they came to my place and wanted to help themselves to my horses. I objected to having them help themselves. I told them they were as bad as the robbers, but I was as anxious to see the country rid of those highwaymen as any other citizen who had any stake in the country. I wanted the privilege of picking out the horses, for I knew them better than they did, and besides that, they were my own property which no man had any right to take without my consent. I picked out fourteen of my horses better able to carry them than the young stallions they wanted to take. I also gave them a quarter of beef and some flour.[2]

1. Conrad Kohrs, in fact, having had "collected quite a little money" in Bannack in September 1863, may well have been the primary intended victim of the robbers. Kohrs, while on his way to Grant's, was deeply concerned about road agents lurking along the trail, and he also recorded the fortuitous meeting with Grant: "I was fortunate in finding the party composed of John Grant, Leon Cannell, Louis DeMar, L.R. Maillet, who were taking home goods they had bought at Virginia City. They were driving a bunch of horses they had purchased behind their wagons. So I removed my saddle and turned my horse into the bunch and took my cantinas which contained the money and rode in the wagon with Grant.

"It seems that [Sheriff] Plummer, after seeing me leave Bannack, suspected I was going to Deer Lodge and notified his gang . . . that I was on the road." (*Conrad Kohrs: An Autobiography*, 29)

About two months later, Kohrs again was pursued after leaving Virginia City for Cottonwood. Kohrs describes the chase from Moose Creek to Grant's as follows: "Going down to Moose Creek and coming up to Divide Creek I saw the two men [road agents] had reached the top of the divide between Camp and Moose Creeks and were rapidly gaining on me. My anxiety can be imagined. I made use of the first brush I found on Divide Creek to lighten my horse's burden, for I realized that my only safety lay in the fleetness of my horse. I threw off my blankets, took off my overcoat, pistol and belt in order to make his burden as light as possible, remounted and then road for dear life. In spite of the rapidity with which I traveled each mile seemed like five. Up hill and down hill I flew, clinging to my horse, fearing that each moment my pursuers were gaining on me and realizing that the breaking of the surcingle, a stumble of the horse would bring me to certain death.

"My good horse's speed brought me in safety to Grant's place, beating George Ives and Dutch John by only fifteen minutes. The sixty miles from Camp Creek to Cottonwood (Deer Lodge) were ridden in six hours." (*Ibid*, 31)

2. Conrad Kohrs served as a guide for the Vigilantes during the famous Deer Lodge/ Hell Gate scout, arriving in Cottonwood late on January "18th," 1864. Bill Bunton was hung the following day. In regard to the exchange of horses, Kohrs provides these details: "Our horses were completely exhausted from traveling through the deep snow and Grant and other mountaineers were asked to furnish us with others. Our request was refused because the mountaineers feared the highwaymen still living would take revenge on them for having given us assistance. We finally persuaded them to drive in their horses and took from the band those pointed out by the herders as being safe, and left our horses in place of them and started the next day for Hell Gate. (*Ibid*, 36)

# 25

## IN WHICH HE TELLS OF THE DECISIVE WAY IN WHICH THE VIGILANCE COMMITTEE RID THE COUNTRY OF HIGHWAY MEN (FROM HELL'S GATE ON THEIR GRIM MISSION OF DEATH TO LAW BREAKERS). THREE OF THEM BEING HANGED TO THE CORNER OF BARON O'KEEFE'S STABLE.

There were thirty-six men forming the Vigilance Committee; and they must have been brave, determined men, for they had to deal with the most desperate characters, but they never drew back. They undertook to rid the country of bad men, and they certainly did so. They spared the American government a great deal of expense and loss of life. For had they undertaken to punish these highwaymen, it would have taken them a long time to do it and would have cost the government a large amount and perhaps loss of life, if one could judge by the expeditions that were sent out, to kill and arrest old men and old squaws as I saw them do.

When the Vigilantes were taking the horses I let them have, they also took a horse which belonged to an old lady, a Mrs. L'Hirondelle, who was camped on the side of a creek. She spied her horse being led away and hurried out, flourishing a butcher knife.

She went to her horse and taking him by the leading rope, cut it loose from the man who was guiding him, shouting at him, "Mean dog of a white man! Leave my horse!"

They laughed at her and went without the horse. Some of this family are now living in St. Albert, Alberta.

The Vigilantes, being now supplied with fresh horses, continued their journey to Missoula where they expected to find seven more robbers, but the day before these men had skipped out of the country. They heard the Vigilantes were hanging every man of the gang upon whom they got their hands, so they left Missoula and went as far as O'Keefe's place, seventeen miles from Missoula. They camped there that night, but in the morning they felt rather shaky, for their supply of whiskey was gone.

Some of them said, "Let us go back to Hell's Gate and raise hell again."

Three of them went back and got on a spree and began to fight. Aleck [Alex] Carter shot Johnny Cooper and wounded him. Carter was lying down sleeping on a lounge in the hotel and Cooper on another when the Vigilantes came in. They tied his hands and then awakened him. When he opened his eyes, he was looking into the barrel of a Winchester [Henry] rifle. He was furious, cursing them and calling them cowards for taking advantage of him when he was asleep. He told them if his hands were free they would not take him so easily and he would kill some of them. They knew him and that was the reason they had him so well secured. The next morning they hanged both men. They hung another man named [Cyrus] Skinner on my brother-in-law's beef scaffold.

Skinner kept a saloon next door to Higgins' store. I do not think he was a murderer, but he was a spy and a member of the robber gang. After hanging these three men, the Vigilantes went to O'Keefe's place and hung the three who were there. One had skipped out. The Vigilantes strung the last three men upon three corners of O'Keefe's stable. O'Keefe objected to having them hanged on his stable, for, being superstitious, he said it was unlucky. They told him to have less to say or they would decorate the other corner with Mr. O'Keefe, or Baron O'Keefe, as he liked to be called.

They then followed Whiskey Bill [Graves] who had left O'Keefe's and caught him at Bitterroot where they hung him.

There was a letter found on one of these robbers by which we learned some of their evil plans. In it Captain Higgins' murder was planned. Skinner, who had a saloon next door to him in Missoula, was instructed to watch him; and as Skinner was in and out of his store every day and got his supply of liquor and cigars from Higgins, they knew he was well posted and able to act when the time came.

Deer Lodge was under Bunton's supervision. He also had a saloon next door to Worden, who was the only man in Deer Lodge who had a safe, and it contained nearly all the gold in that neighborhood, for nearly everyone who had gold put it into it for safekeeping. When the time came, the robbers had planned to put an iron band around Worden's head and tighten it until he opened the safe and then they were to kill him.

There was Johnnie Grant, they said in the letter. They did not know how they were to deal with him. His case was more difficult; he kept so many loafers around him. I had many men, but not loafers. They were my teamsters. When I heard of these plans, I was thankful to my man Reilly for giving me warning to be on my guard against Baker [Wagner], for I suppose his instructions were the same as Skinner's and Bunton's.

The whole country indeed was very grateful to the Vigilance Committee, for they rid the place of a very dangerous gang in a short time without loss of life or expense to the government.

I stated in a previous chapter that I began to build a house in 1862. It was now finished. Although we had none but homemade furniture, the house was comfortable and we enjoyed life. We had a weekly dance in the winter to which I invited my friends. All winter we had only to amuse ourselves. In the spring we had to round up our stock and brand them.

As soon as my house was finished, my carpenter, Alex Pambrun, who was also my wagon master, advised me to build a saloon in town. My house was a quarter of a mile from the town. I did not care about building this, for it was a business I knew nothing of, but he kept coaxing me. At last I consented on certain conditions. I told him I would build it and equip it and give him a half interest in it if he would take full charge of it, for I did not wish to have anything to do with liquor. He agreed to do this. That was in 1864. The whole affair was the most unprofitable business I ever went into; it was only a bill of expenses. I paid him five dollars a day to build it and had to haul the lumber from the Flathead Reservation. I had enough to occupy my time without this saloon, for besides freighting, I had a restaurant and general store and sold beef cattle and horses. I had a man looking after each place, but I had to oversee everything.

John F. Grant (1831-1907), as he appeared in the prime of his life as a "mountaineer" in Montana Territory. He was thirty-five years old when this photograph was taken in 1866. *Montana Historical Society.*

Chief Tendoy of the Lemhi tribe. Johnny Grant's wife, Quarra (ca. 1840-67), was a sister of the famous Indian leader. *Smithsonian Institution.*

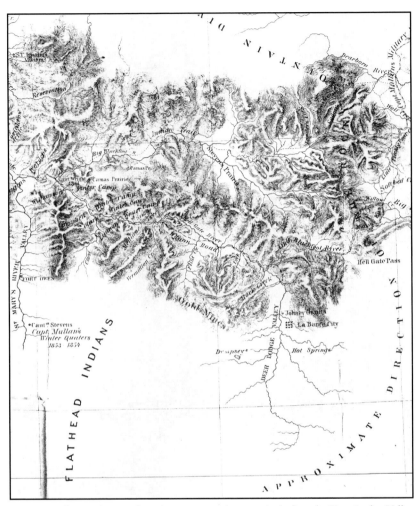

A portion of an 1863 map depicting western Montana, including the Deer Lodge Valley and "Johney Grants," now the location of the Grant-Kohrs Ranch National Historic Site. Other settlements indicated on the map are "Dempseys," and "La Barge City," now the town of Deer Lodge, Montana. *Report on the Construction of a Military Road from Fort Walla-Walla to Fort Benton.*

In the fall of 1862, Grant began construction of the "first good house" in the Deer Lodge Valley. He later sold his home and ranch to Conrad Kohrs in 1866-67. Today, the house and other Johnny Grant structures are focal points of interest at the Grant-Kohrs Ranch National Historic Site. This view of the Grant-Kohrs house was taken in the 1930s. *National Park Service.*

Richard Grant (1794-1862), the father of Johnny Grant. This photograph is of an oil painting of the high-ranking Hudson's Bay Company trader. *Marigold J. Nutt.*

DEER LODGE CITY.

*Conrad Kohrs.*

An old-time lithograph of Conrad Kohrs, the "Cattle King of Montana," with his signature. *History of Montana, 1739-1885.*

Clothild Bruneau Grant (1850-1919), whom Johnny married in Manitoba on May 7, 1868. Clothild painstakingly wrote down her husband's narrative at his dictation in 1906-07. *Audrey J. MacLeod.*

Miss Alice Grant (ca. 1878-1951), a daughter of Clothild and Johnny Grant born in Manitoba. *Audrey J. MacLeod.*

William (Bill) Nutt and his wife, Marigold. William Nutt was the son of Clothild's and Johnny's daughter, Maria (born ca. 1874). As guardians of the Grant memoir, they prepared a valuable typed version from Clothild's original handwritten account. *Audrey J. MacLeod.*

Audrey J. MacLeod, daughter of William and Marigold Nutt. As a great granddaughter of Johnny and Clothild Grant, Audrey has carefully preserved the original handwritten manuscript in recent years. *Audrey J. MacLeod.*

# 26

**WHEREIN HE GOES DOWN TO ST. LOUIS BY STAGE,
SPENDING HIS MONEY LIKE WATER. HE PUTS UP AT
THE OLIVE HOUSE, AND DOES BUSINESS IN
A PLEASANT AND LEISURELY WAY.**

While Alex Pambrun was building, I went to St. Louis and left him in charge of my business. That was my first trip south to buy goods. We had to pass by Virginia City, one hundred and ten miles distant. From there I went by stage. I brought James Arnold with me, as it was the first time that I was going back to civilization since I came to the frontier. I thought I needed someone; but it was not the case, for I very soon found out that I had to look after him.

After we arrived at Virginia City, we were obliged to wait fourteen days for the stage. There were seven dancing halls and there were four of us: Hugh O'Neill, a pugilist; his trainer, Bob Harris; my wagon master; and myself. I paid all the expenses for the four of us. Sometimes we would go to each of the seven halls in one night. We had to pay one dollar for every quadrille we danced, and the last call was a promenade to the bar. We gave one dollar to the bartender and had the privilege of taking two drinks. I did not drink. He [the bartender] kept fifty cents and gave a fifty-cent cheque to my [dancing] partner, which entitled her to fifty cents in cash the next morning when she presented the check. I know one young woman who had got fifty dollars' worth of checks in one night.

One morning my bill was ninety-nine dollars and fifty cents in one house. While in Virginia City I spent fourteen hundred dollars, and the fare for myself and Arnold cost me five hundred dollars apiece. Besides spending all this money, I caught a bad cold which settled into quinsy, and I could not eat my food. It was not much loss, for the bill of fare was not very inviting. It consisted of rusty bacon and beans, not very plentifully served.

The stage horses were very thin for they had had no hay (as the Sioux had burned most of the haystacks along the road [farther east]), but had only corn for feed. When we reached Bannock, there was so much snow that the driver abandoned the sleigh and hitched the horses to a toboggan to carry the baggage and mail, so we were compelled to walk. I tried to keep up to the team as close as possible, for I had eighteen thousand dollars in gold in two boot legs made like saddle bags which I had rolled in a grey soldier blanket with the United States stamp on it. This was all the luggage I brought with me; and I had that bundle at my feet while traveling in the stage; and at stations while at my meals, I placed it on my knee. Passengers seemed to keep at a respectful distance from me. Perhaps they thought there was a bomb or something more dangerous than eighty-five pounds of gold in it. Traveling over the mountain on foot was not very pleasant, but it was not a matter of choice with us. I knew the country thoroughly, so I undertook to make a short cut, and in doing so I had to cross a ravine with the snow waist deep in it.

The next day we reached Box Elder where we again changed our vehicle. The new one was made up of the running gear of the stage with two planks for a box. The road was very rough in places, the snow was melted, and it was icy so that we were obliged to take a firm grip of the planks to avoid being shaken off the rig. At a station about twelve miles from Salt Lake we made a fresh change, this time to a fine coach drawn by four horses. By the time we arrived at Salt Lake, I was thoroughly disgusted with James Arnold and offered to pay his way back to the mines, although it would have cost me a couple of hundred dollars, but he refused. From Salt Lake we had another good drive of twelve miles in a stage drawn by four fine grey horses.

The next relay was four mules. The driver was in no hurry, and at night he said he was sleepy. When I offered my services as driver, he looked at me and asked if I could drive. I replied that I thought I could and would try, for it would help me pass the long dreary hours of the night, so he lay down and was soon fast asleep.

While he slept I made good use of his whip and when he awoke he said to me, "You are driving too fast; we are ahead of time."

He then took his place and drove, to the great satisfaction of the mules.

A little incident which happened on that trip showed how facts are exaggerated. It was after we passed Denver [Colorado Territory[1]]. I forgot the name of the station. The station keeper was afraid to come out as the Indians had stolen the stage horses the night before, so we stopped there. We found a butcher's knife which he said belonged to some Sioux Indians. We remained at his place that night, and the next morning we started. A short distance away we were passing an immigrant camp when the stage driver saw three of the stolen horses near the camp. They were caught and tied behind the stage, but shortly after two of the horses broke loose and the driver decided to go back for them. I told him to go on and that I would bring them, for I was tired riding in the stage and I thought this would be a pleasant change for me. I did not have far to go for them, and I rode one and drove the other behind the stage.

When he arrived at Fort Carney [Ft. Kearny, on the Platte River], the driver reported that I had gone to the Sioux camp for those horses (he thought it was such a brave act). I told the folk it was only an immigrant camp, but they did not believe me. I was looked upon as the hero of the hour. I thought they were trying to spring a joke on me, but I was actually told that I was to have my meals free to St. Joe [St. Joseph, Missouri]. The meals cost one dollar each and not very choice at that. I objected to the free meals, but they persisted. One of my companions advised me to accept what they were doing for gratitude, but I knew better, for I had not seen a Sioux Indian.

On our arrival at St. Joe a telegram was received with news of the assassination of President Lincoln [April 15, 1865]. The mourning was public, every business place was draped in black through respect for the dead president.

From St. Joe we traveled by rail, then by boat down the Missouri to St. Louis. On my arrival at St. Louis I went to the Olive House, where most of the Montana people stayed in those days. My first care was to place my gold in a safe place, so I gave it to the hotel clerk to put it in the safe. I then went to see Mr. Samuel McCartney, a wholesale liquor and grocery merchant. I was introduced to him and to some of his head clerks. There were four or five of them, and by the time the last one was introduced I had forgotten all their names except Mr. McCartney. I knew he was the proprietor, but I did not know which of the four he was.

As nearly everyone who came from Montana was supposed to have gold, one of the four, an old gentleman, asked me if I had brought my gold. I replied that I had and that it was at the hotel.

"Well," he said, "that is not the place to leave it."

He came immediately with me to the hotel, and I got my gold from there. Then we went to the bank, and the same old gentleman was kind enough to see about it being sent to the mint.

He did not ask me anything about my business or want to dictate to me.

1. Although Grant does not give a clear itinerary of his route, the stage line evidently followed a major thoroughfare from Salt Lake City to Denver, in Colorado Territory. From there it utilized a main road across the Great Plains via the South Platte country, eventually connecting with the Central Express route (the old immigrant trail) in the lower Platte region.

# 27

## IN WHICH HE GIVES AN INSIGHT INTO METHODS OF DOING BUSINESS IN ST. LOUIS IN THE SIXTIES WHEN HIS PURCHASE AMOUNTED TO $28,000.

The Olive House where I put up was close to McCartney's warehouse, so I went there often. I usually chatted with one of my new acquaintances, whom I took to be Mr. McCartney. I told him what my business was in Montana. During one of our conversations he asked me what I intended to buy, and I told him a great many things. I am certain he must have noticed that I was a novice at buying; but instead of taking advantage of me, he gave me all the assistance in his power.

He offered to make out a list of what I needed, but I would not tell him.

"I want to see for myself," I said. "I have been so long among the Indians I am not accustomed to dealing with the whites. They may be too shrewd for me."

He laughed and said, "Why, the list will only assist you." He was very pleasant and friendly towards me, and although he did not say anything more about the list, before I realized what I had done, I had told him all I wanted and he had the list made out. It was no small list, for it was to the amount of twenty-eight thousand dollars. I meant to buy a saw mill, grist mill, blacksmith's tools, wagons, harness, saddles, groceries, and every kind of dry goods from a silk dress to a paper of needles.

When the list was finished, he said to me, "Here is a list of all you need. I will send one of the clerks with you to show you all the wholesale firms who handle the goods you need. Do not buy, but just quote prices. You will then see what they would cost you. We can buy those same goods at discount of fifteen to twenty per cent cheaper than you can, but you are to buy where you like."

It was very kind of him, for without their assistance it would have been difficult for me to locate all the firms. I accepted his offer, and the next day he sent a clerk with me who accompanied me to the different firms handling the goods I wanted. I quoted their prices and went back to tell my friend what they were.

While I was conversing with him one day, the same old gentleman who had gone to the trouble of helping me deposit my gold in the bank, and who I supposed one of the employees, came to us every once in a while and spoke as though he was interested in our conversation. I wondered who he was. At last I decided that he was not an employee, for he only walked about from one office to another. I finally concluded that he was a discharged clerk or a friend of Mr. McCartney's.

I felt annoyed at his interference, so I said to him, "Here old man. Will you please go to your office. I am speaking to Mr. McCartney, and you are disturbing us."

The old man laughed and went away.

I turned to McCartney and said to him, "Now we will not be disturbed by him again."

"But that is Mr. McCartney, the proprietor."

I was astonished and said to him, "Then who are you?"

He replied, "I am a salesman, Jack Roland is my name. Call me Jack."

I was quite taken back. I went to Mr. McCartney and apologized for my rudeness, which was not meant. After that little incident, I became thoroughly acquainted with Mr. McCartney and we were the best of friends, as he proved himself to me in all the dealings I had with him. Once, after I had been there four or five days, I was sitting in the office with Mr. McCartney enjoying a chat. After we had chatted some time I noticed the old gentleman chuckle and asked him the cause.

He replied, "I am laughing at you, I have not in all my life seen a man as fidgety as you are. You cannot sit still for five seconds at one time."

Nor could I, for I was unused to chairs and houses. I would get up, then sit down, then cross one leg over the other. I would turn the chair around, then sit straddle on it. At last I would shove the chair aside, and sit on the floor cross-legged in true Indian style. But I would never have noticed my restlessness if he had not passed that remark. I told him the reason I was like a fish out of water, for I had lived in a lodge for fifteen years, and was unused to chairs.

Mr. McCartney said, "Never mind how you sit. Just make yourself comfortable."

After I had gone around to the different wholesale firms and manufacturers besides Mr. McCartney's, from whom I bought my liquors and groceries, I accepted McCartney's kind offer to buy all I needed. Each evening Mr. McCartney used to send one of his clerks with me to visit the different places of interest around the city, and they paid all the expenses. After I had purchased nearly all that I needed and paid for it, I did not have enough money left to buy and pay for my liquors and the fixtures for my saloon which was under construction. I told Mr. McCartney to cut down some of my orders as I could not pay for everything.

"Oh, no," said he. "You buy all you need. You have come too far to go back without getting what you require, I will wait on you for what you cannot pay for."

I bought more, and when I settled with him, I still owed him eight thousand dollars. He did not ask me to give him my note or other security. Had he done so, I would have felt that he mistrusted me or doubted my honesty, and I would not be pleased. Not having done any business with businessmen before, I did not know anything of giving notes or security. He was still more generous before I left. He asked me if I was certain that I had all that I needed. I replied that I did not wish to contract too large a debt.

But he said, "Do not fear. You may purchase one hundred thousand dollars, if you choose."

I thanked him for his generous offer and good opinion of me, but decided not to buy any more that year. I would come again next summer. However, I did not wait till then to pay him, for as soon as I reached Deer Lodge I sent him the eight thousand dollars.

I remained in St. Louis for two weeks, and during that time I enjoyed myself completely. As soon as my goods were packed and ready, I immediately took passage on the steamboat, to Fort Benton, which was one hundred and eighty-five miles from home. My fare cost me three hundred dollars. The voyage was very tiresome and slow. I fancied the boat was always in the same place, and I was at a loss what to do to pass away the long hours, and I was anxious to leave the slow boat.

After we had traveled about one thousand miles we reached Omaha. When the boat was still about twelve feet from the landing, I saw the stage at the hotel door prepared to start. The driver was already in his seat, and like a flash I jumped from the boat to the landing and ran up the hill to the hotel where the stage was and climbed up on the boot of the stage. I had to pay five hundred dollars more for my fare to Virginia Mines, which was one hundred and ten miles from my home. On my way to St. Louis I had traveled thirty-four days on the stage from Virginia City to St. Joe and now again I found the horses still thin, but the roads were fairly good so we traveled faster than in coming down.

We had traveled quite a distance when we reached Dan Smith's station on the Platte River. Dan told us that there had been a skirmish between the whites and the Sioux Indians. There were thirty-five soldiers and as many settlers against thirteen Sioux Indians. Two of the Indians were killed, and the balance of them took the settlers' cattle and crossed the river with them, butchering one in sight of the owners.

Dan added, "I am ashamed to say so, but it is the honest truth. The whole bunch of white men were downright scared of those clever Indians."

# 28

WHEREIN HE DESCRIBES THE TIRESOME STAGE
JOURNEY FROM OMAHA, WHERE HE HAD
ABANDONED THE MORE TIRESOME MISSOURI BOAT.
THE STAGE UPSET ONCE, AND BREAKS THE
MONOTONY. HE KILLS HIS FIRST BUFFALO.

A day or two before we reached Salt Lake we met with an accident. It was at night. I was sleepy, so I made up my mind to sleep on the top of the stage. I shoved aside the carpet bags and the extra harness (kept there because they had only four horses on the stage, although it was a six-horse coach). I placed my blanket around my head and had just laid my head down when I felt a sudden movement. I heard a crash. The stage had turned over. There were twelve passengers, and we could hear them complaining of their injuries. The stage was on its side, and consequently those inside were scrambling out as best they could.

In the rush some called out, "You are stepping on my head."

With another it was his back, and another it was his arm. They were nearly all injured, more or less, for in their rush to get out they stepped on one another.

There was four of us on the top of the stage. I was thrown about ten feet from the stage and got bruised on the heel by the corner of it. I had no time to see how the others fared.

After the stage was put up all right and examined, it was found that the only damage was the broken glass in one door. The stage was brand new and very strong. The cause of the accident was that when we passed a camp of travelers going to Denver, one of them stopped the stage to give a letter to the driver, who stopped on the edge of a ravine. It was dark, and when he started he went too high. The upset was easy then. We continued our journey after everything was righted.

The only article I had brought with me from St. Louis was a small box of jewelry which was worth two hundred and eighty dollars. I had it in my vest pocket, and when I fell, I crushed the box. Then I was at a loss where to put it again so I tied it to a strap on the inside of the stage.

When we reached the next station, the driver called out, "Change stage!"

I was so anxious to get out that I forgot my box of jewelry. I did not miss it until we had traveled two or three miles. I wanted to go back, but the driver said it would be safe and promised to telegraph from the next station and have it forwarded by mail. I never heard anything more about it.

When we arrived at Salt Lake, I was still five hundred miles from home and was tired of the stage. So for seventy-five dollars I bought an Indian pony, a strong, hardy horse, although a miserable looking specimen. I now felt at home. I could ride slow or fast as I wished, but I soon went as fast as my pony could go, for I was very lonesome. I was anxious to get home to my family, and perhaps that accounts for my finding the boat and the stage so very slow.

I could sometimes get meals at stations, but all the provisions I carried for that long journey was one pound of tea, two pounds of sugar, a couple of tins of sardines, and three pounds of soda biscuits. After I had traveled about two hundred miles, I crossed on a ferry boat the Snake River, which was in overflow, and followed its banks for some time. Leaving the river the road crossed the dry bed of a small stream which was between the river and what we called the "Market,"— the dry bed of a lake surrounded by volcanic rocks and level as a table.

It was here that the traders in rendezvous at Fort Hall used to go to hunt buffalo if the meat supply at the fort ran short. There were always some buffalo there.[1]

It was an ideal place for a buffalo hunt or for horseracing. When I reached that creek, I was surprised to find it overflowing also. Still I had no choice but to cross it, although my horse was compelled to swim. Getting out on the other side, my horse's legs mired, and I was pulled down under the water. I lost all my lunch but the sardines. It was noon, but I had no dinner. I remained there that afternoon to dry my clothes. I had nothing to eat until the next day, although I passed stations every twelve miles and had seven hundred dollars with me.

I intended to stop at the first station to get something to eat; but when I got there, I felt bashful and passed on to the next one. I did this for a whole day because there were women at some of those stations, and I was shy about meeting or talking to white women. In the evening I saw a light on one side of the road in the mountain. I was certain these people were Indians, and I knew I would be at home with them. I went to their camp and procured some meat. I then continued my journey.

The next day I reached David Contois' place, which was eighteen miles from my home. There I learned that my son David was dying, and I did not delay there. I had traveled five hundred miles in seven days and scarcely eating anything, for I was so homesick. But hearing this sad news, I never stopped until I reached home. I rode so fast that my poor horse never moved from one spot for three days, he was so tired. I found my son very ill and unconscious. He was only five years old and as helpless as an infant. He got better, but was always delicate afterwards.

I stayed at home only two days, then took some horses with me and left for Fort Benton to join my wagons which had gone there for the freight. At Benton we were obliged to wait for six weeks for the boat on which my goods were.

I remarked to my men, "My oxen will starve here."

There was only bunch grass for them to eat. But I was wrong, for this grass proved very nourishing; and before three weeks the oxen were fat and playing about like calves.

While the wagons were waiting for the boat, Jack Collins and I went along the Missouri River about one hundred and twenty-five miles with the expectation of hearing or seeing the boat, for we expected that it must have grounded on a sandbar. We followed the wagon road until we came about opposite a sandbar where the boat would likely be to go aground. We left the road and followed a ravine which ran down to the Missouri River. After we reached the river, we followed it down four or five miles.

As we were riding along and chatting together, we saw four buffalo coming down a ravine, running down to the river from the badlands. We dismounted and tied our horses and waited until they came within a close range. They were the first buffalo I ever tried to shoot, so I did not intend to miss them. I shot at three of them, one after the other, and they all dropped.

Jack said to me, "The other is a cow. Let me shoot her."

He did, but only wounded her. She went towards our horses and I went ahead, for I was afraid she would scare them, and I did not like the idea of being left on foot. A fallen tree barred the ravine between our horses and the buffalo, so I waited on the side of the fallen tree, which she could

not pass, being wounded. When she reached there, I finished her. We butchered the four buffalo where they fell, only taking away the tongues and
tenderloin.

1. The Market Lake area is located north of present-day Idaho Falls. By about 1840, the
guns of white and Indian hunters essentially had eliminated the buffalo herds on the
ranges of what now are southeast Idaho and northern Utah. In November 1841,
mountain man Osborne Russell recalled: "The trappers often remarked to each other
as they rode over these lonely plains that it was time for the White man to leave the
mountains as Beaver and game had nearly disappeared." (*Journal of a Trapper*, 123)

# 29

## IN WHICH HIS MILLING VENTURE DID NOT SATISFY HIS IMPATIENT NATURE, AND HE IS TRICKED INTO DISPOSING OF IT FOR THREE HUNDRED GALLONS OF HOMEMADE LIQUOR. IN WHICH HIS NEW LIVERY STABLE IS BURNT.

When I recall those hunting days, I now see with regret the reckless waste of killing so many buffalo when we knew we could not carry much meat with us. It was then as now, as soon as the hunting season opens, sportsmen are anxious to kill ducks or other game merely for the sport of it. We enjoyed the sport and the meat too.

When we turned back from there and reached the wagon road, we met several people coming for their goods. They had heard that the boat was grounded on a sandbar at a place called Priest Rapid about one hundred miles from Fort Benton. It was three or four hundred miles from where we were [i.e., back to the Deer Lodge Valley?].

As soon as we heard of the delay of the boat, we hurried back to Benton to notify the teamsters to come with the wagon train for my goods. Our oxen were well rested and fat, so we made good time on our way back to the boat. We loaded the goods on the wagons; and as soon as we were through, I went ahead with the horse train and left the ox team to follow.

We were three days traveling fifteen miles from the river to the wagon road through what is called the Badlands of the Missouri. They are well named. The soil is a soft red clay, and the land is very hilly. The water is alkaline, and the men were all sick from drinking it. The atmosphere must have been charged with alkali, for the sweat on the horses was like a sheet of chalk. The road was very rough. We traveled about twenty miles before we got good water, and we waited here for the ox teams to see if there had been any accident. While we were stopped, a messenger from the ox team arrived to notify us that the wagon which was loaded with the boiler had turned over. The train had reached a place on the road running along the narrow ridge of a hill called a backbone.

The wagon, being so heavily loaded, cut down on the lower side of the hill and slid five or six inches from the wheel tracks. It rolled down forty feet, turning over three times with the wheelers. The other five yokes of oxen fortunately got loose. The only damage the boiler sustained was a crack in the fly wheel.

I sent the other teamsters back to help. There were twenty-seven men and over one hundred head of oxen, so they could not have had much trouble righting the wagon and boiler.

Alex Pambrun and Jack Collins remained with me; and while waiting for their return, Alex took his gun saying, "I am going to see if I can kill a deer," and disappeared behind the hills.

After a little while as Jack and I were among the horses, we saw four buffalo coming over a hill with a rider pursuing them. We caught two horses and started after them, chasing them five or six miles. It was in the direction we had come. We killed one bull, and it took us a good four hours to butcher it, for we had only one knife, a blunt one at that, and the stones were too soft [a]round there to put an edge on it. We managed at last by pulling and twisting. We then left the meat alongside of the road, and when the ox teams passed, they loaded it. They got to us that same evening. In the morning we resumed our journey, and as the road was better, we came through safely.

Once home I fixed up my saloon. In St. Louis I had bought three French mirrors that cost me one thousand dollars and two hundred and fifty for freight. At the same time I got three billiard tables for fifteen hundred and seventy-five dollars, paying twelve hundred and seventy-five dollars for freight. Some might think I was extravagant with my money in buying such costly fixtures for an out-of-the-way place like Deer Lodge was then. I think so myself now, but in those days I was young and healthy and never thought of saving money. The thought of getting old and helpless as I now am never entered my head. While I had the money and saw everything that I desired, if money could get it, I bought it.

While I was away from home to St. Louis, the clerk Pym took a brewery in payment of a debt for about two thousand dollars. He paid two hundred dollars for repairs and was paying a man two hundred a month to run it. I soon put a stop to that business when I came, for it did not pay, so I sold the brewery. Then I outfitted a blacksmith's shop, and I had to get someone to run it. I lost money in that venture too. Indeed in everything

that I undertook besides stock raising and trading I lost money, for I had
to depend on others. I lost quite a lot of money that way, and I regretted it
more than what I lost at cards or other sports, for I was satisfied then I got
something for my money. In the business affairs I often got nothing but
vexation, as in this case.

When I started for St. Louis I had no intention to buy a grist mill, or
saw mill for I had no experience whatever in milling; but on my way to St.
Louis while I was talking to a man named Frederick, one of the passengers
on the stage, who was a mill wright, he remarked to me that he thought a
grist and saw mill built in the Deer Lodge country should pay.

I thought it possible.

He added, "You are going to St. Louis. If you buy all the machinery, I
will put it up and pay one-half the expenses with the produce of the mill."

After a little persuasion I consented.

Now on the Gallatin River, which is one of the forks of the Missouri
about one hundred miles from my home, there was a fine, lush country
which I thought would be a good place to raise wheat. There were people
coming there already and flour was so high, one dollar a pound, that I
came to the conclusion that milling would pay, so I bought the machinery,
as I have already stated.

I sent the grist mill to the Gallatin and set up the saw mill eight miles
from home [Deer Lodge Valley]. Frederick put it up and operated it. He
hired the men and I paid Frederick, as engineer, ten dollars a day. The
sawyer was paid the same, while seventy-five dollars per month was given
to the other mill hand. At the end of two months I had paid all expenses of
the mill and received nothing in return. I concluded that it was only a bill
of expense and decided to make a change.

I offered to sell Frederick my interest in the mill or buy his. It never
occurred to me when I made him the offer that he had not invested one
cent in it. He offered to find me a purchaser and brought me a man named
[A.J.] Davis. He was one of the passengers who had been on the stage
going to St. Louis. He seemed to be an honest man, and I told him I only
wanted five thousand eight hundred dollars for my two mills, the cost
[. . .] in St. Louis.

"The freight you can pay me in lumber," I added.

He agreed and said, "I will give you three hundred gallons of homemade liquor over the bargain."

I repeated the terms of the sale three times so that he would understand them thoroughly.

He sat down at the table and wrote them out in English, or rather pretended to.[1] He read the agreement word for word as I had stated it. I took his word, for I thought it was all reliable, and I signed it without a witness. Davis took passage on the stage and left his bogus document with a lawyer named Brown the day of the sale. The following day James Stuart told me Lawyer Brown had said I had sold my machinery for three hundred gallons of homemade liquor and that Davis agreed to pay me with lumber for the freight. I went to the lawyer to find out the truth of this. Imagine my surprise and anger when he told me it was so. I had been robbed of five thousand eight hundred dollars in the most barefaced and rascally manner.

What aggravated me most in that deal was to think that I had placed the utmost confidence in the man and that he had abused it to such an extent. He deceived me by his seeming honesty.

He was an elderly man and had been a preacher and might be considered above defrauding a man or taking advantage of his ignorance; for if I could have read English, I would not have signed that paper without reading it. I repeat again, lack of knowledge in business dealings and too much trust in others has brought me in my old age to an unprofitable struggle on a northern homestead. So I would advise everyone who reads this: Do not do as I have done. Be always certain that you thoroughly understand a document before you sign it. Trust no one, in business dealings.

I firmly resolved at that time never to be guilty again of such stupidity. I am now seventy-six years old and am sorry to have to acknowledge that I trust others still and have often been deceived since then. The lawyer told me I must abide by that false document. I felt indignant and intended to smash the machinery into bits, but James Stuart warned me that if I did that, Davis could have me placed under arrest.

I disliked trouble of that kind, and as Stuart was a well informed man, I relied on his word. He pretended to be my friend, but he really befriended Davis that time; otherwise, he would have told me that the agreement was not legal, for there was no witness. Davis acted very wisely when he went away at that time out of my sight; for if I had met him, I am certain I would have shot him like a dog; and I believe that I would have been justified in ridding the world of such a scoundrel, for in my opinion he was as bad as any of those highwaymen the Vigilantes had hung.[2]

Twenty-two years later when I went to Montana from Manitoba, that same Davis was a banker in Butte and was looked upon as an honorable man. I was told he was worth several millions and still unmarried. His heart was so contracted I suppose that he could not share his millions with a wife.[3]

To come back to my bargain, I was obliged to accept the liquor and forty or fifty thousand feet of lumber. With the lumber I built a livery stable eighty feet long by thirty feet wide. A few days after it was finished I had four or five tons of hay put in the loft at a cost of fifty dollars a ton. The stable was now ready for business when suddenly the whole place was destroyed by fire [in February 1866]. It was freely said that the fire had been set on purpose, but I could never prove it although I had my suspicions. I had four horses in the stable at that time and the liquors I had got from Davis. We took these out and there was a general drunk, perhaps even the fellow who set the fire was drinking my liquor. The fire took place in the fall.[4]

The winter passed pleasantly. Besides the weekly dances which took place at my house for my friends, there was also a weekly pay-ball given at my saloon so that the whole countryside enjoyed themselves thoroughly.

1. Grant could read and write in French, but not in English.
2. A.J. Davis (b. 4/25/1819, d. 3/1/1890) was scarcely more than a decade older than Grant. He was at various times a merchant, miller, miner, and banker, but does not appear to "have been a preacher." Several years later, an article in *The New North-West* (July 16, 1869) noted that the Deer Lodge area still had no flour mill. The editor pleaded for one to be established: "Wanted—A Flouring Mill. With 30,425 acres of land, officially returned as under cultivation in Deer Lodge Valley, and the largest population of any county in Montana, it is a singular fact that there is not a flouring mill within its limits . . . Some years ago 'Johnny Grant' and others purchased and brought from the States a mill for this point, but litigation ensuing between the owners, before it was erected, it reverted to the possession of A.J. Davis, of Gallatin City, and seems to have carried the old infection with it." (7/16/1869, *The New North-West* [Deer Lodge, MT])
3. Ironically, Conrad Kohrs, who eventually purchased Grant's ranch, was befriended by A.J. Davis after the severe winter of 1886-87 resulted in disastrous livestock losses. In his autobiography, Kohrs states: "One of the bright spots in the heavy losses of this season was the kindness of Mr. A.J. Davis of Butte. Hearing of my losses, he sent for me and offered me $100,000.00 without any security. The confidence of such a friend added to my courage and I was very happy. While I did not accept it then, I made use of it the next year following for the purchase of cattle." (*Conrad Kohrs: An Autobiography*, 86)
4. On February 17, 1866, the *Montana Post*'s "Special Correspondent at Deer Lodge City" reported the conflagration that destroyed Grant's new livery stable: "A FIRE occurred in our place, on last Saturday night, resulting in the total destruction of a fine, large barn, with a quantity of hay, the property of our well known townsman, Johnnie Grant, Esq. The loss is about $3,000. Misfortunes never come singly—and never was this saying more aptly applied than in the case of Mr. G. He has lost

considerably in commercial enterprises, during the last year; and a few days since, almost his entire stock of liquors—some seven hundred gallons—was seized by the United States revenue officer, here. Johnnie declares that he will clear up and go among the Indians again, if his luck don't change. After the fire, those who had aided in saving some portions of the building—among whom were a number of legal gentlemen, and also many officials—were invited into Mr. Grant's spacious billiard hall, to enjoy a 'social drink.' And now began a scene of boisterous mirth—A REGULAR FROLIC, such as is seldom witnessed anywhere. It would be futile to attempt a description; but I will say that certain prominent democrats, among whom was our good natured friend McC_____k, Judge N_____l, Major B_____s, B_____r, and many others, looked like very near relations of Sambo—their faces (and those who were bald also suffered) were as black as charcoal, well applied, could make them. All passed off very good naturedly, and the fun was enjoyed hugely." ("Letter from our Special Correspondent at Deer Lodge City," 2/17/1866, *Montana Post* [Virginia City, MT])

In 1886, the only time Grant revisited Deer Lodge after settling in Manitoba in 1867, he told a newspaper interviewer about his former circumstances and why he had left Montana: "I'll tell you. I had been raised in an Indian country since I was 15 years old. I got along well. My door was open to every one and my table free to all who came. I harmed no man, nor did any harm me. My stock ranged the valleys and hills unmolested, and my money, as much at times as $10,000 or $20,000, lay in my cabin unmolested. I needed no protection. I cost nobody a dollar. After a time the Territory was established, then counties, and then officers were elected. Then came Assessors and the Collectors annoying me with their lists and tax collections and laws for this, that and the other, and I concluded to leave for Manitoba." (4/16/1886, *The New North-West* [Deer Lodge, MT])

# 30

## His pet saddle horse killed by a champagne bottle, and there is seen the beginning of the end of his days in Montana.

In the spring of 1865 Conrad Kohrs offered me thirty thousand dollars for my place and cattle, but I refused it. Three years before he had worked at Bannock mines for the butcher [Hank Crawford] who shot [wounded] the Sheriff Plummer. The butcher ran away [spring of 1863] so Con Kohrs was out of work. He walked from Bannock to Deer Lodge with twenty-five dollars in his pocket to buy beef cattle. I sold him three head, and he gave me the twenty-five dollars on account. When he came back and paid me the balance he took five more. He continued buying from me; and if he could not settle in full at the time, he did so the next time he came. Latterly I advanced him the number he wanted, sometimes as many as twenty. In 1864 when he came to buy his Christmas supply of beef cattle, he paid me eighty dollars a head for them. He told me afterwards that one of the three-year old heifers, dressed, weighed eleven hundred pounds. That was the time we had good beef because I had the whole valley to pasture my cattle on.

Con about this time took a partner named Peel who took a great fancy to my riding horse, a fancy bay called Billy. He was one of the finest little horses I ever had, full of spirit but so gentle that my little girl could ride him. When I rode him, I only used a hair rope for a bridle, but I could make him prance. He was so fearless I could make him face anything and had boasted of it often.

One day I rode him to town and went to my saloon. While there someone said, "I will beat the treats that there is something in town that will frighten your fancy bay."

I had not the least idea what it could be, but I was certain that he did not fear anything, so I took up the challenge and asked what it was. They brought me to the next house about sixty yards from my saloon, and there in the yard were three camels in a shed.[1]

One was led out. I was riding my horse, and as soon as he saw it he was afraid, for neither of us had ever seen a camel before. I urged him on. He touched the camel, but just then the strange animal stretched his neck and sneezed. My little horse wheeled round on his hind legs like a top. He was trembling like a leaf.

I turned him round again and said, "Go on, Billy. Do not be afraid," urging him at the same time with my heel.

He jumped forward and struck the camel with his breast, almost knocking him down. I felt proud of my horse and I had won the bet, so we all went to the bar and it was treat after treat till at last I felt as though I had enough. I started to go home and several of the men came out of the saloon with me. I jumped on my horse, and I suppose being top-heavy, I leaned too much on one side. My horse reared up and I slid down behind him landing on my feet. They all clapped their hands and cheered at what they considered a very clever trick. They called out that this was worth a treat so we all went in and took it.

I started home in rather a hazy condition on a fast gallop; and when I came in sight of the creek which I had to cross on my way home, I saw two riders about to cross. I had just enough liquor on board to make me mischievous, so I called out to them to clear the road. One went on one side; the other was somewhat slower in giving me the road; and I passed so close to him that my horse splashed water clear over him. I believe that my horse would have attempted to leap over both if they had not got out of his way. He always seemed to take on my moods. He was a wonderful little horse, and for that reason I did not care about parting with him.

Still Peel was anxious to buy him. He paid me two hundred and fifty dollars for him and fifty dollars for his passage on the boat. But I heard later that a few days after he arrived home in the East, he gave a champagne dinner, and one of the guests threw an empty bottle through a window opening onto the garden. Fancy Bay was in the garden, then under the window. He happened to raise his head and look up when he was struck in the forehead with the bottle, and my poor little horse was instantly killed. Peel felt his loss keenly, for he was fond of the horse, and besides, it had cost him three hundred dollars.

1. As an experiment, the U.S. government acquired a limited number of camels to serve as pack animals in the West, but the project generally failed, not the least of which because horses and other livestock often were terrified by the site and scent of the strange beasts. Afterward, some civilian packers acquired these camels. For a time, they were utilized in small numbers in the northern Rockies and the Columbia Basin in the 1860s. (See, William S. Lewis, "The Camel Pack Trains in the Mining Camps of the West," *Washington Historical Quarterly* 19 (October 1928): 271-84)

# 31

## IN WHICH IS SHOWN THE RISE OF CONRAD KOHRS, MILLIONAIRE AND ONCE CATTLE KING OF MONTANA, WHO BOUGHT OUT JOHN F. GRANT'S RANCH IN 1865 [1866] FOR $19,000.00.

Con Kohrs,[1] as I had stated, started with twenty-five dollars, and three years after he offered me thirty thousand for my place.[2] If I had known of a place where I could have moved to with my family, I would have sold then, for I was very anxious to take my children away from the bad example there. That country was very rough. There were mines all round and too many of the robbers and gamblers that are generally met with in a mining country. But I did not know where to go, so I decided to put in a crop on a larger scale than before.

A couple of acres of oats that I put in the year before did so well that I was encouraged to try some more. I paid five dollars a bushel for seed oats. I tried a garden too. A French-Canadian there who was a gardener proposed to make a garden on shares if I bought the seeds. I agreed. Vegetables were an unknown luxury there at the time, so he paid twenty dollars for a pound of onion seed and other seeds in proportion. It cost me two hundred dollars for garden seed. That summer Montana was visited by a plague of Colorado beetles or grasshoppers. They devoured everything green as soon as it showed itself above the ground. I was completely disgusted and made up my mind to sell and leave the country.

I concluded to look for a more peaceful place, for my sons were growing up, and as I have already stated, Montana was no place for them. There was bad example continually before their eyes, and bad habits are much easier to contract than to forget.

I told Con then that I would accept his offer, but he would not give me over nineteen thousand dollars. I accepted the offer, and guaranteed him two hundred head of cattle. If he did not find that number I agreed to make good the number missing; and if there were more, he agreed to give my family ten beefs during the coming winter, for I had made up my mind to go and spend some months in the Red River district [in Manitoba]. Con Kohrs told me later that when the cattle [were] rounded up, he found three hundred and fifty-seven head. Con took possession of house and cattle and simply stepped into my shoes, as they say, and became wealthy.

When I sold out to Con, I wrote to my uncle, John Rowan, in Manitoba. He was a step-brother of my mother. James McKay, brother-in-law of John Rowan, being married to my Aunt Margaret (John Rowan's sister), answered my letter. He told me that my Uncle John had died that spring, but he invited me to go to Manitoba, saying that I would be welcome there. After having settled my family for the winter, I started for Manitoba.

I took with me my oldest daughter, who was fourteen years old, to place her in a convent at St. Louis. We left Benton in a Mackinaw boat which carried thirty-two passengers, all bound for points along the Missouri.[3] After traveling a few days, we saw some buffalo about half a mile from the river. Most of the passengers thought they would like some fresh meat, and I was of that opinion too. I offered to go and try to kill one if they would wait for me with the boat at the next point.

One of the passengers named [John] Healy remarked, "It is not safe for you to go alone. I will go with you," and he did.

Healy and I had been good friends since we had first met two years before. That was one day when I was about one hundred yards from my house in Deer Lodge. I met a man who said he had come from the Florence mines. He wanted to buy a horse to go back, so I went with him to the corral and caught a horse that suited him. He had no money, but he promised to pay me when he came back from Florence. I said that would be all right. He took the horse and went away. He had only gone a few yards when I called him back and asked him his name.

He replied, "My name is John Healy."

"All right," I said, "go on, Healy. I suppose I will forget it as soon as you are out of sight, but it makes no difference, for I do not think I will ever see you again."

He laughed and answered, "Oh, yes you will."

About two months later I met a man in about the same place I had met Healy.

He said, "Good day, Mr. Grant." I said good day and passed on.

He cried out, "Hold on! Do you remember you sold a horse to a man, and you said you did not expect ever to see him again?"

"Well," I said, "what about him? Is he dead?"

"No, I am the man, and here are your seventy-five dollars."

After that he always looked upon me as a friend because I helped him in time of need, and I liked him because he was an honest man. So when that day on the boat he said he would go with me, I was satisfied. The owner of the boat, I do not remember his name [. . .] said he would wait for us at the next point, so we started on our buffalo hunt. The animals got scent of us, however, and got away. On our way to the next point we killed four deer anyway. That was not too much for the crowd in the boat. We cached three and took the meat of one with us, intending to send someone back for the rest. When we reached the next point, we found that the boat had passed straight on. We took one-quarter each of the deer meat and traveled on from point to point until nightfall.

We now realized that we had been left in the most dangerous part of the country, for it was the hunting ground of the fierce Sioux Indians.

1. Grant may be said to almost have been a benefactor to the man who subsequently bought him out. According to Kohrs: "Grant commenced giving me some credit and this credit enabled me to pay some of the boys from whom I had borrowed. However, in May, 1863, I received a letter from Grant telling me that he was going to Benton to meet the boats and asked me to send him all the money I could. I complied with this request as far as possible, but still owed him a balance of $1,100.00."

   Later, after cornering the beef market in the gold camps, Kohrs records: "Now having $5,000.00 I told Grant I wanted to finish paying up the old indebtedness . . . Grant was one of the men who never kept books and believed the indebtedness had been liquidated with the last amount sent from Bannack. He was so tickled that he had found an honest man that he actually forced me to buy one hundred head of cattle, giving me the pick of the herd and selling them at a more reasonable figure than I had ever bought from him before, and allowing me my own time to make the payments." (*Conrad Kohrs: An Autobiography*, 25, 31-32)

2. "On the 23rd of August, 1866, I bought out Johnny Grant's ranch, the land of which had not been surveyed and had no title to and the remainder of his cattle, amounting to about 350 head from yearlings up. The price paid was $19,200.00, on which I paid $5,000.00, the balance to be paid the next spring. The fore part of September Grant took his horses and went to the Red River, where he bought a tract of land near Pembina, and I took possession of my property." (*Ibid*, 43)

3. "In the fall of 1866 Henry Kennerly and myself had a mackinaw boat built at Fort Benton for the purpose of carrying passengers down the river to the States. We made big money in the enterprise although only carrying 20 men beside our help, we charged each one about the price of the fare around the world now. I remember the names of some of the passengers . . . Johny [sic] Grant." (John Largent folder, Montana Historical Society)

# 32

## [IN WHICH HE RELATES THE DIFFICULTIES OF TRAVEL BY MACKINAW AND STAGE DOWN THE MISSOURI RIVER TO FORT UNION AND SIOUX CITY. HE AND HEALY ARE SET AFOOT IN HOSTILE INDIAN COUNTRY.]

We made a small camp fire, on the edge of the river under the bank so that it would not be seen by Indians. We felt very hungry after our long walk and we planned to enjoy this fresh meat, but after it was cooked we could not eat it with pleasure. We had no appetite, for we did not know what moment the Sioux might come on us. I did not know Healy's thoughts concerning his wife and the money he left on the boat, but I did feel anxious for my young daughter who would feel lost among strangers. Besides, I had seventeen thousand dollars in the captain's safe. We felt so lonely that we could not talk. We just sat and considered what might have happened to the boat, whether it had sunk and all were drowned or perhaps that all had been massacred or taken prisoners by the Indians. We imagined very terrible things that might have happened.

In the silence of the night we heard the sound of oars. We did not know whether it was our boat or not, but we yelled to them and they stopped to take us on board. It was not our boat. They had really left us behind. The next evening we caught up to them at Fort Union.[1] They had sent two men to look for our bodies because they were so sure that we had been killed in that dangerous place.

We had to pay one hundred dollars apiece to those men, for they had been promised that amount for finding us. I thought afterwards what fools we must have been to pay it, for it was not our fault the boat left us. We never even asked the reason of it.

Healy's wife and my daughter were overjoyed to see us come back. They had been so anxious. Mrs. Healy had even vowed that if we were killed by the Sioux, she would kill the first Indian she would meet, but there is more to tell of the first part of the trip.

Three days before we got to Fort Union an elderly man from St. Louis, one of the passengers, asked if I was not Mr. Grant and he added, "I have been watching you since we left Benton, and you seem to be a respectable man. I heard something concerning you, and I think it is my duty to warn you, as we are getting close to Fort Union."

Then he told me there was a man at Fort Union who had sworn that he would shoot me on sight.

I asked if he was not rather a stout man, giving description of a man who once threatened my life through jealousy. I named him, for I had very few enemies.

He told me it was that man. I thanked him for the warning and was on my guard, although I was not much afraid of the man, knowing him to be a coward. I did not know what he might do at Fort Union where he was home among his friends.

When I arrived at Fort Union, I went to see him and told him what I had heard and added, "You have been threatening to kill me often. Come on now, here is your chance. I am tired of hearing those threats of yours."

He took it all back and said he would never bother me again.

A couple of days after we left Fort Union we saw a camp of Indians on the bank, and one Indian was on the riverside yelling at us. The captain stopped on a sandbar, but I told him it was not safe, for we were just about a gunshot from the Indians, but he seemed bound to stop. So I took the skiff from the boat and together with Joe Kipp, a boy seventeen years old, I set out for the shore with the captain, who said he knew some of this tribe. (The town of Kipp in Montana and in Alberta were, I understand, named for this lad who afterwards was [a] stage driver for many years.) We wanted to make peace with them and be friendly. We took some crackers as we started. The Indians on the riverside shouted, and the others up the hill answered with shouts and yells.

Mac was afraid and said, "Let us give those crackers to this Indian on the shore. There is no use for us to go further."

I was full of fear, but I knew the Indians' ways too well to let them see it and held that we had better go on or the Indians would think we were afraid of them. So we followed a little path through the brush. We felt as if we were going to our deaths. The least little noise, a willow cracking, would give us a start. We would think it was the click of a rifle. At last we got to the camp, and I felt as if my hair was standing on end, for there were fifty or sixty wild Indians shouting and loading their rifles. We went into the first lodge and sat down. After a minute or two an Indian came to the door and called McKay out. Joe and I remained sitting, talking as unconcerned as if we did not know what fear was. After a little while a woman opened a bale, took some dried meat out, and gave us some to eat.

We thanked her in Indian style, and I said to Joe, laughing, "They want to feed us before they kill us."

When we were done, Mac came back and we went down to the skiff. They looked so fierce and kept clicking their rifles and yelling so long after we went that we were afraid all the way down to the river and even on the water. But they let us go without any harm.

If they wanted to scare us, they succeeded to perfection, for after that we were very anxious to get to the end of our journey. But we were not over our troubles. Whenever the boat got grounded on a sandbar, we had to get out in the water to shove it off; and as it was October, the water was far from being warm. We were getting sick and tired of the voyage; and at last we went to the owner of the boat and said if he wanted to travel day and night we would help row, each in our turn, and he agreed.

The first night it was all right, but the second night we passed through a very bad place. The boat struck a snag and sprung a leak. The boat had a deck, and those swells from St. Louis got frightened as soon as the boat struck the snag. They went up on the deck and jumped to the bank one after the other. Some would sink to their knees in the water. I wakened my daughter and untied the skiff and backed to the stern of the boat. Then I told Mac to open the safe and take the little bags of gold and throw them in the skiff and called to my daughter to hurry up, but the skiff was half full of water before she came, partly dressed.

When we got ashore we found there was not one that did not miss some provisions lost in the water, or damaged. We waited on the shore, and after two days a boat came up. They helped us to pull our boat ashore, when we took the deck off and repaired it, and resumed our journey.

At Fort Randell [Randall[2]] four of us left the boat, for we thought it was not safe. After the luggage and trunks were loaded and strapped on the stage, we could not all get in. It was too full, so I went across the river to the stage agent and told him. He offered me a rig that would follow the stage. I went back and tried to take my trunk off the stage, but the driver said it [. . . would] be all right if I follow[ed] close.

The first night we camped together, and I would have liked to take my trunk then, but it was strapped under too many trunks and pieces of luggage. Besides, I did not like to try too much for it, as the bystanders would guess that there was something valuable in it.

So I thought to myself, "Tomorrow I must get it out."

But next day we could not keep up to the stage, and we did not overtake them till we reached Sioux City. They got in Saturday night and we landed on Sunday morning. I inquired for my trunk, but no one knew where it was.

When the porter was questioned about it, he said he had found a trunk down by the riverbank, broken open. There were some clothes in it, he said, and he produced the trunk.

It was mine. The clothes were all there, but my gold was gone. I had two thousand dollars in it—sixteen hundred dollars' worth of nuggets worth from one dollar to three hundred and sixty each. These had been picked out from over one hundred thousand dollars' worth in four years' time. Every time I would get an odd one, I would put it away.

I put the matter into the hands of a detective, and I told him my suspicion of the porter, but I never heard from the detective again, although I knew he must have found out if he had gone right about it. The nuggets were odd and not hard to trace. After giving him all the information I could, I kept on to St. Louis.

I never was so glad to be at the end of a journey, as it had been full of bad luck and annoyance.

1. The American Fur Company had established Fort Union in 1829 at the confluence of the Missouri and Yellowstone rivers, close to today's Montana/North Dakota boundary. Situated in a key geographical location, Fort Union long played a prominent role in northern Plains history.
2. The U.S. Army established Fort Randall in 1856 on the west bank of the Missouri River close to what is now the southeast boundary of South Dakota.

# 33

When I arrived at St. Louis, I placed my daughter at the convent. I called on Mr. McCartney, my old friend. I left him the seventeen thousand dollars in gold and an order for goods to be shipped to Fort Benton in the spring.

While in the city, I met a young man who had been in the mountains a few years. I was acquainted with him, but did not know his family name as was often the case in those days. He said he had come from Trois-Rivières.[1] I then told him I was brought up there; and as it was not long since he had left home, I asked him many questions about my friends. I happened to tell him of the last fight I had there with a young Coffin whose father's place was next to the corner where I used to buy milk. Coffin had whipped me that time.

The young fellow said, laughing, "Why, that was myself."

He asked me if I was going home to visit my old aunt, Mrs. Pelisson, who was now very old and blind.

I had thought she was dead, for I had not heard any news for so long; but if she was still living, I felt I should go and see her, although I did not intend doing this when I left [for] St. Louis. That is how I came to go [to] Trois-Rivières instead of Red River.

Passing Montreal I stopped three days to see my cousins, Richard and Charles de Lafrenaie. Next morning I was very glad to receive the visit of one of my old chums, Louis, who said he had hurried to call. I felt it was very kind of him. I got all the information I wanted from him; and after we had chatted quite a while, he said he was in a bad fix. He wanted me to lend him fifty dollars until the next morning, as he did not want to break his bank account.

That next morning of his never came. When I saw that he was not coming, I went to his house, but I could not see him. His wife saw me. She cried because she felt so bad about Louis' meanness. I felt bad also, not so much for the money as for the way he deceived me. If he had come to me saying he was hard up and needed fifty dollars or more, I would never have hesitated a minute. I would have given him what he needed, and then I would have had the satisfaction of feeling that I was helping a friend in need. But as it was, if he had money in the bank, he did not need it; and if had not, then he lied to me and I had been made his dupe. I always hated a liar and deceiver.

There was one off my list of friends, I thought. That is how I found out there were rogues in the heart of civilization as well as among the miners, so I thought I must be on my guard.

Louis had just left me that first morning when my cousin, Richard Lafrenaie, called. He said he had just seen my name in the papers and he wanted to see me before he went to his office. He was a Queens Counsel, and they called him Professor Lafrenaie because he lectured to some law-students. We had a long talk, and he told me there were twelve hundred and fifty dollars of my father's money in the bank that was not mentioned in his will; and I could get it if I wanted it, but I did not need it. Moreover, my name was not even mentioned in his will, so I did not wish to touch his money. I wanted to be independent, and I was not attached to money. I made it easy sometimes, and some other times it was very hard work, but I spent it as I went.

Richard had lost his wife, so he wanted me to come to his office that evening. I met Charles, his brother, and a young man by the name of Arthur Levesque there. Richard opened a barrel of oysters in the shell, and we passed a pleasant evening.

That young Levesque came to Manitoba a few years after as a volunteer at the time of Riel's rebellion. He remained in the country and married a Miss Deschambeault and was Indian agent before he died. Next day I called on my old friend that used to be Miss Betsy Loranger and found she was married and had eleven children, all strong and healthy.

I called on Charles at the store with which he had been connected for twenty-two years.

While talking to him, a very stylish lady came in and Charles said to me, "Let me introduce you to your father's cousin, Madame de Montignac."

I said, "Oh, no, she is too stylish for me."

I felt myself too much of an Indian then, but I was sorry a few years after that I had not made her acquaintance, for when I moved to Manitoba I was at Archbishop Taché's house talking about old times; and when I told him of that time, he said Madame de Montignac was not proud at all. He was also related to her and used to spend a part of his college vacations at her place.

She was very kind, he added. "I am sorry you did not make her acquaintance, for she would have been like a mother to you."

So I found out that we must not always judge people by their appearance. I thought she was proud because she was so stylish. I could not be if I tried. Once when I was walking down the street with my cousin Richard, he persuaded me to put on a white collar. I wore it just to please him; but as much as I would have liked to please him, I could not stand it.

We had walked about ten yards when I threw it on the street, saying to my cousin, "It chokes me."

He laughed, but I did not care. I never did. I never dressed to inconvenience myself for the sake of fashion or style.

I soon set out for Trois-Rivières, my old home. When I got out of the train, I was with a young man named Gauthier whom I had met on the train. I did not remember him, but I knew his father well, for he was the baker and I remembered him so well, delivering his bread with a yellow dog hitched to a baker's sled. It was eleven o'clock when we left the station.

Passing a large store, I said to young Gauthier, "This used to be Dickson's hardware store."

"Why," he replied, "do you remember that place? It is still Dickson's, but the sons have it now."

I remembered every street and most every store in Trois-Rivières.

Late as it was, I went to my aunt's house. I rang the bell and the door was opened by an old servant, but before opening it, she said, "Who is there?"

I wanted to surprise her, so I said, "Charles Lafrenaie."

I knew she would open the door for him, but what was her surprise when she saw it was not Charles, but only a stranger. I wore my beard in the American style, and once in the house I wanted to shake hands with her and kiss the old lady.

I had recognized her right away. She was the same servant that had been at my grandmother's thirty years before when I first came from Edmonton, so I considered her as one of the family. But I only scared her, and she gave a scream.

I said, "Keep quiet or you will frighten my aunt."

"But who are you?"

I said to her, "Do you not remember John Bull?" for that was the name they used to call me then. It was no use to try and keep her quiet then.

She called out, "Aunt, aunt, it is our dear little Johnny."

I followed her into the room and put my arms around my old aunt's neck and kissed her.

She did not let go my hand, but passed her other hand over my head saying, "I want to feel your curls."

When she felt my beard, she said, "Oh, Marguerite, he has a beard."

"Well, Aunt," I replied, "in twenty years a beard has time to grow."

She could not speak for a moment. She was overcome and I could not say very much, for I felt grieved to see her blind and so deeply moved.

After talking a little while, I told my aunt I would see her in the morning, as it was then late. I began to think. If I intended to be in Manitoba for the first of January, I had to hurry, for I had a great many friends to visit, so next morning I was up early, and right after breakfast before my aunt was yet visible I went out to begin my round of visits.

After I had made a few steps, I stood still for a while, looking at the peaceful town of Trois-Rivières, the place of my childhood. What a contrast it was with the busy towns I had left behind and the noise and bustle of mining towns. Twenty years before I had said goodbye to the town, and I scarcely noticed any change. It seemed but yesterday since I had looked on it. I let my memory take me back to my school days, to the thought of how I hated them and misspent them. Time had surely avenged my old teachers, for often when I saw myself deceived or at a loss through my ignorance, I thought of the wrong I had done myself in deceiving my grandmother.

Twenty years could work so little change to a town, and yet so much to an individual, and I wondered at it as I looked over the town lying quiet and unchanged in the morning sun. Twenty years before, I had left Trois-Rivières a child, I might say; for although I was fifteen, I did not know as much as a modern child of seven or eight years. Now I was a man of family and had amassed a fortune without education, it is true; but I had found out [. . . I] needed learning to take care of it against unprincipled people. That little incident in Montreal had shown me this need, not only among ruffians in Montana, but right here in the heart of civilization; but where I missed schooling the most was in the dealings with my own clerks.

Standing on the quiet street of Trois-Rivières where I had lost the chance which is given to a man only once in a lifetime, I thought of these things a long time. I had done little of account, while my old comrades had already made a name either in law or commercial life. From my cousin, Charles Lafrenaie, when passing through Montreal, I learned that all our relatives (the De Nivervilles, the Cressys, the Beaubiens, and Lamothes) had either one or two lawyers in their families and they had all been educated in that little town of Trois-Rivières or the surrounding schools, while I could hardly tell the months of the year. I did know them once, but I had forgotten them in my Indian ways.

All that passed quickly through my head while I looked at the town that morning. Then truly I regretted the way I had spent my young days, but I hurried to put the bitter memories behind me, for I had something to do.

My cousins whom I was coming to visit were lawyers, and I imagined what kind of wives they would likely have. I was almost ashamed to present myself and afraid to make blunders. However, I tried to forget those fears along with my regrets, for I was certain that mood would not be agreeable to my friends.

At any rate, I could not look dull for long at a time, so going to visit one of my cousins, I made myself as pleasant as possible. I went to Mr. Niverville's house and asked for him.

The servant said he was dead.

I had anticipated that; for he was very old when I left; but I asked for his daughter; and when she came in, I thought once more I was back to my childhood days, for my cousin Celina was the very image of her mother, large and fat like her. I went toward her to kiss her, but she drew back, indignant. I told her she need not make such a fuss because I would kiss her anyway, and it would not be the first time. She looked shocked, for she did not know me. That was the place I used to go for my New Year's gifts and New Year's kisses. But when I told her who I was, she got up quickly and caught hold of me and kissed me herself, laughing and welcoming me in a breath.

Another of my cousins, Marie de Niverville, who was then Mrs. Daignault, was visiting there with a Miss St. Clair and another young lady. I had dinner with them and chatted quite a while, but the time passed quickly in the company of such pleasant women. I do not believe that in the world over more charming women can be found than French-Canadian women, the upper class. They are gay, witty, and friendly and without affectation. I had a really good time while there. I tore myself away and promised to come and spend the next evening with them. I went back to my old aunt, for we had a great many things to talk about.

Next morning I rose early and went to see Joe de Niverville, Celina's brother. When I went in, his wife did not know me; and in answer to my inquiry, she said her husband was still in his dressing room. I knocked at the closed door and walked right in.

I said, "Good morning. How are you?"

He looked embarrassed, for he did not know what to make of me. It was enough to make a man nervous, to invade his private room that way. His wife I do not know whether she had any idea who I was or if she found her husband comical, but she smiled at him.

I put out my hand saying, "Are you not going to shake hands with me?" He shook hands with me but still could not place me.

At last I told him who I was, and his wife said, "I thought so. Something was telling me you were some of our relations."

Joe was a good deal older than I was but quiet, and although he was glad to see me, he was not fussy like his wife. After a while Joe drove me to his brother Charles' place about three miles from town at the Coteau (the ridge). There again sad thoughts forced themselves to my mind. It was my brother William's hunting place. When we were young we often went there. My brother killed squirrels with arrows in the top of large Normandy poplars which lined the way. When they were not too high up, I climbed up the poplar to get them. I could not linger very long on those sad memories, for I was in a friend's company.

When we reached Charles' place, he did not know me, but they soon welcomed me warmly and time passed on wings there. When the time came to return to town, it seemed as though we had just arrived and did not have time to say anything.

I kept my promise and spent the evening at Celina's (Mrs. Bourdage) where there were quite a few of the fair sex. They were very inquisitive, and I had many questions to answer about myself and family and my life in the West. I was very truthful in my replies, so true that they could not believe me and they laughed heartily. I felt like laughing too. Marie de Niverville played the piano, and the others danced to her music. I enjoyed it all thoroughly, and I was sorry I could not stay longer in their company.

The next morning I was out early to see my cousin, Auguste Cressy, whose wife I met that day too. She was a charming woman, one of those women you do not meet every day.

I left there in the afternoon and just had time to go and say goodbye to the others. I called at Celina's and thanked her for her kindness. They all kissed me goodbye but Miss St. Clair, so when I went to Montreal and I was sending back presents to all my relatives, I had a gold ring made for her and "For a kiss" engraved inside. She afterwards used it for her wedding ring, I heard years later.

The last person on whom I called was my aged aunt. She did not want me to leave her and spoke to me as if I were yet a child. She wanted me to go back and get my family and live in Trois-Rivières. I told her it would be impossible for me to live in the city now. I left her in tears, the good old lady.

1. Three Rivers, Quebec, where Johnny spent most of his boyhood, is located on the St. Lawrence River about equidistant between Montreal and Quebec.

# 34

## [WHEREIN HE VISITS HIS FUTURE HOME, MANITOBA, AFTER A TEDIOUS WINTER JOURNEY FROM ST. LOUIS.]

I remained a couple of days with my cousins, the de Lafrenayes [Richard and Charles de Lafrenaie], when passing through Montreal, and while there I got some souvenirs for all my cousins made of the gold I brought from Montana. Twenty-two years later my wife went to visit them, and they still had the gifts. It may be they have them yet in remembrance of their cousin on the frontier.

I went back to the Red River by St. Louis. I went to see my daughter and called on my old friend, Mr. McCartney. I went by train as far as St. Cloud, Minnesota, and when I arrived there, the stage was gone. If I waited for the next trip of the stage, I would have to remain there three or four days, and I did not want that. I hired a man to drive me to Fort Abercrombie.[1] He charged me six dollars a day and we were sixteen days on the road, which cost me ninety-six dollars besides the other expenses. Driving in a buggy with one horse in the latter part of December, traveling through seven inches of snow and in bitter cold weather, was not very pleasant; but I did not mind the cold much. The stage would have cost me only twenty-two dollars and would have been more comfortable.

Once at Fort Abercrombie I did not know how to make the rest of my trip, for the stage did not go any farther north. I enquired of a Mr. McCauly, who had a saw mill and a little store there, if there was any way to go to Georgetown.

He told me he was driving a young lady, a Miss Fergusson, there next morning, and if she did not object he would take me also.

So I went with them. The trip was only forty or fifty miles, so we reached Georgetown in one day.

I do not know what he charged the young lady, but he charged me ten dollars. It must have been a cold drive for her. McCauly had two ponies on a double cutter and the young lady sat alone on the back seat, with the driver and myself on the front seat. The young girl (she looked like a very young one) was very cold. About noon we caught up to a Mr. Hallet, a man from St. James, Manitoba, who had a load of freight. As he stopped to feed his horses we had a cup of tea with him.

In the afternoon I asked Miss Fergusson if she would allow me to wrap her up from the cold in the Indian style, as I was not accustomed to looking after white women. She agreed, and I took a pair of blankets, put a rope about the middle and tied it around her neck with the upper portion about her head. Then I took another and wrapped it about her. I took a rope and made a belt of it for her. Wrapped up like that she could not sit upright, so I had to sit beside her to keep her from falling. I put my hand through the rope belt to hold her steady, and she did not complain of the cold after that. She would ask occasionally to have the covering opened so she could breathe a little fresh air, so she was comfortable for the rest of the way.

We reached Georgetown the same night, and next morning Mr. Hallet took Miss Fergusson to the Red River. He had a kind of a small caboose fixed up for her on one of the sleds in his freight train and there were a couple of men with him. He continued his journey to the Red River, and Mr. McCauley went back to Fort Abercrombie, and I was left once more.

When I got up in the morning, I said to the man who was in charge of the Hudson's Bay post, "I suppose I can hire a team from some of the livery stables to continue my journey to the Red River."

He looked at me, smiling at me, and said, "There are no livery stables here."

A little surprised, I asked him if this was Georgetown.

He said, "Yes, that is the name of the place, but there is no town. It is only a Hudson's Bay store and warehouse."

"Well, well," I said, "I am worse off than ever, no stage to wait for, no freighters going to the Red River in the winter." (For Mr. Hallet had come expressly for Miss Fergusson.) What was I to do?

I asked the man if there was anyone from whom I could hire a team.

He said there were only some half-breeds across the river, but they had no horses.

Just then a man came in with freight from Fort Abercrombie, and I bought a fine team of sorrel horses from him for three hundred dollars.

The Hudson's Bay man went across the river and got me a little sled. He put a pole on it and charged me six dollars and fifty cents for it. It was quite an outfit, but at any rate I reached the Red River with it. (I overtook

Mr. Hallet the first day. The little lady was very comfortable in her caboose. Mr. Hallet had a large, flat tin can full of hot water under her feet; and he was very attentive, and she was very sociable.)

On Christmas we were still on the road. Miss Fergusson treated us to some butter and cakes, so it seemed more homelike. This lady afterwards married Doctor John Schultz, who was later Governor of Manitoba and was knighted, so she is today known as Lady Schultz. I thought on the journey when we traveled together that she was a very nice young lady, and my better acquaintance with her afterwards justified my good opinion of her. She was a fine helpmate to her husband, and he was a fine man, a very good-hearted man, especially to the poor. He was a warm friend. He was a friend of my late father-in-law, François Bruneau, and was very kind to his family.

1. Fort Abercrombie, located south of Fargo, North Dakota, stood near the Red River on the southeast border of the state.

# 35

## [WHEREIN HE VISITS RELATIVES IN MANITOBA, AND OBSERVES CANADIAN HALF-BREED LIFE.]

When I arrived at Red River, and before I reached Fort Garry, I passed several settlements along the road.[1] As I was passing the houses on the way people came out and stared at me. I wondered what made them so curious. It was my big team hitched to that small sled. They were not admiring me, but my team for there were very few in the country then who drove double.

It was on the seventh of January [1867], my thirty-fifth[2] birthday, when I arrived at my aunt's house. The holiday season was on and I had been regretting I had not stopped at Three Rivers until after the holidays, but the kindly way in which I was received by Mr. and Mrs. McKay made me soon forget that. I remained there three months and made the acquaintance of a number of relations I had never seen before. My uncle Pascal Breland had a large family, one of whom was married that winter. I went to the wedding and as I was fond of dancing I enjoyed myself thoroughly. The Brelands lived in a place called St. François Xavier (White Horse Plains) twelve miles from Deer Lodge, as the McKay's home was called. (This place, which was one of the finest of the old homes of Winnipeg, later became a well-known inn just outside the city. The old buildings were burned down in 1907.)[3]

Mrs. Ross, another sister of my mother's, lived at the Stone Fort which was called Lower Fort Garry. But besides my relatives, I made a number of friends, some of whom came from the United States. One group that kept a kind of bachelor's hall across the Assiniboine River at Fort Rouge was made up of Jack Nevins, Bob O'Lone, Scott and Lyon, and Tom Spence who died a few years ago in Edmonton. Every time I went to the fort I was sure to meet some of the men. We went around the country to dances together and enjoyed ourselves. Among James McKay's friends, was one Pierre Leveillier with whom I became warm friends, as also the three Genthon brothers.

I spent my time visiting from one place to another. This did not take so long for there were very few white people in the country at that time except those who were or had been in the employ of the Hudson's Bay Company. These men had married Indian women and the population was largely half-breed. The half-breeds in general were not wealthy, but a few were in good circumstances. They were all comfortable and the money they made remained in the country. Some were farmers, but they did not grow very much grain, nevertheless nearly every one of them had a few bushels to sell of wheat and barley. Wheat was generally worth ten shillings or two dollars and a half a bushel and barley was sold for one dollar and twenty-five cents a bushel. I did not see any oats grown, but some farmers raised a few acres of peas and corn. Wild ducks and wild pigeons were very plentiful, especially the pigeons, which were as numerous as blackbirds and as destructive. The farmers were obliged to destroy them and to do this they set traps to catch them.

The traps were made of [a] square frame about six feet square covered with netting. One side rested on the ground and the other was raised and supported by a post five or six feet high to which a long cord was attached. One end of the cord was held by the hunter who sat in a safe hiding place. He scattered wheat under the trap and, as soon as the ground under the trap was covered with pigeons, the hunter would pull the cord and down the trap would fall with sometimes as many as twenty and thirty birds caught at one time.

Their flesh was delicious and they were so plentiful that they were sold for six pence a dozen dressed. The Red and Assiboine rivers were well stocked too with good fish, the sturgeon, gold eyes, and cat fish. The poorer classes among the half-breeds hauled fire-wood and occasionally, a load of hay and sold it to the people in the town.

The buffalo hunters and traders came in early in the spring from their winter quarters so that they could be at Fort Garry for the twenty-fourth of May, the Queen's Birthday. Although it was far from civilization the people of the country told me they celebrated the birthday of their Sovereign as royally as possible. This meant with sports and merry making, horse and foot racing being the chief amusements. Everyone was interested, rich and poor, old and young. It was a day of excitement, even the Americans brought fast horses across the boundary to race. Sometimes the Americans won and again the Red River horses took the prizes. The hunters and traders sold their furs, meat and leather to the Hudson's Bay

Company and to the store keepers, exchanging some with the farmers for flour, vegetables and other provisions.

They remained around the fort about a month to rest their horses and get their supplies for another year, and then returned to their winter quarters. On their trips to the plains they were always accompanied by some Catholic missionary who kept the fear of the Lord in them. The Hudson's Bay Company and other store keepers had their goods freighted by half-breeds from St. Paul, Minnesota, and later from St. Cloud, to the Red River at a cost of four dollars for each hundred pounds. They often freighted furs to Minnesota and brought goods back, so they had loads both ways. What money there was in circulation remained in the country which was probably the reason that everyone had some.

The settlers all had buffalo meat to eat the whole year round. Some of the farmers went out to hunt every spring after seed time and brought back dried meat and buffalo tongues as well as pemmican which is made of dried meat, crushed and mixed with hot grease and put into sacks made of buffalo skins. Meat put up in that way would keep for years. Sometimes sugar and berries were mixed with it. The fat used was marrow fat and the whole dish was delicious. In my old days I have often wished to have a piece of it again. I would prefer it to the best plum pudding. The half-breed farmers sometimes made a second trip after harvest and returned about the fore part of November with fresh meat for winter use.

They tanned the hides and got leather to make moccasins. The women had pleasant rivalry as to who made the finest garments for their husbands. They embroidered the moccasins with silk or beads and also ornamented pieces of black cloth or leather which were used to carry a powder horn and a shot sack. Besides this they trimmed leather coats and gun covers, using porcupine quills sometimes with the silk and beads. The half-breed never wears boots or shoes, but only moccasins and in wet weather they wear rubbers over their moccasins. Very few wore stockings, only a piece of flannel nip around their feet. The women did not wear embroidered moccasins and, instead of stockings, they wore leggings made of cloth embroidered with beads or ribbon of different colors in a wavy zig-zag pattern four or five inches high from the ankle. They did not wear coats or cloaks, but a piece of fine black cloth about two yards long which they wore in cold weather over a couple of shawls. A colored silk handkerchief covered their heads. Dressed in that manner they would face any wind or cold. They often walked six or seven miles to church and sometimes farther after a week of hard work. The women worked harder then than now for besides the embroidery, all their sewing was done by hand, and in summer they helped in the hay-field and then in harvesting the grain.

The men too worked harder to raise the few bushels of grain than a farmer does to raise thousands now. They used plows which were all wood except the steel stock eight inches wide. They cut all the grain with sickles and threshed it with flails and winnowed it by hand. That was one reason grain was dear. They cut all their hay with a scythe and raked it up by hand. Very few had steel pitch forks, nearly everybody using wooden forks. There were no wagons and every man made his own cart and sleds of wood.

1. Following here (in chapters 35 and 36), Grant describes the mid nineteenth-century frontier settlements of southeast Manitoba. Today, this vicinity is dominated by Winnipeg (population 560,000), which is the capital of the Province of Manitoba.
2. Grant is mistaken in recalling his age at that time; he actually was thirty-six.
3. These two sentences appear to have been added to the text by Clothild Grant or her grandson, William Nutt.

# 36

## [IN WHICH HE TELLS OF FRENCH CELEBRATIONS, FETES, AND CONDITIONS IN THE RED RIVER COUNTRY.]

Notwithstanding all the drawbacks of life on the Red River the people enjoyed themselves, especially during the holiday season. New Years day was the great fete for the French half-breed. In the morning those who lived far from the parish church left home at three or four o'clock and, even before daylight, stopped at every house they passed to wish the people a happy New Year. A carriole would leave each house and by the time the church was reached for High Mass at ten o'clock there would be as many as twenty carrioles in the party. This is for one road only, but it was the same along every road leading to the church. They all had bells or ribbons of different colors on their horses' bridles, vying with each other as to who would have his horse most gaily trimmed.

After Mass they began to visit friends and they kept up a round of visits for a week or longer. They went from house to house wishing everyone a happy New Year. The housewives prepared for a week beforehand for every one; white or Indian expected refreshments as soon as they came in. These consisted principally of buffalo meat, plum pudding and cakes, and it was a poor house where there was not a bottle or two of rum to treat the men and a bottle of wine for the ladies.

If there was any ill-feeling between families in the settlement this was a day of reconciliation. Every one was expected to be happy; past grievances were forgotten and buried. Christmas was also a day of joy and of merry making for them, but not like New Years day. It was mostly a day of prayer on which they attended the midnight Mass and other religious services. The English and Scotch half-breeds however celebrated Christmas as a season of rejoicing.

Weddings were great events to which all friends and acquaintances were invited. This was a favorite season for weddings. Among the French half-breeds dances were ordinarily forbidden, but at weddings they were allowed to dance for even three or four days. The old folks went during the day, the young folks in the afternoon [and] for the balance of the night to dance. If the wedding lasted more than two days some of the guests remained home the second day to rest, and if it lasted four days some would rest on the third day to be fresh and ready for the fourth. The marriages usually took place on Tuesday, [and] dancing lasted only for three days because these people never danced on Friday. After the marriage ceremony they had a breakfast of meat cooked in different ways, plum and rice puddings, doughnuts and a wedding cake built in either two or three stories.

An extra good and sweet Bannock about two inches thick and as wide as a dinner plate formed the first story. A round stick was inserted in the center and one or two more bannocks mounted higher on this. Small sticks were pushed into the cake and streamers fastened to them. There was also a small piece of cake on the end of each of those sticks and any of the guests who wished to sing a song took one of those sticks from the cake.

The bride, if she could sing, sang first either a good bye to her family or to her girlhood days, and while she was singing an elderly man, a friend of the family, would go under the table and take one of her moccasins off and auction it off. Sometimes it brought a high price which was then used to pay the fiddler or some other expense of the wedding. The bride who had used her best skill to make her moccasins pretty and attractive listened blushing to the bidding and was always relieved when the moccasin was returned to its place. Weddings took place from time to time between New Years and Lent. Besides this, all during the winter people visited from one friend to another, the young people playing cards, the old folks playing checkers.

During the summer there was plenty of work and little play, until the harvest was over and then there was another merry time at the corn husking, which was always followed by a dance in the evening.

When I came to the country there were five or six traders' stores as well as the Hudson's Bay Company's fort. There were more people in Point Douglas than at Fort Garry. From the point to the Stone Fort (or Lower Fort Garry as it was sometimes called), English and Scotch half-breeds were settled and two Presbyterian churches as well as St. John's Anglican Church had been built for their worship. Across the Red River from Fort Garry was the Catholic Church, the bishop's residence, the old convent and the college. The bishop's residence which was built of stone a couple of years before I came to the country was the best building in the settlement.

There was a small hospital too kept in what had been the home of Louis Thibeault, a brother of the late Vicar Thibeault, an early Saskatchewan missionary then in charge of the White Horse Plain.

Below the church for a distance of three or four miles, St. Boniface was settled by French settlers, mostly all descendants or connections of the Lagimodières, the first French-Canadian couple who came to the Red River. On the south side of St. Boniface Church there was a settlement of French half-breeds who had a convent at St. Vital, six miles from Fort Garry and another twelve miles farther at St. Norbert with the late Monsignor Richot as parish priest.

From St. Norbert south along the Red River for a distance of about twenty miles to Scratchiny River (which is now called Morris) the country was sparsely settled. West of Fort Garry along the Assiniboine River it was settled by English and Scotch half-breeds and for a distance of six miles it was called St. James. There was an Anglican church there. The next settlement was St. Charles settled by French half-breeds. Farther on was the settlement of Headingly, settled by Scotch and English half- breeds. Then came White Horse Plains (or St. François Xavier) where Pierre Falcon the singer still lived. From this place to Bay St. Paul the prairie was very sparsely settled; then there was Poplar Point, then High Bluff, and finally Portage la Prairie, where there was quite a settlement. East of St. Boniface there was a French half-breed settlement at Oak Point (now called Lorette); farther on there was Oak Island (or Ste. Anne); these parishes are on what was formerly called the Dawson Road. There were quite a number of Indians settled and scattered over most of the parishes, especially around Fort Garry, and the Stone Fort as they were older places than the others.

One pleasant feature of the country was the general friendship that existed between all classes, rich or poor, and of any nationality or creed. Everyone was as friendly with his neighbors as though they were members of one family. But with the coming of the surveyors and new settlers from Ontario there was a great change. Good fellowship and harmony came to an end. A number of the half-breeds began to take on the manners of the whites. Others held back and a division grew. The poorer families mingled less with the well-to-do. Still there were not any so poor as to be compelled to beg. Wages were small and men worked for ten and fifteen dollars a month, and girls who earned four dollars a month had to be very capable. The average wages for girls were two and two and one half dollars a month. The natives were generally honest and trusty; if they made a bargain they always abided by it without a scratch of a pen. Their word was as good as their bond, and if any one ever acted dishonestly he was scorned by the others. They even sold land without having a deed drawn.

I can vouch for this because when I bought a valuable piece of land near what is now the Louise Bridge in Winnipeg I did not get a deed of it for two years after, and I am certain that the party I bought it from had been offered twice what I paid for it. He would no more think of accepting the new offer than of taking money from a man's pocket. That was the condition of the country when I came to it and I was perfectly satisfied with it and I considered it a good place to bring my family to live. Besides being so peaceable, there was a college and a convent where I could educate my children, so I made up my mind to make my home along the Red River.

# 37

## [WHEREIN HE ORGANIZES A PARTY TO CROSS THE PLAINS TO MONTANA. THE SCOUNDREL GUIDE STEALS FOOD, CAUSING DISCONTENT.]

After a winter of pleasure and amusements I began to prepare for my return home to my family in Montana, but before I went I found it hard to say good-bye to one young lady. It must not be supposed that I passed the winter there without noticing the fair sex. That would be impossible for one of my nature. I saw quite a number of pretty and friendly girls, but there was one I met at my aunt's home who took my whole fancy. She was the first white girl that I had really found attractive since I left the little Louise in Machiehe. Like her, she was fair with yellow hair and brown eyes and she was very charming in my estimation. We were very great friends.

I would have certainly looked at her in a different light if the thought of my Quarra had not put a guard on me. Although I might have done like many other white men, leave my Indian woman and take a white one, I do not think my heart was hard enough for that especially after the answer mine had given me before I left home.

I said to her, "Quarra, I am going to the Red River to see some relations and some friends. If the country suits me I am going to move there. Will you leave your people to come with me?"

With fear in her eyes she said, "If you will take me I will go to the end of the world with you to be with you and my children. Will you take me?" she asked, in her pleasant way, but with trouble in her voice too for she was afraid to be left.

I assured her I would take her.

She was only a poor Indian woman, but she knew how to show her love and her gratitude. Poor little woman, since I had taken her at the age of thirteen she had been a good wife and had done all she could to please me. How could I leave her if she was willing to come. But she was weak and consumptive, and twice had nearly died, so when I met this young girl I am afraid I forgot my poor Quarra for awhile. Quarra might die soon, the tempter said, and I thought if she does, my first choice will be this young girl. But there seemed lots of time as she was only nineteen or twenty, so I did not compromise myself. I did not say anything to her; just treated her as a very dear friend.

After I was ready to leave for home I went down to her home to bid her good-bye. The ice was very bad on the Red and Assiniboine, but I did not know the danger of the ice in the spring. It only appeared as though no one had been crossing for awhile. I crossed anyway, although I soon found the ice was very rough and rotten. I had to drive a couple of miles after crossing the river. I could not stay very long and as I hurried back over the ice the wheels cut down to the axle, the water coming to the horse's flank. I heard later that the Sisters in St. Boneface Convent, seeing that reckless driver, knelt down and prayed for his safety as he crossed the Assiniboine River. Their prayers were granted. When I reached the other side of the river, I looked back and shuddered at the danger I had escaped. I had not seen it in the same light before I crossed. It may be I was a little blind with a love that is said to bring blindness, but I remained true to my Quarra. I left without telling my secret, but with the hope of coming back.

So on the sixteenth of April [1867] we started for Montana. I hired twelve French and Scotch half-breeds, also Malcolm Ross, my cousin. I had an American named Jackson and his wife who was the half-breed daughter of old Munroe, a noted character through the whole West. Mrs. Jackson was as good on the trip as many men are and even better than my guide, Decotean (Shoshigh) to whom I paid twenty dollars a month. I paid only sixteen dollars to the other men. They did not have much to do, but to look after one cart each. Angus McKay, brother of James McKay of Silver Height, came with me for company.

I had to buy horses, carts and harness but I was not long preparing for my trip. People were plowing when we left. Mr. McKay and Peirre Leveille came with us as far as Bay St. Paul. We stopped at noon on the bank of the Assiniboine River near the home of Faillant Leveille's father-in-law. The old gentleman had still three daughters unmarried who were at the time across the river busy making maple sugar.

I spoke to them from across the River, but the old gentleman said to me, "Mr. Grant, don't you want to go and bid good-bye to my daughters, I will take you over."

I said, "Of course I would like to go."

There was open water on both banks and ice in the center of the river so he got a canoe to cross the water, but I was not accustomed to canoes and I jumped in it from the bank and it upset giving us a cool bath.

I knew I was in the fault, but I laid the blame on the old gentleman, laughing at him for trying to drown me because I wanted to go and see his daughters. We had to put on dry clothes, so I was then too late to go across to see the daughters and was compelled to leave the place without bidding them good-bye. At Bay St. Paul, Mr. McKay and P. Leveille after wishing us a safe journey and quick return bade us farewell and we traveled on our way.

We had fair weather until we reached Moose Mountain.[1] About fifteen miles from it we met George Fisher and his party returning from their winter quarters. He told us the mountain was fifteen miles away, and we traveled all that day, but did not reach it. Our guide was leading us astray going too far south. Towards evening a storm came on. I went ahead to look for water and I found a small lake or rather a mud hole. There was about fifteen yards of grass around it and the rest of the country was all burnt. I made signs to my party to come there. It was raining and before they had reached the place, it was pouring down. We placed three carts together and spread an oil-cloth over them to make a shelter.

Jackson was in a quandary as to what would become of his wife in such weather, but she simply had to crowd in under the shelter with the men. I was nearly suffocated and those outside were praying for daylight to appear. Jackson was a very thin man and during the night he was crushed almost to death.

He exclaimed, "Oh my God, I wish I was in Hell," but he immediately added, "for the same length of time."

Perhaps he was afraid he might be there before morning.

When morning came every one was alive and well, but we had to do without breakfast, although we had had no supper. There was no wood to make a fire. After traveling for some time we reached the foot hills and stopped to cook some breakfast. Our flour was nearly exhausted and we were obliged to divide the pieces of bannock.

While we were eating someone said, "There is a flock of geese passing."

One of the party took a gun. Decotean, the guide, advised us to bow down our heads so as not to frighten the geese, and nearly all took his advice. I did not, so as soon as they bowed their heads I saw him reach out for their pieces of bread, capturing by his deceit four or five pieces. The rest of the party were furious.

There was some very loud talking, but I did not understand what they said for they spoke Cree. It was a most contemptible act for the meat allowance was also running low. The second or third night after, we reached an abandoned camping place. Shoshigh was prowling about the camps looking for something to eat when he suddenly exclaimed joyfully, that he had found two or three pieces of meat. There was about half a pound in each piece, but it must be remembered it was the refuse of an Indian camp. The man was a glutton; he did not care, he just shook the dirt off those pieces and cooked them, and made a good meal.

We went to bed without any supper and to make matters worse we experienced another storm that night. One of my horses died. I had a few crumbs of dried meat left next morning and gave each a pinch keeping as much for myself. I did not eat anything for I was not hungry. Towards evening the weather cleared up, but it was too late to start, so I told the men that they had better go and get some of the horse meat, for we had no idea when we would see any buffalo. They took the hint and went and got a hind quarter of the dead horse. As soon as they had it in camp Shoshigh put some of it in a kettle to cook. He watched it and as soon as a piece was cooked he ate it, at the same time telling stories and feeling quite happy. The next morning I was in no hurry to get up for the Bill of Fare was not very tempting.

I could not eat that poor horse meat, neither would any of us nor Mrs. Jackson. After I got up I took my telescope and scanned the country around us. I fancied I could see objects moving and we concluded they were buffaloes. I told one of my men, Augustin Racette who was an expert at buffalo hunting, to take my horse and to kill a buffalo.

1. Grant's party had proceeded westward across Manitoba, entering what is now southeast Saskatchewan. Today, Moose Mountain is protected as a provincial park. Grant's route soon led south across the U.S./Canadian border to the Milk River drainage of north central Montana, and on to Fort Benton.

# 38

## [Wherein he leads the party to the Milk River buffalo range after the cowardly guide, afraid of Indians, takes them astray, causing hardship.]

The men were about to have their breakfast. We saw Racette nearing the buffalo. He did not chase them very far before we heard the report of his rifle.

The next minute Shoshigh kicked the kettle of horse meat over saying, "To the devil with the horse meat. It is good only for dogs, not for men."

One of the party said to him, "You glutton you ate nearly all the horse meat last night, and drank the broth too. I wish Racette had not killed any buffalo so that you would not have any breakfast." But Providence was in his favor.

The fresh buffalo meat was very welcome and we certainly did justice to it. We loaded the cow on the carts and while it lasted for three days, we were all meat eaters. The next day our guide again went astray. In fact this fool was the cause of our running short of provisions for he told McKay the time it would take us to reach our journey's end and Mr. McKay had outfitted us accordingly.

I told him he was going too far north and pointed out to him the direction we should go.

He followed my advice for some time but he again turned aside from the right direction.

I went to him and said, "Decotean, you are going astray again."

He pointed to a bluff of poplars. "There are Indians there," he said, "and I am trying to avoid them."

I told him there were no Indians there, and if there were any it is the very reason we should go there to show that we were not afraid of them. "It is better for us to go to them than let them come to us."

He went in the direction where he supposed the Indian camp was, but he only found a bluff of poplars.

I think it was the next day he came to me and said he was lost.

I told him to go back and that I would guide.

Mr. Jackson said we had to go South West and I set my compass accordingly. Angus and I went ahead nearly in the opposite direction from the one Shoshigh had been traveling in.

We traveled a mile or two when he came to me with tears in his eyes and said, "You are going in a dangerous direction, we will all be killed by the Sioux Indians."

I asked him what difference there was being killed by the Sioux or Bloods (Blackfeet) or to starve. "Where ever I am going," I said, "I will go straight." So I went on.

The next day after traveling on high land for sometime, we began to go down, and presently at the bottom I saw Milk River and the wagon road going to Fort Benton. I wanted to know if my ex-guide knew where he was and so I went back and told one of my men to tell Shoshigh we were lost.

He called out, "I knew they were lost." Then he put on an air of great importance, "You see that knoll," he said, pointing to it with his hand, "that is the Tiger Hill, a days travel on the other side is the Milk River."

We traveled a couple of hundred yards further going down the hill, and came to the wagon road.

I said, "Hello, what road is this?" but he was ready.

"I do not know it, that road must have been made since I was here before."

"What about this river?"

He could not answer, so I said, "Never mind who made the road and the river, let us go on."

We followed the road and in about fifteen miles we reached the crossing of Milk River.

We traveled until eleven o'clock that night in the bright moonlight. After we had set up camp Angus McKay, Boniface Plante and I went for a stroll to look up a watering place for our horses. We were startled on the way by the sound of a dog growling and as we had seen some Indians with dogs th[at?] day we thought it was well to go back to camp. We tried to get Shoshigh out to parley with the Indians because he claimed to know every language from the Red River to Fort Benton. He was a coward as we knew. He would only go when Mr. Jackson took his arm and brought him forcibly, but they did not go far. The next morning we found out it was a she-wolf and her whelps we had disturbed as they ate a buffalo carcass.

We watered our horses next morning and resumed our journey, keeping a sharp look-out for buffalo as our larder was empty. The river bank was all cut up by buffalo trails, crossing the river coming from the south and passing north. There were antelope trails too about six inches wide and an inch deep. Being ahead I noticed a buffalo, chased him and shot him. Just then the men called me; they were pointing north to a big herd of buffalo so I left the old bull at once. One of the men named John Swain rode up to me and as he was a good hunter I gave him my horse and he went after the buffalo killing a cow. I came up to him then and took my horse to join the men while he remained to butcher the buffalo.

As I was going I saw another cow and following her into the bush, shot [at] her six or seven times, but did not hit her. I was no expert shooting on horseback. She crossed a small stream called the White River and I got off my horse and shot her with my revolver. I broke her back just as she was coming out on the other side. I overtook my men about a mile away where they were camped for the night and sent them with a cart to get the meat of the two cows. It was fortunate that we killed those cows for we would have been hungry without them. We remained there the following day to cut up and dry the meat, first cutting it into slices about half an inch thick, one foot wide and as long as it can be made.

We built a scaffold out of small poles covered with willows,spread the meat on the willows and then kindled a fire under the scaffold to dry it. My guide Shoshigh had a good fill and then fell asleep. But before closing his eyes he put a fine piece of meat on the end of a stick by the fire to eat when he woke up. During the night the other men disposed of his roast. When he woke up he rubbed his eyes with one hand and reached for his roast with the other, but to his disgust it was gone.

He was furious, and called the men gluttons.

I said to him, "Decotean, there is the meat of two cows, do not worry, take some more," but that was not the question; the roast they had taken was a choice piece which perhaps could not be replaced.

For two days we saw large herds of buffalo crossing the road ahead of us. We were traveling west and they were going north; we must have passed thousands during those two days. When we reached the last crossing of the Milk River the water was very high and as the weather was windy and cold we camped there, for I did not want to see the men get wet in the water on a cold day.

# 39

## [IN WHICH JOHNNY IS SADLY INFORMED OF DEAR QUARRA'S DEATH, AND HE ARRIVES IN DEER LODGE TO CLOSE OUT HIS BUSINESS DEALINGS.]

While there we saw a buffalo passing, so four of us went after him on foot. We all shot at him and broke his hip. He was furious but helpless. We had often heard that a bullet would not penetrate a buffalo head and now we tried. We found that only the Henry rifle bullet went through. I brought the animal's tongue to the camp and the others brought enough meat for a couple of meals. We would have taken more, but we now saw a herd of buffaloes across the river towards Bear Paw Mountain and as this was an old bull we left the rest of the meat. When we got to our camp, Shoshigh who was then eating his supper asked if the marrow was good. I threw the tongue to him telling him at the same time to see for himself as he was an old hunter.

He looked at it and added there will not be very much left by morning. He was very fond of marrows, but wanted to be sure it was good, as he had sickened himself during the trip eating the marrow of a buffalo we found dead on the plains. He went out to the fresh carcass that night, got the four marrow bones, the kidneys, and a part of the insides. He cooked these and ate it all in one meal.

After supper as he was walking along the bank of the Milk River picking his teeth, he kept telling us, "Shoshigh's stomach is well braced."

It certainly must have been after eating such a meal.

The weather grew fine, and the men finding a crossing, we forded the river next morning. The buffalo we had seen the day before were gone, but we had enough of the meat of the two cows still left to last us until we reached Fort Benton.

After four days traveling, as we were about one mile from the fort and camped on the Teton River, I said to my ex-guide, "Decotean, now we are near a place where you can earn double the wages I am paying you. I have no more use for you, a man who has lied to me as you have done all the way. You have told us there would be water and wood in places, where we found neither. We nearly starved on the road because you made us travel farther than was necessary. I would not on any consideration trust such a man as you to guide me back with my family and my stock. Now we are a mile from Fort Benton and you can get work there."

After that he was satisfied to go.

Next morning we continued our journey and before long I met my clerk who said he was on his way home. He gave the sad news of my wife's death.[1] She had died four months before, leaving a boy five months old. I was deeply affected as I had lost a good wife. She was a thorough Indian woman and not handsome, but a better and more clever woman could not be found, without education. She was a good mother, industrious and gay in her moods and friendly with every one regardless of nationality or color. She could speak several Indian languages as well as English and French. She was expert with her needle too and could ride horses that many could not. My little Quarra, when I heard of her death my first thought was the great loss our children sustained. She had been such a good mother. My own loss I realized more and more as time passed.

With a sad heart I went to my home and to my motherless children. I arrived at night, but the baby's aunt had him. I went for him, but he did not want to come to me. After a few days he cried when I would leave him. I was told that Quarra had said she was resigned to meet death, but she would have liked to see me there when she breathed her last. Her last request before she died was to see her children. She took the baby in her arms and pressed him to her heart until he cried. She did not want to let him go, her children were so dear to her.

After a time I thought of how I was going to take those motherless children to a strange country [and] memories came to my mind of some one that I had left back there. She had seemed to me of kind disposition and would likely be a good mother to my little ones and a good wife. So I wrote to her sending the letter in care of a friend.

That clerk that I had met on his way home with one of my horses in payment of a claim of one hundred and fifty dollars, which he had against me, came back to Deer Lodge at my request and together we looked into all the business. I settled with him first, but I found that instead of my owing him he was in my debt over two hundred Dollars. He told me then he had no money to go home so I lent him two hundred dollars. I had no idea what he could have done with his wages for he was getting one hundred dollars a month. A French woman who kept a stopping place at the Divide told me afterwards, however, that his saddle bags weighed about eighteen pounds, so I had my suspicions. He was not the only one indebted to me; my partner in the saloon owed me twelve thousand dollars and there was fifteen thousand on the books, and besides my liquors and groceries were all gone. The only cash on hand was eighty dollars of which I gave half to my partner.

Fortune had once smiled upon me, but now all luck had turned against me. When I sold my place to Con Kohrs he had given me his note for nine thousand two hundred; it was due, but I could not find it. I told him that I thought the note was lost. I offered to publish it in the newspaper so that if it was presented by any one but myself he would not be obliged to pay it. He insisted on getting the note before he would pay it. I was in a bad predicament with no money to get ready to return to the Red River. I had notes for the fifteen thousand dollars which were on the books, but they were not worth the paper that they were written on for the men who made them were penniless, and should never have got so much credit.

I searched for Con's note, but could not find it. I thought it might have been in my pocket book when I was robbed at Sioux City. One day I wanted to shave and asked for my razor case. They handed me an old one which had not been in use for some years, one that had belonged to my father. I sent it back, but when I again asked for a razor, that same razor case was brought to me. While they were gone to get it, I opened the first one they had brought to me and I saw a folded paper in it. I took it out and it was the identical note I was looking for. I immediately went to town where the money was ready for me in Worden's safe. With that I began my preparation to move to Manitoba.

1. The *Montana Post* reported: "On the 24th instant, at her residence, Cora [Quarra], wife of John F. Grant, Esq., closed her earthly career and started on her journey to the happy hunting grounds of the nation, or the white man's destiny, as the case may be. The Deceased died as she had lived, strong in the faith of Jesus Christ, and the Virgin Mary. Her funeral was well-attended by both whites and natives, who mourned her untimely departure. She was much respected by the former, and her memory will be fondly cherished by her countrymen and women. Her disease was consumption [tuberculosis] and her death slow and easy." (3/12/1867, *Montana Post* [Deer Lodge, MT])

# 40

Before I left Deer Lodge I made another blunder. A man named Captain Finch had come to Montana to organize the militia. He bought horses and supplies from those who had them to sell and in payment he gave vouchers on the American government. I sold him horses to the amount of ten thousand, six hundred dollars, then brought the vouchers to St. Paul, Minnesota, and placed them in the hands of a firm of lawyers. All I received out of those vouchers was eleven hundred dollars. The reason they gave me for not paying the full amount was that the government had not authorized Captain Finch to buy those horses, so I was again the loser, of nine thousand, five hundred dollars.

I remained a couple of months at Deer Lodge to prepare for my long trip and during that time I settled some old scores with a fiery Mexican. I had a little trouble with him before I left for my first trip to Manitoba. It was not much, but I nearly paid for it, with my life. He was always in my debt; he kept a restaurant and got his goods from me; he would pay what he owed, and take more, and sometimes he would borrow money.

In the short winter days, I did not generally take any midday meal. About noon this man would hunt me up, when I was in town, and ask me to come, and have some dinner with him. I could not always refuse for he would say, that his wife, a bright Blackfoot half-breed, had some nice soup, or some other tempting dish and after dinner they were smart enough to get round me to borrow some money. I had it and I could not refuse them and he would generally pay me, all right.

Things went on that way until a few weeks before I left for Manitoba. Being so much in their company, we were all pretty friendly and one day after dinner we sat talking by the window. The woman was sewing, the man rose and went out by one door, but coming back in the same direction passed the window just in time to see his [wife] near me. She had dropped the sheepskin glove she was sewing and both of us bent down to pick it up and as our heads were very close together he thought she kissed me. The Mexican came in by the other door, furious and struck his wife a blow right on the face, before I could prevent him.

He packed up and set out for Mexico with his wife and son, but as they stopped at noon a few miles from my house, she said to [her] husband she would come to bid farewell to her friend, Isabel,[1] another Blackfoot half-breed who had taken shelter at my house some time before. I was away at the time, but I was told that the woman did not remain very long. Still when she went back to the road the Mexican was gone. She followed his tracks for a time, but when she could not catch up to him, she turned back, and having no place to go, she came back to the house and remained with her friend for a while. Shortly after that I left for Manitoba and when I came back I learned she had gone off with a French-Canadian trader.

But that spring when I sold those horses to Capt. Finch, I drove them one night to a corral from which we intended to deliver them in the morning. After we had the horses secured, I went in the owner's house where there were a number of men. Among the crowd I noticed a Mexican who had just come from Mexico.

I was sitting on the bed, as seats were scarce, when I asked if that other Mexican who had deserted his wife had come back. (Something was telling me that he was near.)

The man said he had not.

I asked when he was coming and the fellow told me he was not coming at all.

I knew he was telling a lie. I told him so, and added, "I know he is coming."

"Well, yes," he said then with a guilty air, "he is on his way."

I left after a little more speech with the man of the house. My home was near and before I went to bed, I left with one of my men, to see the horses again. As we neared the corral, we saw a dark figure sneaking away along the fence. It was so dark, we could not see, if it was an Indian, or a white man, but we found my horses all right. Next morning some of old Lame Tom's horses were missing, but mine were all right.

A few days later someone told me that the Mexican was back from the south and wanted to see me. That same day or the next, I met him [and] he asked me to go to a vacant barn that was close by as he wanted to ask me something. I went, but once inside I put my back to the wall; if there was going to be any treachery, I would have only three sides to guard.

Then I said to him, "What do you want?"

"I want to ask you a favor," he said, "but first I will tell you why I went away. I went to Mexico to take my boy away and I came back to kill you. When you were asking that man that night, if I was back, I was under the very bed where you were sitting. I was going to steal your horses that night and you saw me along the fence later on, but thinking over it, I knew if I stole them you would follow me to Hell, so I stole old Tom's instead. Now for the last three nights, I have watched for you, in that bunch of willows, near the creek by the the foot bridge."

"I had my revolver not three inches from your temple every night to shoot you."

"Then why didn't you?"

"The thought of all the kindness you did me held my hand."

So his gratitude was stronger than his jealousy.

"And now," I said, "what do you intend to do?"

"Well, I made up my mind not to try to harm you any more."

"And what is the favor you want?"

"I want you to tell my wife to come back with me."

"I have nothing to do with your wife. I have not seen her since I came back. I will send her word, but I do not promise you that she will go."

He offered to shake hands. I shook hands with him and he went his way and I went mine.

That day or the next I met a woman who lived near his wife.

I said to her, "Tell Lucie that I said for her to go back to her husband."

Lucie did, so the Mexican got his wife back.

In settling up my business affairs, I left an agent by the name of Pemberton to take charge of my property there. It included $25,000 worth of goods that had come from St. Louis that spring and $15,000 worth of notes to be collected; the saloon, which with its fittings had been valued at $19,100; four town lots; the blacksmith shop; the restaurant; [and] the site of the livery stable. The lot where the brewery was built, and which had cost me $2,200, was sold for $1,800. All I received out of this property, including the $25,000 worth of goods, was $11,800, which came to me in various amounts during the next few years.

When I started for the Red River quite a number of people came with me from Montana. Some were going to the States and others to the Red River. There were sixty-two wagons and twelve carts with about five hundred head of horses, two hundred of which were mine. There were one hundred and six men besides the women and children. I fed about sixty of the men and furnished most of them with horses and some with rifles. I had about thirty rifles, some shot guns and a rifle cannon. I was the leader of the party, the men being divided into squads of ten with a captain over each squad.

We stopped at Fort Benton a couple of days to get some horses shod and also to do some repairing. After we finished the work that was to be done, we resumed our journey. About seventy five miles from Fort Benton, near the Bear Paw Mountain, an Indian scout came to us and told us that he belonged to a band of Blackfeet who were going to Fort Benton to the treaty. He spoke for some time to our interpreter, Isabel, who had come to look after my baby. She spoke the Blackfoot and Assiniboine languages as well as English, and the Indian told her that he was going back to his band to tell them that there was a party of whites going east and to tell where we intended to camp.

1. Catholic Church records indicate that Grant had a daughter, Emma, by "Isabella Ruis" in about 1863.

# 41

## [WHEREIN THE BLACKFEET SAY FAREWELLS WITH TEARS AND WHISKEY, AND TWO BRAVADOS FALSELY ALARM THE TRAIN.]

When we reached the camping place on Butter Creek, the Indians were there already camped, so we passed on and camped on the other side of the creek. We made a corral for the horses by driving the first wagon to the right, and the next to the left, and so on alternately until the last wagon was fitted in close to its companions and the circular corral was formed. The scout we had seen was the band's spokesman. He came out and told us to wait until he put on his uniform.

Presently he returned dressed in a suit of white underwear. It was a funny contrast with his black face, but he imagined he was royally attired. There were several others with him for it was a large camp, of about eighty lodges. I told the interpreter to tell the chief that I was also chief of my party and that when I said anything to my men they did it, and he should tell his young men to drive their horses across the creek from our side, for we wanted to let our horses go to feed.

In a short time there were a dozen nearly naked Indians with only breech cloths on running over the prairie yelling at their horses, and in a few minutes they had their horses on the same side as their camp. So we let our horses loose and before going to bed we hobbled those we used, and placed a guard over them. The Indians offered a guard of ten men to watch our horses while they fed, but I thanked them and told them we had enough men to watch. At the same time I warned the men of our party if any of them had any liquor and wanted to trade with the Indians they must wait till morning, and after the rest of our party had gone the interpreter and I would remain with them. I thought this caution necessary for the majority of our party were strangers to me. Next morning at daybreak I was awakened by the shouts of drunken Indians. I got up and saw eight or nine naked braves riding around and yelling fiercely. I started our party immediately and told my men to unload a barrel of whiskey I had brought with me.

There were only twelve or thirteen gallons remaining in it. It had evidently been tapped for it was full of reeds. I also had a five gallon keg of Madeira wine. When it was produced I saw it had met the same fate, for the hoops were falling off. I told the men I could guess the guilty parties and I reproached them for not treating me before they drank it all.

After the party was gone I asked Baptiste Champagne, whose father was interpreter for the American Fur Company at Fort Benton, to tell the Indians that I was now leaving the country, but I would come back again. Then I treated them with whiskey.

One of them led up a horse and put the rope in my hand saying to Baptiste, "Tell him that I am the one who stole his horses, but I did not know him then. I am sorry and I would like to make up for what I have done. If he comes back to trade with us we will do all we can to help him, we are sorry to see him go."

I told Baptiste to tell them that I was also sorry to leave them, but that I would return the next year when the grass was a foot high to trade with them.

They told me to bring a good supply of liquor and I replied that it was not good for them, that it would only cause their families to starve, but that I would bring them something better such as groceries and ammunition. I traded all of the whiskey except two gallons. That was the only time I gave liquor to Indians. I got six horses, twenty-two buffalo robes, eight dressed elk and deer skins, and six bales of dried beef. When I wanted to leave, the braves came one after another to shake hands with me, some of them with tears running down their cheeks. I could hardly get rid of them. They told me I was the only white man who had treated them right, for they still recalled the morning I had fed those who had come to my house on the Little Blackfoot.

I again told them I would come back the next year, [but] they did not want me to go. I took those two gallons of whiskey which were left in a keg and, putting it down, I told Baptiste to tell them that I gave them that liquor to drink to my health after I was gone. They wanted to give me another embrace, but I dodged it as it was not very pleasant.

I got away at last. I had four horses on my wagon and drove very fast, but I had traveled only half a mile or so when I saw the Indians coming. I drove faster, but they overtook me. I stopped my horses and getting out shook hands with them again and had the interpreter tell them that my men were quite a distance ahead of me and that I was obliged to hurry to overtake them. So I got away after another farewell. After I had traveled a short distance, the interpreter looked back and saw them coming again. I whipped the horses and drove them as fast as they could go. Finally they went back when they saw they could not overtake us, but I was glad to be rid of them.

On that same trip they had some trouble with the whites and war was declared. What caused the rupture, I could not say. I knew however that the summer before about a dozen whites from Benton followed eight or nine peaceable Blackfeet and killed them in a ravine about one and a half miles from the fort. The Indians were asleep without guard, as they did not suspect any treachery while they were in their own territory. The following year they did not go to Benton to trade, so if I had kept my word to them I would have realized a large amount of trading that year. I heard afterwards that they spoke of me as their friend.

After that meeting we traveled a day or two very quietly. Two Americans through bravado rode far ahead of the party in spite of my warning to them. They declared they were not afraid of Indians and would kill the first they saw. One day along the Milk River we heard them firing so many shots that we believed they were having an encounter with the Indians and we hastened to their rescue. When we reached the place, we found it was nothing more or less than an old buffalo bull at which they fired about twenty shots. He was still standing, pawing and snorting, but he was only wounded and we soon finished him.

Just then we saw a band of buffalo coming from the river where they had gone to drink and, as a few of us went after them, my little son David who was not over seven years old rode on after us. He chased the buffalo, even following them through some bushes. I was very anxious about him, but before long he rode back to us safe and happy. One of the party killed a cow and we took the meat along with us.

# 42

We were still along the Milk River when we met the mail carrier coming from Fort Union and going to Benton and he told us there was a big camp of Indians ahead. Three of our party went to see where that camp was, as we had so many horses there was great temptation for the Indians, and we preferred to ride far out to avoid them. We had not gone far when to our great surprise we saw about fifty Indians between our scouts and our party, they had just got up from the tall grass where they had been hiding. They were keener than we were for they had seen us before we were aware of it. It was a sight not easily forgotten to see those Indians loading their guns and whispering to one another. Our braves who had boasted that they would kill the first Indian they saw were as mute as mice, and I believe trembling with fear. The Indians were Assiniboines, a tribe with which I was not familiar. They were noted as horse thieves.

When we met them we stopped and made a corral and drove our horses in it. They asked us where we were going and I told them we were going to the Red River. As we were leaving the road then they asked us to follow the road and camp near them. Indians like to have the whites camp near them so that they may beg for something to eat.

By following the road, we had to pass a risky narrow place between a steep hill and a river near their camp and there would be no chance of escaping if they choose to attack us. On the other hand, if we continued our journey away from the trail we might not find water, as we were in a part of the country which is not well watered. I decided to pass through their camp and of the two evils I chose the least.

There were some in the party opposed to it, especially the Americans who formed the majority of our party. Our two braves were the most strongly opposed. They said it was an ambush and that we would all be killed. I told them ambush or not I was now going to follow the road. I had considered the situation and decided to go, so we went by the road. The two who had been so anxious to lead before there was any danger now preferred to keep in the rear. Anyhow the sight of those wild-looking Indians was enough to strike terror into the stoutest man. They were all painted and walked on each side of our wagons talking to one another and looking at the men, and all the time they were carrying loaded guns.

When we reached the camp in which there were about eighty lodges, we saw a strange sight: fully one hundred and fifty dogs were running across the flat to the top of the hill, each dog with a tripod fastened to him to prevent them from fighting each other. Those tripods are used by the Indians to hang kettles on to cook and some of the kettles were still tied to the tripods. The noise of those dogs sitting on the hill barking and howling was deafening. Some of the women were crying and lamenting, I suppose for some of their relatives who had been killed. It was a mournful scene. We passed through their camp and went to the next bend of the river about one quarter of a mile from them where we formed a corral and camped.

That night we passed a double guard over the horses, for we had to turn them loose to feed. My brother-in-law McLauren, who was one of the party, was captain of one squad, nearly all Scotchman, and it was their turn to guard that night. I told them not to allow an Indian among the horses on any consideration. I also ordered that if any of them wanted to trade horses with the Indians they should fetch their horse to our tent and interpreter Isabel would speak for them.

In spite of my warning and the double guard there was a horse stolen in broad daylight. Our men let a couple of Indians go in among the horses and they kept behind the guards looking at the animals and petting them. Beaupre, one of our party, had a quiet riding mare and one of the Assiniboines got on her back and rode around. Presently another Indian got on behind him and they continued to ride around gradually edging nearer until they came to the outside of the herd, then they soon disappeared in their own camp. The mare had no bridle on, but she was so gentle she could be guided by the hand any place they wished to drive her.

At night when Beaupre came to catch his mare, she was missing. He inquired of the men on guard if they had seen his mare and they replied that they saw two Indians riding her off, but they thought he had traded with them. They looked so unconcerned riding her through the herd that the guard did not interfere. That was the last trace of his mare. Beaupre was on his way home to a place in the neighborhood of St. Cloud, Minnesota.

The next morning as our party was leaving the camp, I was the last one to leave. I saw a group of five or six Indians talking to an Irishman of our party. I found that the Irishman in spite of my warning had traded horses with an Indian, because the Indian's horse had a feather on his head, the sign in those days of a prize winning horse. The Indians were playing with our man, chasing his horse away and trying to take their own back. They would soon do him out of both horses.

I shouted to him to take his saddle off that horse and catch his own before they chased him away.

He tried to hurry then, but he was so excited he could hardly unsaddle the horse. He was so nervous that the Indians were making sport of him, whipping the horse and scaring him. When they saw me coming near, they laughed and let go the horse. He saddled his own as soon as it was caught and I believe he learned a lesson he did not forget in the future.

We gladly left those lively Assiniboines behind, though we hired a guide from their camp, a Cree Indian. He brought his family with him and another Cree and his family came too. They had five or six dogs hitched on to travails [travois], made of two poles crossed over the saddle and dragging behind. Two or three feet behind the dogs, there were cross pieces of wood in the travails to carry their baggage and children. I lent a horse to the guide and David Contois lent one to the other.

On the second day we saw our guides, and the half-breeds with them, ride back from the front at full gallop. The guide said that there was a large band of Sioux Indians ahead.

We immediately formed a corral. Some of our party were so terror stricken they could not drive the horses into the corral. As I did not believe the guide, I sent two scouts out and they returned in a short time, saying it was only a false alarm. The guide, I suppose, wanted to test our nerve in case of an unexpected attack, to see how we would act. He would have a poor opinion of the party's courage, for as soon as the alarm was sounded they were all frightened. Some ran to me for a rifle, some for balls, others for caps or powder; they were thoroughly upset.

I told them they were not very brave or they would always be prepared for an attack and ready to defend themselves. I do not pretend to be very brave myself, but kept my weapon by my side ready for any emergency.

As soon as we saw it was only a false alarm, we continued on our journey. The third day the guide seemed to be traveling in the wrong direction. I asked one who could speak Cree to tell him he was going in the wrong direction to Red River.

Angus said the the Indian was looking for water.

"Looking for water?" I said, "it is an Indian camp that he is looking for to get us robbed."

That same day we broke the axle of a wagon, but a mulatto blacksmith I had named George Lawson repaired it.

# 43

## [WHEREIN HE FALLS AND IS INJURED IN A BUFFALO HUNT, AND CALLS THE BLUFF OF THE GUIDE, A CLEVER HORSE-STEALING CREE.]

As the cook began to get dinner ready that night, we could see in the distance a black spot that seemed surely a buffalo herd. The guide, mounted on a spirited horse, set out to drive the buffalo near us. After dinner we saddled our horses, ready to chase them, and when they came toward us we saw it was a big band of about eight hundred. About sixty riders rushed on them and started them in another direction. This was fortunate, for had they come closer they would have stampeded our horses. As we rode out of the camp I told Augustin Racette that I would like to kill a fat cow. Augustin soon managed to drive off four or five buffaloes from the herd and, as they were going down a hill, he shot one and motioned to me with his revolver to come.

He had gone down the hill at an incline; I went straight down and as there were badger holes aplenty, my horse put his foot into one and fell on me. I was stunned for a time, and when I looked about and reached for my rope-lariat, it was gone along with my horse after the buffaloes. Augustin was [gone] off too. I tried three times to rise, but always fell back. I had injured my back and neck. I looked around and called to a rider passing up the hill. It was my son Billy. I mounted his horse and killed the cow that Augustin had wounded. She was very fat, so I had my wish. When I got back to the camp I found that L'Hirondelle had caught my riding horse. While he was among the buffaloes, he saw him and picked up the dragging lariat with his ramrod. My saddle was smashed to pieces, so it was not surprising that my back was injured.

We took some of the meat of that cow and continued our journey. The next day the Cree stopped to eat some cherries and we passed on, stopping a short distance to camp. When he reached the camp he told the half-breeds to tell me we would have to put on a good guard that night, for he had seen enemies, five Sioux. They made signs to him to go to them, and he added that I had better let him keep guard that night. I told Angus to tell [him] that he was a liar, that he had not seen any Indians. I knew Indians well enough to know if they had seen him and were enemies, they would have killed him on the spot, instead of letting him go to give the alarm. I would not let him guard that night and sent word that if he came out of his tent he would be killed.

I said to the whole party, "If you see either of those Indians come out of their tents to night, shoot him on the spot, for they intend to steal our horses if they have a chance."

The Crees took the warning and were very careful to remain in their tents. Every morning Contois and I were in the habit of saddling the horses we lent the Crees, because we were afraid they would hurt their backs, but next morning the two men caught the horses and saddled them [and] they were very jolly about it.

I said to Angus, "Those Indians mean mischief to-day and they will try to steal our horses."

He did not agree with me.

All morning the guide and his friend lagged behind, and at last when I sent Angus Mackay back to look for them he found them eating the liver of an antelope they had killed and they refused to come on.

I was furious for I was driving four horses and was obliged to stop at every creek or wash-out to find the best place to cross. Now the guide was paid for this work, not to remain behind. I did not even know where to stop for water, but two men I had sent out in search of it found a place and signalled to us to go there. We camped there for noon. As the wagons came in [one] after another, I enquired of the drivers, if they had seen the guide.

"Yes," one would answer, "one mile back"; another said, "Two miles," and so on.

It was quite a long train of sixty wagons and twelve carts, and when the last one came in the drivers said they had seen the guide two miles back in the "bad lands" where it is very hilly.

That Indian was shrewd, coming along the wagons back and forward as he did, sometimes remaining behind for a short time.

I could see by what the men told me that they were simply blindfolding us. I sent Angus and Augustin back to look for them, though I felt he was by that time far from there laughing at our simplicity and enjoying a joke at our expense. They returned that night about eleven o'clock without getting a glimpse of the Crees, though they discovered that the squaws must have left our party in the morning, for they saw the men's tracks where they joined their wives. Next morning Angus and Augustin took fresh horses and started after our wayward guide and his companions.

The Americans in our party were running short of provisions and, as it was not far from St. Joe, they went on to that town, while we kept on our way. When Angus and his companion returned two days later, he gave me an account of his unsuccessful trip. They followed the guide and his friends to a big Assiniboine camp and, when they arrived there, the guide told them that the camp they were in then was what he had been looking for and not water.

"If you had allowed us to keep guard the night I asked you, we would be well provided with horses, but we did not have the chance. Now you came all that distance for this little mare?" He said laughing at them, "You must be very thoughtless or you would had brought a pack horse loaded with provisions, for you have spoiled us feeding us on bread and good bacon with coffee and sugar. Now we must live on buffalo meat straight. It is lucky for you that you are half-breeds or I would send you back on foot."

So our ex-guide had some sympathy for half-breeds it seemed. Our supply of flour was getting short, as we had been delayed so much on the way, and we were obliged to leave without paying our Indian friend a visit or trying to get even with them. The remainder of our journey was more quiet, but one day we traveled late to reach water. We had a French doctor for cook; his assistant, an American boy, was a thorough-bred blackguard. The doctor who spoke broken English complained that his assistant was very impudent and I advised him to use force to make the lad more respectful. That night we caught the little doctor shaking the lad desperately and threatening to cut off his head with the coffee-pot if the boy ever tried to provoke him again. Fifty or sixty men gathered around them watching the fight and their laughter shamed the little man. But he was not used to frontier life and he was actually afraid of the boy.

The first settlement we reached was Fort Ellice and from there to the Red River all went well with us. But a disappointment was waiting me on my arrival. That young lady who had been so particular a friend of mine was married to one of the leading young men in the country. The friend in whose care I had sent the letter to, received it two weeks before her marriage, but kept it back from her for fear of making trouble, because everybody knew how warm our friendship had been, and the older people had told her I would never likely come back to the Red River district again.

# 44

## [Wherein he starts a new life in Manitoba.]

My first duty on reaching the Red River was to place my three daughters in St. Boniface Convent and my three sons in the college.[1] I intended to keep the two others at home, including the baby, who on all that long trip had been fed on condensed milk. But I had brought a half-breed as nurse to look after him. I rented from John H. McTavish a house which was the property of the late John Rowan, my uncle, and I left that woman there in charge of the little ones while I started for St. Louis to get my eldest daughter. I had promised to go after her as soon as the family would be in Red River.

I left my horses and twelve thousand dollars in cash in a relative's care. I brought Angus McKay with me for a companion. We drove to Fort Abercrombie with four horses which we left at the fort, going by stage to St. Paul, and from there to St. Louis by train. Coming back we remained at St. Paul a few days and I bought there a double cutter, a single one, and a light buggy and shipped them to Georgetown. When we arrived there we met Mr. McDermott's men coming for some machinery and we traveled with them back to Red River.

I was told when I first came to Red River that the half-breeds were good travelers, but Mr. McDermott's men were not of that class. Whether it was ignorance or carelessness, I do not know, but they took no care of their horses. There were fat animals that had not done anything all summer. My horses had come from Montana that summer, and for this trip I did not even have hay or grain as the half-breeds had. It was a hard winter and the snow was deep. The first day [when] we camped, as soon as I unhitched I went to look for feed for my horses and was not satisfied till I had found the best to be had; then I made a track by tramping the snow and made a water hole through the ice the depth of my axe handle.

At the camp, I told the drivers where this water hole was if they wanted to water their horses, but the brave fellow said, "Never mind, the horses will eat snow while they eat their feed."

They simply threw the feed on the snow, tied the horses to their loads, and threw an old robe over each. By morning the robe would be down under the horse's feet, wet and frozen. I told them if their horses could take their loads home after that they were better than mine. However fat as their horses were, they did not take their loads home. The men were obliged to walk from the Pembina and drove their horses ahead of them without sleighs, while I reached home with all I set out to bring. In general, I believe half-breeds are good travelers, but careless with their stock, especially in the winter time. On my return to Mr. McKay['s] I placed my daughter in the convent with the others.

Turning my attention to my stock, I found only thirty-seven head of horses left out of two hundred. The man in whose charge I had left my horses had an Indian who was in his debt looking after them, but, as I had left him so much money, he might have hired more men. He had made so many declarations of friendship for me that, in proof of it, he might have given more thought to my interests. I came to the conclusion later that it must have been my money that prompted his affection.

Seven of the thirty-seven horses that were left to me were down with sickness and needed extra care. Among them was a brown stallion called Shangkhigh, who two weeks after my return brought me over six miles to St. Boniface Church in just nineteen minutes. I had trouble with these horses, but finally brought them all around. The men I sent out to look for the one hundred and sixty-three strayed found only forty -five, so when spring came I had only eighty-two head, and one colt which I called Black Hawk. This splendid little animal never fully recovered from the hardship of that winter after his mother died, and he was not more than thirteen and a half hands high when full grown. Still, he held the championship of Manitoba for eight years from one half to a mile and most old timers along the Red River will recollect him.

As soon as spring opened I went in search of a place to locate. I selected the Carmen District which was then called Riviére aux Islets de Bois. Three other families who had come from Montana with me also settled there. The men were Alex Pambrum, Thomas Lavatta and David Contois and Bill Cosgrove. There were Cree Indians about who stole a horse from David Contois and killed another belonging to Billy Cosgrove. These men feared more trouble, so they made up their minds to leave the place. I called on Governor McTavish of the Hudson's Bay Company and asked for protection. He told me it was out of his jurisdiction. I then asked for permission to protect myself and he told me to do as I thought proper. I went back and held my ground.

I took up land that I thought would suit myself and family and I located, [and] also for two boys whom I had adopted—a Bannock Indian and a mulatto. I adopted these boys a few years before.

When I was in Montana, on one of my trips to Benton, a big Negro came to me and said, "Mr. Grant, old Phil Barnes is dead and you are kind hearted. You better take his children for they are starving around here."

There was a boy and two girls. The boy was about four or five years old. I told the fellow to put the boy in my wagon and that I would take him anyway, but, when he took the boy, the two girls hung to him and cried so for their brother that I had the Negro put them all in the wagon. When I came to Manitoba, I left the oldest girl in Montana and brought the other two, so I had to provide for them as well as my own children. The girl died when she was young, but the boy still lives. In fact, he married his fourth wife not many years ago.

The Bannock Indian was an orphan too whose parents had been killed. I found him playing one day about the mill at the Jesuit's Mission of Pend d' Oreille. He told me how he had been ill-treated by a man named Craft. I asked him if he would come with me. He was willing and I took the poor lad home with me, and I brought him to Manitoba. I had also selected a piece of land for him as well as for my own boys, but at the time of the transfer they were still too young to take homesteads, so the people from Ontario got the places. When they were old enough to take land, they were obliged to go further where the land was not so good, but I secured scrip for them later.

In the winter and spring of eighteen hundred and sixty eight before my baby died, I made up my mind to get married. I was going to start a new home and I could not do it alone. I had to get a companion who would also be a mother for my children, and, as a Galician widower was saying the other day, it is not difficult to get a wife, but it is not so easy to get a mother for my children. I was like a grandmother to my motherless children. I loved them so much and I wanted a kind woman for their sake.

I was helped in my choice by my eldest girl, who every time I called to see her at the convent had something to say in praise of Clothilde Bruneau, one of her school mates. She said she was so patient and kind to her. After hearing about her so often, I inquired about her and found she was an orphan whose parents had died some years before. She was only eighteen, one year older than my oldest child. I wrote to her asking if she would let me see her and, as she imagined what it was for, she refused me. The number of children I had, with the three adopted, was enough to frighten any girl. I found that His Grace, the late Archbishop Tache', was her guardian.

I went and asked him to use his influence in my favor. He said he could hardly do that, but, if she was willing, he would not object, so I wrote to her again and, well to make a long story short, after some correspondence and visits she consented to marry me.

The day we got married I said to my children, "Here is my wife, she will be your mother after this and the first one that disobeys her or is impudent to her I will punish severely."

They knew I meant it for I used to be very stern in those days. However, we have always been a very happy family, and I had reason to be satisfied with my choice.[2]

My wife was the daughter of Francois Bruneau, a county judge in Manitoba at the time of his death. As he was one of the most prominent figures among the first French Canadians on the Red River, I will speak of him at some length. His father, who was a member of a French family of some note since the days of Francis I, emigrated to Canada in the latter part of the eighteenth century. He was married and then came on to Red River.

In eighteen hundred and ten, [. . .] Francois was born, and his father, dying soon after, he [Francois] was brought up and educated by Bishop Provencher. He studied for the priesthood. In the meantime, Edward Harrison, a Chief Factor of the Hudson's Bay Company, had died suddenly leaving a wife and three children. Mrs. Harrison did not understand business methods and became the victim of unscrupulous people, so that she was soon penniless although her husband had left property. Bishop Provencher took them also under his protection and gave them a home. The youngest daughter, Marguerite, was a pretty girl with fair hair and blue eyes and so different from the other girls of the country that, by the time she was twenty years old, young Francois Bruneau fell violently in love with her, and changed his mind about his calling. Instead of continuing his theological studies, he married her. Although they were both poor, they were willing to face the world together. He taught school and studied law, and in time became a magistrate and then a county judge.

He was so big-hearted that, a week or so before the High Court met, his house would be full of people asking advice. They got the advice and free board as well. He always tried to affect a settlement between litigants; his usual way being to appoint a day for one party to state his case, then he would hear the other side, then he brought the two together and in nine cases out of ten affected a settlement between the litigants. He explained the law to them and they would leave well satisfied and good friends. In cases which came up in court, if he was obliged to sentence a prisoner, he was just, but very tender hearted, so he was highly respected by all classes. He and his wife died of the Red River fever in 1865 and were buried on the same day.

As he was too hospitable to have saved anything out of his small salary, he left his five daughters with little means. At Judge Bruneau's funeral, Archbishop Taché began to address the congregation, but he was so deeply moved he could not continue his address. The two pioneers were buried on the twenty eight of June. In the following month, the archbishop in a strong sermon advised the fathers and mothers of families to send their children to school. He recalled to them how often he had told them this, but they had not heeded his good counsel. He added how Mr. Bruneau is no more and there is no one among the people of the country to replace him. There is one who will soon come, however, and I hope he will prove himself worthy to fill the important and responsible position left vacant by Mr. Bruneau's death.

The archbishop had reference to Louis Riel who was then being educated in Montréal. He did not at the time have any idea that his hopes centered on a very poor substitute. There was as much difference between Riel and Francois Bruneau as there is between day and night. I am nearly certain from what I have heard of the judge that if he had been living at the time of the transfer there would have been no rebellion. He would have tried to get the people's rights without rebelling.

Talking one day about Riel's rebellion to a Manitoba old timer who was personally acquainted with Mr. Bruneau, I asked him if he thought Mr. Bruneau would have joined Riel if he had been living.

"Oh, no," he said, "Mr. Bruneau was too loyal." That was all, but it meant a good deal.

After my marriage in May [May 7, 1868,] my bride and I lived with the McKays at Deer Lodge for a few weeks and then I set out for St. Paul again. I wanted to get supplies for a store which I intended to open at Sturgeon Creek. Before starting for St. Paul, I sent a Mexican to the plains to get buffalo meat for the family. I fitted him out completely with seven horses and carts, and two race horses for hunting. But instead of coming back, he kept on to Montana with my outfit, and left two of his children for me to look after. That fall I got two of my race horses back from a hunter who had traded with the Mexican. I wrote to my agent Pemberton in Montana to take the horses from that man, but he had only three mares left. Pemberton took these, and it was not long before I had quite a few head of horses out there.

I had left some gold dust with Mr. McCartney in St. Louis the previous year and, now that I wanted it, I did not know how to write in English for it. In the meantime at St. Paul, I got acquainted with Joe Roberts who introduced me to Jim Hill, his partner, I believe.

I asked Mr. Hill if he knew Mr. McCartney's firm in St. Louis.

He said he did and [. . .] I asked him if he would kindly write to him and ask him to send me the money he had of mine.

He gave me a searching look, but just said, "All right I will write."

Next day as I was walking on the street, some one gave me a tap on the shoulder.

I turned and found Mr. Hill. "You got the best of me yesterday when you came in to the office," he said; "I thought you wanted to borrow a few dollars and tried to make me believe you had money in St. Louis, but it is all right, your money is coming."

He had telegraphed to St. Louis, I suppose. I did not blame the man; I was always so commonly dressed. I got better acquainted with Hill, and he always treated me as a friend after that.

When I returned to Red River I found that the grasshoppers were there again. There had been a plague the year before and now there was great fear of famine, if the settlers did not get relief. They did get help from the Hudson's Bay Company and the Canadian government, and I heard too from the United States.

I went with twenty-one sleds for some of that relief wheat and pork, taking a sub-contract for it from Mr. Bannatyne. I took some hay with me, leaving some at points along the road concealed under the snow. I was very glad to find them all right coming back. When not far from Riviére Salé, I met my nephew, Richard Grant, who had come from Montréal the year before to join me at Red River. My wife, when she saw the snow going so fast, sent him with the hired man to bring me a wagon and four horses.

Although because of my recent arrival in the country I was unaware of any trouble threatening, I learned later that for some years the half-breeds and other settlers along the Red River had been dissatisfied with their position under the rule of the Hudson's Bay Company, and, now that the North West had been transferred to the Dominion of Canada by the Company, the half-breeds were more than ever troubled because their rights had not been assured in the transfer, and the Canadian surveyors coming through the country then were treating them contemptuously, making light too of their claims to the land they held. So the French half-breeds rallied around Louis Riel to assert their rights. The English half-breeds sympathized with them, but the new comers from Ontario were in strong opposition to them.[3]

1. One of the Grant children, Mary, remained in Montana, being adopted by Robert Dempsey and his wife. Dempsey's wife was related to Chief Tendoy, as was Johnny Grant's Quarra. "Mary, who was a daughter of Johnny Grant, was adopted by Robt. & Mrs. Dempsey. She married a Dr. Cline of Twin Bridges. I doubt whether the Dr. title meant anything." (Henry G. Ruppel to Paul Gordon, 8/19/1975, Grant-Khors Ranch National Historic Site, National Park Service)
2. "Clothild Bruneau the wife of John F. Grant (my mother) was born June 8th, 1850, at St. Boniface, Manitoba, and died in the General Hospital at Edmonton Oct. 17th, 1919. My mother is buried in the same grave as is her husband, my father, John F. Grant." (Excerpt from letter of Alice Grant to Frederick John Shaw, in Shaw letter to T.C. Elliott, 4/14/1935, National Park Service copy
3. This concludes Grant's reminiscences of his years in Idaho and Montana (1847-67), which he dictated to his wife Clothild in 1906-07. Grant's memoir, of course, does not end here, but also includes a description of his subsequent four decades in Canada (1867-1907), which he continued in dictation to Clothild. This latter part of Grant's manuscript, yet to be published, is somewhat longer than the part focusing on his years in Montana and Idaho. What follows here is a brief synopsis of Grant's life in Canada after leaving the northern Rockies. Included are some direct excerpts from the handwritten memoir:

Grant settled in the Carman, Manitoba, area where he ranched and kept a store. By 1869, considerable unrest had arisen among the local population over the transfer of the Red River region to the Dominion of Canada. Though Grant had strong ties to the French Canadians (Metis), he allied himself with the government rather than Louis Riel, the leader of the rebellious Metis. The people of St. Charles and St. James parishes selected Grant to be their delegate to the "provisional" government, but Riel refused to let him serve.

It was during this first Riel Rebellion that Grant felt that the Canadian government, and particularly Donald A. Smith (later Lord Strathcona), had become indebted to him. However, the exact nature of this indebtedness remains unclear because the pertinent 10 pages of Grant's handwritten 1906-07 manuscript apparently were later lent to the Canadian government and never returned. Perhaps it is irretrievably lost.

Years of comparative peace followed the first Riel uprising, while Grant continued to farm and trade. His narrative in this period ranges from focusing on the political to the personal. For example, an attack of rheumatism made his right arm nearly useless and the treatment he described is memorable: "I killed a skunk. I remember my father use to use the oil and [it] did him good. I thought that was not powerful enough for me, I would try the skin. I got one of the men to skin it, then wrapped my arm with the flesh side to the skin. It did not smell nice at all, but I slept; next morning my arm was well and the part of the hide next to my skin was as black as coal. The smell is awful, but the relief one feels of getting rid of that annoying pain of rheumatism, it is worth trying."

He also described the many dances and social events he enjoyed attending. But when his favorite son, David, fell ill after a dance in early January 1877 and died some days later, a deeply sorrowful Grant declared "no more dance for me." He danced just once again, several years later, only to avoid offending a woman who asked him to do so during a "ladies choice."

Agriculture, trade, sawmill, gristmill, and hotel ventures all had ups and downs, but it was speculation in scrip that caused his greatest financial misfortune. As the Metis pressed their claims for farms, they were issued scrip for land that they would be able to redeem at some future date. A boom period ensued and land prices rose. In the meantime, many poor claimants, including some on the brink of starvation, conducted a brisk trade in scrip, largely to just survive. Sometimes as an investment and sometimes out of compassion, Grant bought scrip. Some of the scrip was valueless to begin with, but, when land values plummeted, even valid scrip became worth less than what he had paid for it. Despite his troubles, however, Grant retained his capacity to enjoy life, and his story is filled with anecdotes detailing social events and practical jokes.

In the spring of 1886, he traveled to Montana's Deer Lodge Valley for his only return visit to the haunts of his younger years (see following appendixes B and C).

In 1889, after reading a government pamphlet proclaiming Vancouver Island, British Columbia, to be a paradise on earth, he borrowed money to travel there, but found it to be a wild goose chase. Returning to Manitoba with some horses he hoped to sell, he passed through Edmonton, Alberta, and thought it a fine country to make a home. After selling everything of value in Manitoba, he left for Alberta on September 11, 1892. Much of his family went with him, but two sons and a married daughter stayed behind. He reached Edmonton on November 11, and stayed the winter with friends.

(In late 1906 or early 1907, when dictating to Clothild at this point in the narrative, Grant's health was failing rapidly and he knew there was little time left to finish the story. Consequently, his description of the last 14 years of his life in Alberta is shockingly brief, when compared to the lengthy and detailed accounting of his life up to that time:)

"In the spring [1893] we took homesteads at Bittern Lake, Alberta. We lived there eight years, then went to Grande Prairie. I took sick and had to return to Edmonton. [missing word] went on to Athabaska landing, the third place went to Deep Creek, now called Waugh, Alta. Kept a stopping place. I never got my health back. I said spring is coming, I am getting worse; beginning of April [1907], I am done, I have not long to live. I was then in Edmonton, not to get doctored, but to prepare to meet my Judge. I knew in a few weeks it would come, the end of my life."

In the final sentence, Clothild closes the story: "He died the first of May, 1907, near the old Hudson Bay [post] where he was born in 1831."

# Appendix A

Fort Garry R.R. S
July 17th 1868

James Stuart Esq
    Dear Sir.
Will you be so kind as to go to the Post Office at your place, get all letters and papers there are for me and forward the same to me
The address is
    F. H. Burr
    Fort Garry
    Red River
    Care of Hudson's Bay Co., B [?] A

My family are well, but very homesick. I have done tolerably well since I have been here and may remain for some time.

Dave Courtois & Alex Pambrun are disgusted and curse J. Grant. they will leave here as soon as possible. Alex is "broke" has not a cent. Tom Ackinson, Baptiste Quesnelle & Lou Pambrun all left here on their way back to the land of "sun flowers" - ie Montana. McLa[rrin?] has gone to Minnesota, but intends to return & go across the [?] on a trading expedition for fur.

Have you been able to realize anything for the property I left in your hands. I may come back one of these days, but it is doubtful.

John Grant has run himself pretty near in the ground. His great friend Jas. McKay has soured on him. Isabella is in the convent & Aggie also, as well as all his children. John has married a Red River "half breed" girl about 16 yrs. old and I suppose is enjoying all the felicity and happiness of the "Honeymoon" . . .

Grasshoppers have eaten all the crops. Pemmican is "rare" and times are hard generally. I have done well and if I have no bad luck will make money. But at the same time would not advise any of my friends to come here. One can do nothing to make anything except by trading in furs, and it is "one devil of a country." Musquitoes, flies, bedbugs, lice and all kinds of vermin abounds.

I have not received a line from any one from home or Deer Lodge since I came here, which I think is rather strange, as there should be a letter at your place from my Folks. I have been off and have had very few opportunities of writing, so that my friends may think I had forgotten them.

How is Quartz.

If you can spare a few moments to write me a line or two I would like to hear from you.

My wife sends her love to "Aubonny" the children and all the folks. Dixie & Jennie are growing fast, going to school & doing well generally.

Give my best respects to all my friends. I would write to some of them but am hurried as you may see by this scrawl. Please write to me and write soon, when I have leisure I will write a long letter and try to give you an idea of this country and its surroundings.

John F. Grant is now at St. Louis or St. Paul but is expected to return soon. Bill Cosgrove went him & I think will not return.

How did the Election go? My best respects to Granville, Reese, Judge Dance and [Nordeau?]

Yours truly
F. H. Burr

# Appendix B

## MY FIRST TRIP TO MONTANA [1886[1]]

### [BY JOHNNY GRANT]

In my trouble [bankruptcy in Manitoba], I thought of Montana friends. I had notes of some of them. I knew they were outdated, but I thought when they hear[d] of my misfortunes they very likely [would] pay me something on those notes and there was one especially to whom I had given back his note for three thousand dollars. I had heard that he was in pretty good circumstances. He had said with [?] when I had given him his note, ["]Johnnie, I will pay you sometime,["] and as I had helped him in many different ways he would surely help me, but it takes money to get there. I had a few scrips left and a small bag of gold dust, that I had brought with me from Montana in 1867.

In 1882 Mr. J.J. Hill had said if I ever wanted a pass on his [rail]road to write to him. It was very kind of him, but I hated to impose on his kindness, but I thought if I could get to Montana without spending my scrips and the few dollars in gold dust, I could buy [a] few head of horses so at last I wrote and told him what I intended to do. Well, he was generous, sent me two passes, one for a companion if I wanted one. I would have liked to have taken my wife, but the children were small and the place to look after, we could not both leave at the same time. As my nephew [Richard] was well educated I thought he would be some help to me. I took him along. The journey was not extra pleasant, as I had been begging my way. I felt discontented. The only incident that happen[ed] worth mentioning was the acquaintance of two middle age widows. They were selling some books as agents, [both were] very nice persons. We had quite a few friendly chats together, it enlivened the journey, made the time much more agreeable.

When I arrived at Deer Lodge, Montana, [on or about April 14, 1886] there was quite a change, but it seemed familiar to me. The first place I went was at Conrad Kohrs, who I had sold out to. He was still living in my old house. The only changes he had got the shingles renewed and had trees planted in the front of the house. I rang the door bell. He came and answered it himself. I recognized him right away, but he did not [recognize me].

I said good morning, sir.

Good morning, he answered, and asked me what I wanted. When I saw he did not recognize me, I did not tell him. I answered do you want to hire a man?

He said, no, I have all the men I need. I have no work for more.

Oh! I said, I am not particular if you have work or not, as long as you have good beef to chew.

He did not know what to say.

It was raining a little. I said to him, can't you ask a fellow out of the rain.

I beg your pardon, come in.

He took us in the sitting room, gave us chairs. I pretended to be very green. I sat on the cushion chairs, making the seat spring, and looking all round. I said, you are pretty well fixed.

Yes, he answered slowly, I am all right. I could see he was puzzled. I looked at him saying[,] and you do not know me.

No, he answered.

Yes, I said, you do know me very well.

No, he insisted, I do not think I ever saw you.

I said, think of long ago. You had a friend.

Surely he exclaimed you are not Johnny?

Yes. I said, that is who I am.

He caught hold of my hand with his two hands, and shook it pretty hard. Well John, I am glad to see you. You are well come.

Then he excused himself, and went out of the Parlor to come back with his wife and daughter. His wife looked young enough to be his daughter, and his daughter was a very nice girl, both very pleasant. Con treated us to some wine and asked us to remain for dinner.

During the conversation that followed he said, "Well, John, it is twenty years since I bought you out.["]

And you done well since, I said.

Yes, he answered, then told me that he had twenty eight thousand head of cattle, [six] hundred head of riding horses and two hundred Brood Mares. He said I will show you my stallions after dinner. We had many things to talk about, old times and old timers.

Con was rich, in fact he was a Millionaire. He had climbed the ladder and I had went down. I did not regret it. I expected it. I preferred poverty rather than to run the risk of seeing any of my sons meet with a tragic death which was the lot of some poor boys out there [i.e., in the rough Montana mining camps]. He had more stock than anyone. He was called the Cattle King of Montana.[2]

After dinner he took me to the stable to see his stallions. He had beauties, all Thorough bred. He had fine imported bulls also. I said to him, Con, tell me, do you raise as large cattle as I raised in the valley? That yearling bull, I added, that was among the milk cows when I sold out to you could eat his feed on that bull's back, pointing to one of his.

Yes, he said, he was a fine one.

Tell me truly, I repeated, do you raise as fine cattle as we did then?

["]No, John,["] he replied, ["]we have not got the feed,["] and it took quite a bit to feed all his stock.

I learned from him that there was some of the old timers still living there. After a while I went to Town. I recognized all those that were there, but none of them seem[ed] to know me, but after I had made myself known to some of them those called out to others on the streets, come here, here is John Grant the man that fed us all. In no time there was a crowd gathered around me. There was hand shaking for a while, a word to this one, then to another. I did not know which way to turn. There was people of all classes, Judges and Lawyers, Bankers and Merchants, as well as miners and working men. They all talked to me. No ceremony.

After I had been talking with the crowd, in fact we still [were] talking, [when] Mr. Sanders, a very nice and pleasant man, took me by the arm, saying, excuse me gentlemen, I want Johnnie to myself for few minutes.

We went to his office. There was three or four others there. He said to them, will you please go out for a while, and then asked me all about my life from the time I came to the Frontier till then. Next day [April 16, 1886] there was one column and a half in the Montana paper.[2]

After I left his office I met my old friend Grove. He used to be a miner in my time. Every winter or whenever he was not mining he would work for me. We all liked him. He was so kind to the children, would do anything to amuse them. After shaking hands with me, he invited me to a saloon to treat me.

He leaned his elbow on the counter and looked at me, saying, ["]well Mr. Grant, I am so glad to see you, I do not know what to say,["] and repeated those words so often, he was really pleased to see me.

I was also, but I could not talk for there were so many to answer. After a while Grove found something to say, he was married, and invited us to his house. We went.

Before we left next day I went to see some more friends that lived about the town. A Mexican came back with me at dinner time. I asked him to come and have dinner with us, [and] on our way to the Hotel we met one of the Judges. After talking for [a] few minutes, he said to me, come on Johnnie to dinner with me. I did not like to refuse him, but I hated to leave that man on the street.

I said, your honor will excuse me for this time. I am taking this man to dinner.

Oh, let the darn Greeser come along, so we all went with him to the hotel.

As I was saying before there were not very many of the old timers that I knew there but now that I had been a day with them they all seem to have known me for years. They were all so friendly, when Mr. Sanders had asked me the first day about my affairs I had told him that I had speculated in land and had lost everything. Mr. Sanders at the head of others wanted to take up a collection for me. If I had let them I am nearly certain that they would not have taken very long to make a purse of a couple thousand, but as I had not seen those people from whom I had those notes I thought if I could get even a part of the amount I would be more contented.

I thanked them for their kind offer, but when I saw my debtors they were too poor to pay anything, and the one that I had given back his note for $3,000.00, he seemed to be pretty well off. He had quite a few head of horses, some cattle. He had a farm, thrasher and different kinds of machinery.

I said to him, you done pretty since I left.

Not bad, he answered.

Well, I added, it has been different with me. I told him about my land speculation, and all my losses, that I was about ruined. I said I have [brought a] few scrips and those notes that had been given for debts while I was in Manitoba. I was in hope I could raise some money on them and buy [a] few head of horses, but I could not get a cent for those people are just as poor as they were then. If I had been home they['d] never had got in my debt so much.

He never said anything and I thought I had said enough.

I intended to tell him he ought to let me have few head of horses. Before I left he loaned me a horse to go away from his place, as it was too far to walk to the station.

He said, you can leave him with such a one, I will get him later on.

When he said that, I saw it was no use to expect any help from him. All my bad luck did not make any difference to him. I left there with a sore heart. If I had been in his place he would not have had the painful trouble to tell me so much before I would have offered him assistance. I will not mention here all I have done for that man, but the fact only that I had given him back his note for $3,000.00 when I thought he could not pay goes to prove the friendship I had for him. So I came back without getting a cent of what was due me.

It was different with Con. I got help from him. He was very generous. [He] Took us to several places on the train, paid my way and expenses all through and loan[ed] me horses whenever I wanted to visit around.

Early one morning, about five o'clock, I rode to the Little Blackfoot, now Livingston [actually, Garrison] where I had built my first house with rough cottonwood logs. I was surprised when I got there, not so much of the change wrought by civilisation but the natural beauty of the place which I had not noticed while I was living there. All that was left of my house was about a couple of feet of the old fireplace. As it was early in the morning, everything was quiet. I stood a while looking at it and let my memory go back to that time.

Since I had come [back] to Deer Lodge I had been in several places, different company, [and] different ground. The first meal that I had taken there was in the [Kohrs] house I once owned but [in] no place I had felt as I did [now] at the sight of [my] old chimney. My heart came up to my throat. I could have set there and wept like a child at the recollection of those days. Some of my first children were born there and they and their mother were dead and gone. But I was a man, not a child. I repressed my emotions and kept the survey of the place. What a change the advent of the railroads make in a place, and right there [tracks] are so numerous.

There was many places to visit that we had never seen. We went to Butte and to Anaconda. We saw the smelters. They were very nice, but awful things to look at. I will pass over the description of them, for I could not describe them as they should.

### Visit to my friends the Snake Indians

After we had been in the Deer Lodge for about ten days, I mentioned my intention of going to the Snake Reserve [in Lemhi County, Idaho]. Con offered us a team when I was leaving. John Bellingburg [Bielenberg] Con's brother (they were in partnership I believe) said[,] Mr. Grant, you may keep those horses if you are in need. You may sell them if you want to.

It was very kind. I brought them back.

On our way to the Reserve, we went astray often, for the old roads that I knew so well were all fenced and what was worst with wire so it was impossible to go through. Some places we had to travel a couple of miles for nothing.

The first night we reached Silver Bow where Grove kept a sheep range. We remained overnight with him. He could not do enough for us.

Next we came to a Chinaman, but different from many others. He had been raised by an American. His father had been killed in 1847. He was very hospitable. He had [two] white men working for him. He was well fixed. He was already in bed when we got there. The men put our horses in and as it was late we did not say anything about supper.

The Chinaman was not pleased next morning. He said you are not going without breakfast, and he gave us a first class meal.

When I asked him how much for our horses and ourselves. Ah! Nothing, nothing, when you see a Chinaman, he added, in need, give him a meal.

After thanking him and [I] said I will return the kindness to a Chinaman but I never had the chance. That was not all. He knew we would have to pass the night out. He gave us a bale of good timothy hay. That night we travelled as far as we could till we got on the summit of the Rocky Mountains. The sun being down we could not see our way very well so camped right on the Summit. In the morning we saw we had gone the wrong road for there was some people camped on another direction but we had done right to [have] stopped when we did for we were on the edge of a 200 foot cliff.

That day about noon we came to Mexican Joe's place. (He had come to Manitoba with me in 1867, had worked for me for a few years and had married there and gone back.) We remained with him for dinner. In the afternoon he came with us to show us the Big Hole, where Joseph the Nez Perse years ago had trapped the American soldiers [Battle of the Big Hole, August 9-10, 1877], and nearly a whole American Company got [downed?].

We remained with Joe till next morning. Before we started we got all the information we wanted about the Reserve.

We got to the Agency that same night, going into the Indian store to find out what chance there was to get lodging. I met a Snake Indian. I recognized him. I said in his language, How do you do! naming him.

He was passing me when I spoke. He wheeled around astonished. After a second's look he knew he did not know me as one of his acquaintance[s].

He said who are you?

I said you must find out.

I know you well, he answered, you must be Johnny for he is the only white man that used to speak like us.

Yes, I said. I am Johnny.

He came and shook hands with me saying he was so glad to see me. [He] Invited me to his place to see his wife and children.

I told him I was in a great hurry. I could not go. It was getting late. I had to get a place to camp. So shaking hands again we parted. I got the accomodation I wanted from the agent.

The next day we resumed our journey. We had gone just a few rods when we met another Indian. I put my hand out saying in Snake, How are you?

He shook hands with me, still holding my hand he said in a puzzled way, who are you?

I said, how is that. I know you, naming him, and you don't know me.

Well, he said, as the other one had said, you must be Johnny.

I said that is who I am.

My! He said sadly, you are changed.

I must be when you did not recognize me.

Yes, you are very much changed. I am very glad to have met you.["]Come here,["] he addressed his little six year old boy, who was riding a two year old pinto colt, ["]come and shake hand[s] with this man. He is an old friend.["] the boy who's head was on the same level with the colt's head came up with much importance to shake hand[s]. "How do you do sir."

I spoke [a] few words to him. He answered alright, not bashful at all. I talked a little longer to his father. He wanted me to go and see him. I told [him] I was sorry, but I could not go. I was in such a hurry to go back home. Well, goodby, he said. I am glad I have seen you anyway, and we parted at last.

It was not long before we got to Tyndaille's [Tendoy] lodge. I said in English, how do you do!

He answered in English also. Come in, he added.

I went in, sat along side of him, while talking still in English. I notice[d], although he was not changed very much, he had grown quite older. He had two wives. I knew the oldest for he had her before I left. She did not look much older, but the loss of one eye made quite a difference in her for she had pretty eyes. She was sitting opposite to us reclining sideways on some packs. She did not seem to notice us very much. In the meantime I was talking with her husband on different subject[s]. I could see he did not have the least idea who I was. After a little while one of his boys, about 13 or 12 years old came in, looked at me, then sat down alongside of his mother, the oldest wife.

He whispered to her[,] that man can talk like us.

As he said that his mother sat upright and looked at me and with unshed tears in her eyes she exclaimed[,] oh, that is Johnny.

The last word was hardly out of her mouth. Tyndaille turn[ed] towards me in surprise. ["]Well, brother in law, I would never had recognized you but you are changed. Your hair are nearly all white.["]

Yes, the past years were hard on me.

By that time I was shaking hands with him and his wives. He said that young woman was his wife and all his children. It was not long before dinner was ready. They could not do enough to show how pleased they were to see me. After I was recognized, the English language was put aside and the Snake language came back to me as natural as if I had been speaking it all along. We had many things to talk about. We remained there two days. The old people that used to know me came in to see me, talked about the past, present and future. Everything was changed they were saying.

How forcibly those conversations I had with my Indian friends recalled my young days, the days when I had no anxiety for the morrow. Why should I? I was like an Indian as I said before. We just lived for the day, for food, and clothing. All we had to do was to go and kill an antelope or a mountain sheep or any other kind of game, for they were plentiful. The Indians kill game when they needed it only. Let them have a chance to [increase] and if the locality of my home did not suit, was getting too old, all I had to do was to pitch my lodge in a new fresh place. All the country was ours. I was not greedy for land. Real estate did not annoy me those days as it had in Manitoba since I had the misfortune to speculate in that uncertain business.

But what I regretted the most of those by gone years was the feeling of absolute trust I had in my fellow beings[,] for an Indian is not deceitful. If he is a friend he will be true. But certainly if he is an enemy look out. You must be on your guard. But since I had been dealing with the whites, that trust was so often abused, for I was repeatedly deceived by them under the mantle of friendship, but it was very hard to destroy that feeling in me. I am convinced that it will never be entirely destroyed for it is too strongly impressed into my heart, for as I said before everytime I was imposed upon I promised never to trust anyone, and I am still trusting and often deceived and I fear I will trust in others and be deceived till death and I believe it is that [conviction] that made later on such a changed man of me, for I want to get away from civilisation as far as I can, for outside of my family and few friends, I would be contented to live in the wilderness.

I must not get away from my subject. Those recollections of the past were more painful than useful. The Indians themselves felt sorry of the change. They said they felt as if they were in bondage, could not go hunting and fishing where they liked. ["]We are driven, you may say, out of the world by the whites. We have hardly any fish.["]

["]Why did you not ask for a place where there was fish for your Reserve.["]

Tyndaille answered[,] there used to be plenty here then, but there is none come up now. I do not know why.

I said, perhaps you have [ruined?] them.

Oh! no, he answered, we could not.

I imagined that the river must have been dammed somewhere above, but I did not speak my thoughts. I could not help them. What was the use to make them feel bad.

I asked him, why do you not speak to the agent about it.

What would be the use?

Why, he might help you, I suggested. Tell him about the fish.

After some reflection he said I wish you were agent for us.

I said I wish I could, but it is impossible. I could not leave Manitoba just now. So I told him about the fall in the price of land and the loss I sustained.

When I was through he said with real grief, I am sorry. No wonder you got old, he added.

I wish I could help you, and I continued[,] they might not give me the Agency and another thing the present generation might not be like the old timers.

Oh! that is certain the young people are not as we used to be, and for my part I am nearing the end of my journey, he added with a sigh. The young folks will get used to the ways of the whites by and by. It will be better for them to learn to work like them. Game is getting scarce.

I said, yes.

He answered they have to work like the whites if they want to live. If they do they will be all right. Just then, as if something struck him, he turned towards his wife. He said, give me that rifle. After taking it in his hand, he handed it to me saying, brother in law, what do you think of this gun.

I examined it. It was a breech loading rifle. All the mountings were of silver. An inscription written on it, the different occasion[s] that he had helped the American Government. It had been given to him as a reward for several services that he (Tyndaille) had done for the Government. It was a neat piece of work and valuable. It had been made purposely for him. He considered [it] as a great gift, so it was. I told him it was worth keeping. He meant to keep and leave it to his children.

The third day, I said I am sorry, but I must leave you, and I was really feeling grieved to leave forever the friends of my young days. They all gathered around Tyndaille's lodge to bid me goodby, and between 200 to 300 riders escorted us as far as the agency.

They insisted that I should come back and see them.

I told them frankly I could not come back. It was farewell forever.

They came one after the other to shake hands and say goodby in so sad a fashion it took us quite a while to shake hands with every one of them. I did not want to slight any of them. At last we parted [Tendoy and Johnny were close in age, and died the same year, 1907].

We came back to Deer Lodge in a shorter time than we went for we knew the road.

From there we went to Missoula to see my sister Julia, Mrs. Higgins and family. She recognized me right [away] although it was nearly twenty years since I had seen her.

She said I looked so much like our father.

They were all surprised to see me. Captain Higgins was still living then. They had a large family of big boys or rather big men. They made us both very welcome. We remained there ten days. I met Frank Worden, an old friend. He was very kind to me. I saw my sister, Mrs. McLaren's son. I had not seen him since he was a baby. He was quite a young man now. He was visiting his aunt. His father and mother were dead.

While there, we went to the Coutenay [Kootenai] Reserve where Pablo and Charles Allard had their ranch of Buffalo. Charley recognized me right away, for it was only eight years since I had seen him in Manitoba. We could not be better received. Charley looked as young as I saw him last. Fearless rider as ever, he took me to see the herd of buffaloes. They had then 16 pure bred cows and some mixed with Galways. Some were quite tame. It was so strange to see them tame, they used to be so wild. They had other cattle and were paying $5.00 a head to get a cow broke to milk.

We remained there three days. If I had listened to Charley I would have stayed a week and more, but we were in a hurry. I visited some other old friends I knew around there. I went back to my sister's and remained [a] few days more. When the day came to leave my sister forever I felt sorry. I think this second parting from her was more painful to us than the first. I suppose it was because we knew it was likely to be a last farewell, for I knew I could not go again, nor did I. Her eldest son John got married not long after I left.

## My Return Trip

I bought a few head of horses and sent my nephew back on the train. I hired two men. When we got to the crossing of the line, we could not come any further, for the Custom office was sixty miles away on one side and the prairie was all [? burnt?] to go there. Consequently no feed for our horses, we left them in charge of some people that were living there. It was late in the fall when we got home . . .

1. In the spring of 1886, following his financial ruin due to land speculation failures in Manitoba, Johnny Grant returned to Montana. For a month or more, he visited with white and Indian friends and relatives, while attempting to collect old debts. He recorded his reminiscences of the trip in this short manuscript, titled "My First Trip to Montana." This was the only time he returned to Montana and the Deer Lodge Valley after relocating to Manitoba in 1867—an interlude of nearly nineteen years.
2. Grant's visit preceded the famous and disastrous winter of 1886-87, which devastated Kohrs' livestock herds. Had Grant arrived the following spring, he then might have felt himself the luckier one, since the Cattle King of Montana's spring branding dropped precipitously from 3,000 to 900 after that brutal winter.
3. The article Grant refers to, titled "Camping on the Old Trail," appeared in *The New North-West*, April 16, 1886. See Appendix C for the entire text of the newspaper account.

# Appendix C

**JOHNNY GRANT REVISITS MONTANA.**

**NEWSPAPER ARTICLE IN *THE NEW NORTH-WEST,***

**DEER LODGE, MONTANA, FRIDAY, APRIL 16, 1886.**

**CAMPING ON THE OLD TRAIL.**

———

**THE PIONEER OF DEER LODGE VALLEY**

**REVISITS OLD SCENES.**

———

**RETURN OF JOHN F. GRANT.**

———

In the fall of 1859 John F. Grant, with a little band of cattle, came up here from Fort Hall, at which his father, well known as Captain Grant in Pioneer History, was agent of the Hudson Bay Company. Young Grant had come from Lower Canada with his father in 1847, and in 1859 concluded to strike out for himself. He located at the mouth of Blackfoot, near where Cline's dwelling now is. There he cut down his first tree and built a cabin. The next winter he went to Fort Bridger and induced a number of people there, including Leon and M. Quesnelle, Louis Demers, —— Duchesne, D. Courtois, R. Boisvert and L. R. Mailette to come north, which they did that autumn, he returning early in the spring to Blackfoot and they locating here at the mouth of Cottonwood next spring. His nearest neighbors in 1860 were at Fort Owens, distant 130 miles, and Fort Benton, distant 180 miles. He had several hundred head of cattle and horses ranging in the valley, and seven nations of Indians passed his cabin going to and from Buffalo, but he said, "I never locked a door then or since, never was hurt or threatened, and never lost a dollar or a hoof." In 1863 he moved to where the residence of Conrad Kohrs, Esq., stands, and built a cabin just under the bluff, and remained here until 1867, when, selling his property, he pocketed a nice fortune and removed to Manitoba, taking with him 200 head of horses, locating at St. Charles, seven miles from Winnipeg, and in 1868 removed to the Boyne river, 58 miles from Winnipeg, where he has since resided.

Quite unexpectedly Mr. Grant, or "Johnnie Grant," as he is known to all old-timers, reappeared here Wednesday morning and began inquiring for old friends, few of whom at first recognized him, as he has grown quite gray, but all of whom were glad to meet the hale, hearty and genial old pioneer, who is enthusiastic in his expressions of admiration for the town that has grown up near his old home.

Our reporter, of course, met him, and was surprised to learn the veteran frontiersman is in search of "green fields and pastures new" toward the setting sun. He became a large land-owner in Manitoba, owning at one time 35,000 acres of land, of which he retains 8,000 acres, but values have depreciated, owing to the frontier troubles, and times are very hard. The climate where he resides is colder than here, but land is productive, wheat yielding an average of 20 bushels and the ruling price ranged this year from 60 to 75 cents. Cattle have to be fed six months in the year, but hay land will yield from two to five tons per acre, and is plentiful. Cattle are cheaper than here, but his herd has never exceeded 257 head. He has, however, grown tired of the country, and is going to look up the country along the Cascade range in Northern Washington Territory, with a view to finding a location for himself and other colonists who would accompany him.

Mr. Grant tells many interesting incidents of early times, and is evidently enjoying his visit to the old home. In reply to the rather abrupt inquiry, "Why did you leave Montana?" he said: "I'll tell you. I had been raised in an Indian country since I was 15 years old. I got along well. My door was open to every one and my table free to all who came. I harmed no man, nor did any harm me. My stock ranged the valleys and hills unmolested, and my money, as much at times as $10,000 or $20,000, lay in my cabin unmolested. I needed no protection. I cost nobody a dollar. After a time the Territory was established, then counties, and then officers were elected. Then came Assessors and the Collectors annoying me with their lists and tax collections and laws for this, that and the other, and I concluded to leave for Manitoba." He did not say so, but we thought we could see in his countenance an expression of the thought that occurred to us— that if he had remained here he would to-day have been one of the millionaires of Montana.

Mr. Grant has a wife and eleven children living, and is quite wealthy, his lands alone having a value of $8 per acre. But he has become imbued with a desire to find a climate better adapted to him. He is now only 54 years of age, and if toward the Pacific he finds a locality suitable, he has yet the prospect of many years to enjoy the new home on the sunset slope of the continent.

Mr. Grant is accompanied by his nephew, Richard. They expect to visit Butte to-day and proceed westward to-morrow.

# SELECTED BIBLIOGRAPHY

## Archival and Unpublished Sources

(Catholic) Diocese of Helena [Montana]. Records.

Grant, Richard. File, Montana Historical Society, Helena.

"Grant, Richard." Unpublished biography by William Wheeler, Montana Historical Society, Helena.

Hudson's Bay Company Archives. Winnipeg, Manitoba.

Largent, John. Unpublished biography, Montana Historical Society, Helena. [This account by John Largent (1839-1919) donated to MHS, 12/21/1904]

Lindeman, Glen, and Keith Petersen. "The Kittson Legacy: Family, Culture, and the Web of Northwest History," Department of History, Washington State University, Pullman, 1988 [15 pages].

Maillet, Louis R., to William F. Wheeler. Manuscript 65, Montana Historical Society, Helena.

Prichet, John. Unpublished diary, Bancroft Library, University of California, Berkeley.

Ruppell, Henry G. Correspondence, National Park Service files, Grant-Kohrs Ranch National Historic Site, Deer Lodge, Montana.

Shaw, Frederick John. Correspondence, National Park Service files, Grant-Kohrs Ranch National Historic Site, Deer Lodge, Montana.

Stuart, Granville. Collection, Brigham Young University, Provo, Utah.

Woodruff, Sandra K. Correspondence, National Park Service files, Grant-Kohrs Ranch National Historic Site, Deer Lodge, Montana.

## Printed Government Documents

Harney, Brevet Brigadier General William S. 9/5/1855 report, in *House Executive Document 1, Part II, 34th Congress, 1st Session, 1855* [841], pp. 49-51.

Mullan, Captain John. *Report on the Construction of a Military Road from Fort Walla-Walla to Fort Benton.* Washington, DC: Government Printing Office, 1863.

Stevens, Isaac I., et al. *[Pacific Railroad] Reports of Explorations and Surveys, 1853-4, Vol. 1, House Executive Document 91, 33rd Cong., 2nd Sess., 1855* [791].

_____. *[Pacific Railroad] Reports of Explorations and Surveys, 1853-5, Supplement to Volume 1, Senate Executive Document 46, 35th Cong., 2nd Sess., 1859* [992].

_____. *[Pacific Railroad] Reports of Explorations and Surveys, 1853-5, Vol. 12, Book 1, House Executive Document 56, 36th Cong., 1st Sess., 1860* [1054].

Wool, Major General John E. 9/4/1855 report, in *House Executive Document 1, Part II, 34th Congress, 1st Session, 1855* [841], pp. 78-80.

## Newspapers

*Acantha* (Choteau, MT), 12/4/1912.
*Gazette and Courier* (Greenfield, MA), 3/18/1922.
*Montana Post* (Virginia City, M.T.), 12/16/1865, 2/17/1866, and 3/12/1867.
*The New North-West* (Deer Lodge, M.T.), 7/16/1869, 8/17/1883, and 4/16/1886.
*Washington Statesman* (Walla Walla, W.T.), 6/28/1862.
*Weekly Missoulian* (Missoula, M.T.), 8/17/1883.

## Published Sources

Anglin, Ron. *Forgotten Trails: Historical Sources of the Columbia's Big Bend Country*, ed. by Glen W. Lindeman. Pullman: Washington State University Press, 1995.

Barry, Louise. *The Beginning of the West.* Topeka: Kansas State Historical Society, 1972.

Bird, Annie Laurie. *Boise: The Peace Valley.* Caldwell, Idaho: Caxton, 1934.

Birney, Hoffman. *Vigilantes: A Chronicle of the Rise and Fall of the Plummer Gang of Outlaws in and about Virginia City, Montana, in the Early '60s.* Philadelphia: Penn, 1929.

Blanchet, A.M.A. *Journal of a Catholic Bishop on the Oregon Trail,* ed. by Edward J. Kowrach. Fairfield, Washington: Ye Galleon, 1978.

Branch, E. Douglas. "Frederick West Lander, Road-builder." *Mississippi Valley Historical Review* 16 (September 1929).

Brown, Jennie Broughton. *Fort Hall on the Oregon Trail.* Caldwell, Idaho: Caxton, 1932.

*Catholic Church Records of the Pacific Northwest,* 2 Vols. St. Paul, Oregon: French Prairie Press, n.d.

Dimsdale, Thomas J. *The Vigilantes of Montana: or, Popular Justice in the Rocky Mountains.* Virginia City, Montana, 1866.

Elliott, T.C. "Richard . . . Grant." *Oregon Historical Society Quarterly* 36 (March 1935).

Fleming, Harvey, ed. *Minutes of Council, Northern Department of Rupert Land, 1821-31.* Toronto, Ontario: Champlain Society, 1940.

Glazebrook, George de. T., ed. *The Hargrave Correspondence.* Toronto, Ontario: Champlain Society, 1934.

Goodhart, George W. *Trails of Early Idaho: The Pioneer Life of George W. Goodhart . . . As Told to Abraham C. Anderson.* Caldwell, Idaho: Caxton, 1940.

Hafen, LeRoy R., ed. *The Mountain Men and the Fur Trade of the Far West,* Vol. IX. Glendale, California: Arthur H. Clark, 1972.

Hamilton, Ladd. *This Bloody Deed: The Magruder Incident.* Pullman: Washington State University Press, 1994.

Hargrave, Letitia [Mactavish]. *The Letters of Letitia Hargrave,* ed. by Margaret Arnett MacLeod. Toronto, Ontario: Champlain Society, 1947.

Josephy, Alvin M., Jr. *The Nez Perce Indians and the Opening of the Northwest,* abridged ed. New Haven, Connecticut: Yale University Press, 1971 [1965].

Kohrs, Conrad. *Conrad Kohrs: An Autobiography.* Deer Lodge, Montana: Platen, 1977.

Langford, Nathaniel P. *Vigilante Days and Ways: The Pioneers of the Rockies,* 2 Vols. Boston: J.G. Cupples, 1890.

Leeson, M. *History of Montana, 1739-1885.* Chicago: Warner, Beers, 1885.

Owen, John. *The Journals and Letters of Major John Owen: Pioneer of the Northwest, 1850-1871,* 2 Vols., ed. by Seymour Dunbar and Paul C. Phillips. New York: E. Eberstadt, 1927.

Palladino, L. B. *Indian and White in the Northwest: A History of Catholicity in Montana, 1831 to 1891*, 2nd ed. Lancaster, Pennsylvania: Wickersham, 1922 [1894].

Purple, Edwin Ruthven. *Perilous Passage: A Narrative of the Montana Gold Rush, 1862-1863*, ed. by Kenneth N. Owens. Helena: Montana Historical Society Press, 1995.

Robertson, Frank C. *Fort Hall: Gateway to the Oregon Country*. New York: Hastings House, 1963.

Ross, Alexander. *The Fur Hunters of the Far West*, ed. by Kenneth A. Spaulding. Norman: University of Oklahoma Press, 1956 [1855].

Ruby, Robert H., and John A. Brown. *The Cayuse Indians: Imperial Tribesmen of Old Oregon*. Norman: University of Oklahoma Press, 1972.

Russell, Osborne. *Journal of a Trapper* [1834-43], ed. by Aubrey Haines. Lincoln: University of Nebraska Press, 1965 [1955].

Settle, Raymond W., ed. *The March of the Mounted Riflemen: First United States Military Expedition to Travel the Full Length of the Oregon Trail from Fort Leavenworth to Fort Vancouver, May to October, 1849*. Glendale, California: Arthur H. Clarke, 1940.

Stuart, Granville. *Forty Years on the Frontier, as Seen in the Journals and Reminiscences of Granville Stuart, Gold Miner, Trader, Merchant, Rancher and Politician*, 2 Vols., ed. by Paul C. Phillips. Cleveland: Arthur H. Clark, 1925 [University of Nebraska Press, Bison Book editions, 1977].

Utley, Robert M. *Frontiersmen in Blue: The United States Army and the Indian, 1848-1865*. New York: Macmillan, 1967.

Van Kirk, Sylvia. *Many Tender Ties: Women in Fur-trade Society, 1670-1870*. Norman: University of Oklahoma Press, 1983.

Watson, June M., ed. *The History of the R.M. of Dufferin in Manitoba, 1880-1980*. Carmen, Manitoba: Rural Municipality of Dufferin, 1982.

Weisel, George F. *Men and Trade on the Northwest Frontier as Shown by the Fort Owen Ledger*. Missoula: Montana State University Press, 1955.

# INDEX